55 Winning Seasons In 61 Years Of Coaching Kiss Basketball

WINNING BASKETBALL GAMES BY FINDING LOST POINTS

BY NATHAN TERRY CALHOUN
(AN EXPERIENCED COACH OF SIXTY SEASONS)

Steve Buhler

"I enjoyed the concise and detailed way KISS is written. The true-to-life examples of the game situations are well done. It covers everything needed to be a successful coach. "

Steve Buhler retired teacher and basketball coach, father of four awesome kids.

Ron Jones

Terry's unique interpretation of the "KISS" principle and acronym should draw coaches to the concepts. Terry's perspective and lessons makes this book valuable for other coaches, especially new coaches." The chapters move easily from practices to games; the best way to get a team ready to perform. From the importance of organizing practices to diagrams, to plays and drills, this book is designed for coaches to succeed.

Ron Jones played basketball at Oregon State and coached basketball for 35 years.

John Francis

"This book is a great spin on how to coach: a complete handbook. I enjoyed how Terry ran the KISS principle through his whole system. Terry's experience shows in how he makes learning faster and easier for coaches and players. If followed this book will lead to success."

John Francis basketball coach for 56 years at all levels 7th grade to college

Robert Key

"KISS is very unique in a lot of ways. Everything was well thought out, spot on and clear. This book is a NEW coach's dream to sharpen skills for the future. I will share this book with the up and coming young coaches I know."

Robert Key high school basketball coach for 30 years, currently at Nelson High School.

Callie Molloy

"In this book, Terry exudes a generous spirit and passion for coaching and mentoring both coaches and players. Sixty years of experience distilled down into a complete and useful guide. The wisdom displayed via philosophical discussion and anecdotal insights are unique and appreciated. A clear, well thought, and organized . . .extremely useful blueprint to developing systems that can be continuously refined and expanded as players advance in knowledge/skills.

Callie Molloy, U.S. Air Force Academy Athletic Hall of Fame Inductee, NCAA 10 x All-American, 6 X NCAA champion.

Ismeal Rosario

The drills, ideas, and plays in KISS are clear, organized, and easy to follow. I liked the explanation for offense and defense strategies and the quick guide makes it easy to find a drill or play in the handbook. From building your program, to selecting players, any coach can learn more details from Terry's experiences. Terry includes interesting plays with unique ideas on how to win hard games and upset good teams.

Ismeal Rosari, coach at Nelson High School, played basketball at Murry State College.

Acknowledgement

I would like to thank my parents, Bonnie and Nathan Calhoun, for their support and push for me to get a college education, so that I was able to teach and coach the game I love so much. Coaching for 61 years was possible because my wife, Geri, who was all for me chasing my dream of coaching basketball, and my 4-kids, Troy, Mark, Michelle, and Callie, who I used on our home court to work on skills and plays.

During my 61 years of coaching basketball, I worked with many special coaches and each taught me something of value such as; Dick Puhl-organization, Bob Bartlett- keeping things simple, Larry Black- take care of all your coaching staff, John Francis-build a bench and use those players, Steve Buhler-working on skills and staying calm, Lyle Carter- defensive tactics. Thanks to the many coaches who have increased my knowledge with the books they have written and the knowledge they shared at basketball clinics. Also, thanks to all my past players who shared their lives with me as we enjoyed our passion of basketball.

I extend my appreciation to Kim Vestal, who encouraged me to move forward with my book idea and lined me up with Amanda Green, who worked many hours on my basketball notes and organized them into a book. She also gave me the confidence to keep moving forward with the project. Lastly a thanks to Parker Publishing who took on the book and finished it to completion.

Dedication

I dedicate this book to Lyle M Carter, a Green Beret soldier, from World War II who became my high school basketball coach in 1957. Lyle demanded discipline while coaching my high school basketball team to the state tournament. He instilled in me a love and passion for the game of basketball. Lyle changed my life by inspiring me to finish high school, go on to college and become a high school basketball coach.

Table of Content

ABOUT THE AUTHOR	1
ABOUT THE BOOK	2
THE KISS SYSTEM	3
PREFACE	5
FOREWORD	6

PART 1 PREPARING FOR THE SEASON — 7

CHAPTER 1 SELECTING PLAYERS	8
CHAPTER 2 TYPES OF PLAYERS ON A TEAM	10
CHAPTER 3 COACHING DECISIONS	13
CHAPTER 4 PRACTICE PLANNING	16
CHAPTER 5 SCOUTING YOUR TEAM	23

PART 2 DEFENSE SKILLS, DRILLS, AND STRATEGIES — 34

CHAPTER 6 DEFENSIVE PHILOSOPHY	35
CHAPTER 7 DEFENSIVE SKILLS AND DRILLS	39
CHAPTER 8 1-2-2 ZONE PLAYER ROLE	46
CHAPTER 9 DEFENSIVE PLAN "B-C-D"	53
CHAPTER 10 PAW THE HALF-COURT TRAP	59
CHAPTER 11 FULL COURT MAN CENTER FIELD	63

PART 3 PLAYER ROLES AND FAST BREAK — 68

CHAPTER 12 NUMBERED BREAK	69
CHAPTER 13 EACHING RUNNING ROLES	75
CHAPTER 14 8.5 SPRINT BREAK	81
CHAPTER 15 KEYS TO SPRINT BREAK	85

PART 4 OFFENSE — 90

CHAPTER 16 OFFENSIVE PHILOSOPHY	91
CHAPTER 17 OFFENSIVE SKILLS AND DRILLS	92

CHAPTER 18 DELAY GAME POINTERS	96
CHAPTER 19 STALL	102
CHAPTER 20 HALF COURT MAN OFFENSE	105
CHAPTER 21 ZONE OFFENSE	113
CHAPTER 22 GAME POINT SAVERS	123
CHAPTER 23 OFFENSE VS. PRESSURE	131

PART 5 CONCLUSION — 136

CHAPTER 24 STATS	137
CHAPTER 24 THREE MORE FEET	141
CHAPTER 26 CONCLUSION	146
QUICK GUIDE CHARTS, DIAGRAMS, AND PLAYS	155
REFERENCES	159

About the Author

When I started grade school, I didn't know I had ADHD and that my brain was wired differently with Dyslexia and Anomia as well. I mixed up 3's and E's, b's, d's and 6's, the number 57 was often 75. This made spelling and reading impossible. My Anomia would cause me to say "stove" when I meant "refrigerator" or "Sam" when I wanted to say "Bill." School was hard and I was at the bottom of the class all through.

I was 4'11' and 98 pounds when I started high school, but I still played sports. Basketball soon became my best. By my junior year, I was the varsity starting point guard. My senior year we finished in fourth at the State Basketball Tournament. My grades were in the high D's, but basketball kept me in school and onto graduation.

I wanted to continue to play basketball, so I went to Lower Columbia JC and Linfield College, where I played hoops and got a BS and Masters Degree in education. In the fall of 1963, I started teaching math and science in a junior high school and coaching eighth-grade football, basketball, track and baseball. Little did I know my learning disabilities would force me to make detailed yet simple practice plans and to coach in a manner that would produce so much joy and success.

When I was young, we didn't have TV. Besides, there were few basketball games on TV in the 50 & 60's. Because of this, most of my basketball knowledge came from trial and error. I went to many games and coaching clinics. I also visited every used book store in the cities I traveled through and slowly built a basketball library. Some of the basketball knowledge I use today came from that reading, but over the years, it has mainly been from trial and error.

Email: ntcalhoun@comcast.net

About the book

This book shares a system that will help coaches build their own basketball philosophy rather than just take ideas from coaches they played for or watched. Beating bad teams on your schedule is usually easy, but this guide will help your team win hard games and upset very good teams. The Kiss system is more about odds, angles and percentages than X and O's. The offensive and defensive strategies listed in the book have been tested at state tournaments and when playing good teams up 1-2 classifications with success.

Winning with KISS will help young and new coaches speed up their knowledge and experience. It will also help coaches who need some fresh or different ideas to jump-start the upcoming year, regardless of your team's ability, age or experience.

This book can make you a better coach, helping you experience joy and success as players reach their full potential. With an open mind, you will gain new ideas to apply and teach to your team.

The KISS system

After coaching for a few years, I went to a basketball clinic where the speaker used the acronym KISS: "Keep it Simple Stupid." I liked keeping things simple as a coach because of my learning disabilities. However, the word "stupid" didn't sit well with me. When you struggle in school people label your difficulty as being stupid. I still like the Acronym KISS and keeping it simple, but for me, it stands for: "Knowledge, Interest, Scouting, & Strategy."

K for KNOWLEDGE:

Success in basketball as a player and coach depends on knowledge. The coach and players must know their craft, which takes time, effort and study. With knowledge and experience it is easy to anticipate changes needed and make adjustments. If the player knows and understands the plan and this philosophy, they will be one step ahead.

That is why we talk about how coaches can gain knowledge through scouting their players from the beginning and throughout the season. We also talk about how coaches can adjust their game plan based on their players' growing abilities and skills. Last of all, we talk about how coaches can gain knowledge by scouting other teams. With this information, coaches can prepare a practice and game plan custom to beat that team.

We also suggest ways for coaches to explain drills and plays as well as their purpose. We discuss how to create team and personal player goals and train players to be thinkers on and off the floor.

I for INTEREST

When a person has a strong interest or investment in basketball, they will exhaust all energy to get better. With a strong interest both players and coaches will give their all physically and mentally. Their performance will show this to be true.

Players have a high interest when they feel team chemistry, build rapport with their coach, and are a part of helping make decisions on and off the floor. This guide will explain how to implement this in your team. Confidence and interest are built with success: winning games, learning from mistakes and overcoming them. As explained in this book, game and end-of-the-year awards and evaluations can encourage interest and performance. As teammates learn to help and encourage each other, they build friendships and have more fun; this builds team chemistry and keeps players interested in the game.

S for SCOUTING

This book shares how scouting your own team and an opponent's live, off film, from the media, from a friend or talking to other coaches is very beneficial. The intel gained about the opponent's players, their strategy and movement helps you to build a defensive and offensive game plan. This book will show you how. Scouting helps you choose your team well and helps you know your team's strengths and weaknesses from the beginning.

Watching film and scouting your team in the middle of the season can help you make adjustments to your offense and defensive plans, as discussed in this book.

S for STRATEGY

In this guide, we also work on strategy, which is skillful planning. The strategy will build the players' faith in your plans. Always make a strategy plan and work your plan, because to not plan is to Plan For Failure. A strong strategy requires knowledge, interest, and scouting to be successful. The drills and plays discussed in this book will help you, as a coach, create and adapt effective basketball strategies.

Today, at age 83, I still operate with the KISS system to keep basketball simple and organized down to the last minute of practice. In sixty years of coaching, this system has produced 55 winning seasons, 989 wins, and a 70+% success rate. I have successfully used the KISS system at all my coaching stops regardless of age and ability levels (from Jr. High to High school varsity boys and girls) because it is simple, organized and disciplined.

Preface

When you are done with this book, you should have a better understanding of pre-season planning and how to create and apply a defensive and offensive philosophy. The KISS system covers practice drills, plays and tips for being more effective and efficient as a team. Also included are communication and organization tips for your team so they will talk better with each other and coaches while being in a defined role.

This book is organized so that it is best to read it before the basketball season starts, as it explains several things a coach must know before starting the season. The chapters of this book are in order of importance. If you skip to a back section and overlook the early chapters, you will miss the essential foundations for success.

With today's shot clock, organization and discipline are key. KISS explains ways to give players roles that will free up their minds so that they can perform constantly at a fast pace. This book also includes how the fast break can be run normally or as a speed break, along with secondary scoring options.

Coaches always talk about how defense wins championships, yet most teams spend their practice time on offense. The book will explain defensive drills that need to be done daily so that the defense can move quickly while aggressively dictating the offense's action.

God gives each of us a passion and God gave me a love of basketball. Basketball is where I honor God with how I treat others, the players, coaches and everyone connected with the game. I try to coach with Zeal: Ecclesiastes 9:10: whatever you do, do it with all your might. I try to coach with Patience: Galatians 5:22: patience is one of the fruits of the spirit. I try to coach with inspiration: Job 32:8: the spirit in man gives him the strength and wisdom to keep going forward. After reading and using this book, I hope you will feel prepared to coach with zeal, patience, and inspiration.

Foreword

As a young man Terry Calhoun played basketball with more enthusiasm and dedication to the game than most other players. As a coach, he believes defense wins games and coaches like a dictator, psychologist and salesman all rolled into one.

Terry's drive to win is strong. To him, losses are to learn from, while wins are expected. Terry's coaching book will go into detail on what he has done to make defense effective with drills, footwork details and his own on-the-floor rules that make a difference, regardless of the type of defense he uses.

Besides the JUG defense and successful drills, you will learn how he teaches his players footwork so they can cover ground faster and fulfill their role in the defense. He explains the type of players to select for your team so that coaching is fun and rewarding. Most importantly, you will be exposed to the old-school experienced traits that a successful coach should have to be a winner on and off the floor.

During my eight years of coaching alongside coach Terry Calhoun, I was able to see his magic work with his teams and defensive play. We went into each game with plans A, B and C. With sound defense, Terry coached a program that excelled, produced upsets and over-achieved while making winning players on and off the floor.

I had fun coaching with Terry, as the team played in the District finals and sub-state all eight years and we took several trips to the State Tournament. The success of those eight years was due to great discipline, off-season work, and time spent on the fundamentals while using many different defensive gimmicks and tricks. Terry is a great friend and my best golf and pool-playing buddy who, at age eighty-three, is still filled with a passion for coaching basketball.

<u>Steve Buhler</u>: Assistant varsity basketball coach at Damascus Christian HS with coach Terry Calhoun for eight years.

Part 1
Preparing for the Season

Chapter 1
Selecting Players

As mentioned in the KISS philosophy introduction, observing the personality and character of potential team players is important. When picking players for your team, you must think about speed, size, skill, quickness, strength, endurance, coordination, and coachability. Most coaches will play their five best players regardless of their size by running an offense and defense that fits their personal philosophy. When choosing team players look also at their discipline, attitude, and effort. Choosing your team should also factor in their toughness or grit. In this chapter, we will talk about what to look for in team players and how you can tell if they have the character and attributes you want for your team.

Discipline

When choosing players, an important aspect to consider is whether they have good discipline. Disciplined players are able to follow directions and love rules that set boundaries. This type of player is focused, eager and they learn fast. Discipline saves time, keeps things organized, and makes directions meaningful. Discipline helps players build confidence, reach goals, become highly productive, and consistently play. Discipline also goes a long way in producing good behavior and a strong attitude.

I advise contacting the player's past coaches and teachers for their opinion on their discipline. In try-outs also make your own observations of how the player takes corrections. Do they make eye contact when given directions, talking or listening? This will help you find disciplined and focused team players.

Attitude

Disciplined players seldom have a bad attitude. Players with a good attitude stand out because they want to please the coach and see corrections as a chance to improve. You can change a lot of things about a player and his game, but it's hard to change a poor attitude. Choosing a player with a bad attitude isn't fair to your team and can make for a long season. A great attitude is contagious and will spur others upward. Players with a good attitude often smile, show joy and work hard. Players can control their attitude and effort so accept only one hundred percent in these two areas.

Effort

When you select players with a great attitude and discipline, they will be more likely to give second and third effort on all plays. The coach must demand effort, but it's best if it comes from within the player. It is important to choose basketball players who will put forth all their energy, focus and effort into the game.

When choosing team players that have discipline, attitude and effort, you need to also factor in their toughness (or grit) and whether the player is an anticipator or reactor. Next, we will discuss what to look for in team players and how you can tell if they have the character and attributes you want for your team.

Toughness/Grit

If you look in the dictionary, under the word: "toughness," there are several examples:

Handling adverse conditions, enduring hardship, not being intimidated by an opponent and staying with an activity until a goal is reached, no matter how long it takes. A tough person is defined as being confident, determined, daring, having tenacity, spirit and perseverance.

Players with grit will bounce back from a turnover, a missed free throw or any missed shot, missed assignment, poor call by the officials or a teammate screw-up. These players can put the bad things out of their minds and move forward with confidence to the next play. Tough-minded players want to guard the opponent's best player and take the possible game-winning shot.

Players with toughness stand out because they have a strong desire to win. They are usually the first players and most often the only players that you will see getting on the floor after the ball. If a player takes charges more than once during a game, it will be by a tough-minded player.

Players with grit love to play the role of an underdog and because they are so competitive, they don't miss practice. Tough players are self-driven and want to be pushed by competition. These players don't take correction personally and their body language reeks of confidence. The size of a tough player's body doesn't matter, as they are all heart. I once heard it said, "A heart of a deer led by a lion would defeat a heart of a lion led by a deer," or as Mark Twain said, "It's not the size of the dog in the fight but the size of the fight in the dog." (reference)

Team Chemistry

If players have the things listed above: discipline, good attitude, effort and grit, they are well on their way toward being players who build strong team chemistry. Chemistry is important at both ends of the floor, in the locker room and away from the gym. It is vital to winning. When the team plays hard to win and everyone is happy, you know that there is good chemistry.

Players who put the team first and are quick to build up their teammates are chemistry builders. Players who compete for their glory, minutes played, shots taken, starting, etc., will cause chemistry problems. Those players put themselves before the team; they don't make others better, and this will divide the team. Players with lesser ability may get fewer points or touches on offense, but if they get positive feedback for setting good screens, passing, rebounding and defense, they will feel valued. This builds good chemistry and prevents players from losing interest or slacking.

Conclusion

Players will learn from, imitate and migrate toward teammates with traits discussed in this chapter. These players will lift everyone up and build good team chemistry. Players with these traits are fun to be around and make a basketball season a joy.

Chapter 2
Types of Players on a Team

If you have selected players with good discipline, effort and toughness, then you need to evaluate how these players perform on the floor, which is usually one of the following four ways.

Soft Players

Soft players play off their man by three to six feet, whether they have the ball or not. When they are off the ball, they don't give gap help and they let the person they are guarding cut their face when breaking across the court toward the ball. When shots are taken, they don't screen out in a physical way. When guarding the post, they play defense behind the post and let passes be made into the post. You never see these players getting 50-50 balls. If a soft player has the qualities mentioned in Chapter 1, then their gameplay can be greatly improved with drills and exercises in grit and perseverance.

The Dictator

The dictator is always pressuring the ball. They force the dribbler to pick up the ball or determine where the ball goes. When off the ball, the dictator gives gap help and is quick to double-team the ball. They take charges and give a physical forearm to the chest of any cutter that tries to make a straight line cut to the ball or cut their face. When guarding in the low post, the dictator plays in a three-fourths denial or full front position, they deny passes into the post. If a dictator has the qualities mentioned in Chapter 1, then they can make a team strong. However, drills and team goals are necessary to give this type of player boundaries to keep them in check.

The Reactor

The reactor is always late on all rotations on defense, so they end up out of position. They often stand in a tall stance, try to block shots, and don't talk on defense. They have to process with their eyes before their muscles will tell the body to move. If a reactor has the qualities mentioned in Chapter 1, then they need additional help to be a beneficial part of the team. Their slow reaction time can be hard to fix, but drills can help.

The Anticipator

Anticipators will be quick on all defensive movements or rotations. Their brains process quickly. They often move before the ball is passed or dribbled based on what they think will happen next. Anticipators move their bodies in advance because they have a good idea of what will happen before it happens. If an anticipator has the qualities mentioned in Chapter 1, they will need drills to help them communicate with their team, especially reactors and soft players.

Type choices on a team

Basketball is a fast-paced game and it requires a lot of quick decisions, so try to fill your team with anticipators. In order to use soft players and reactors on your team, they need special skills to stay on the floor for long periods of time. Dictators can be useful but have to show a good level of trainability.

You will need to coach all these different types on your team differently in order to create team success and chemistry. Chemistry + Attitude + Effort = Team Success. Success isn't winning but getting the most out of your players and team. Here are some tips on how to coach the reactors vs anticipators differently.

Coaching a Reactor

Reactors need extra time for drills, as they may not understand directions the first time or need corrections. Reactors are more likely to stand tall with knees locked and will need practice to have a lower stance with bent knees. Experience has proven to me that reactors are more likely to let people drive past them; they make more reach in fouls and when they try to block shots, the effort is late. These are areas they need a lot of practice in.

Reactors are naturally non-talkers, as things happen too fast for them to communicate. So, coaching them to communicate in the moment is important. A reactor is slow to screen out, more likely to get tied up if it gets a rebound and slow to chin its rebounds. Most of the rebounds they get are the ones that fall into their hands. So rebound practice and drills are needed with a lot of reps.

A reactor is more likely to dribble than pass or pass without seeing the defense; practicing passing to a moving target is needed as they often fail to lead the cutter. Reactors should be places where they are not expected to pass often because they will hold the ball too long while trying to read the defense. This will cause the window for a good pass to close and leave the offense stagnant.

Reactors often over-penetrate and drive into double teams instead of pulling up for an open, high-percentage, 12-foot shot. Practicing these skills and shots will be helpful. Reactors also are often poor at using screens because they don't scrape off the screen, don't wait for the screen to be set or fail to read the defense, so focusing on screening with them will benefit your team as well.

Overall, reactors are best as rebounders on the backside of the offense, spot shooters or post players. Focus on these roles for reactors and their strengths. Do not yell or get mad at a reactor when you get less than one hundred percent from them. Show the reactor what needs to change if they want playing time, point out their strengths, weaknesses and encourage them while knowing growth will be slow. The reactor will be a great cheerleader for your team with a "gung ho" talk, which is great for building team chemistry.

Coaching an anticipator

Anticipators can make an educated guess from scouting reports, practice drills and experience before the play or action happens and respond. The anticipator's first move on a driver or guarding the ball is to be up and into the driver and not take retreat steps. If they make a foul, it is often with their body. If the anticipator is one pass away from the ball, they are thinking gap help, so their body is down, wide, and bluffing, while wanting action to happen toward their direction or area of the floor. The anticipator makes fakes and can read the defense, so they are better passers.

An anticipator is better at moving without the ball; with basket cuts and ball cuts, they will set screens and then roll or fade away to improve floor spacing. They will be in the proper location to steal a jump ball tip 90% of the time. The anticipator will talk, giving guidance and information to improve team play. They can update teammates on the next play or what might happen.

Anticipators do great with floor play but they will need to work on team skills. They can also be very smart but impulsive and struggle with listening or following instructions. If this is true, work out the values and discipline of the team expectations with them. No matter what, they will be competitive and aggressive. Because they always go hard, this type of player raises the bottom and expects more from them. They are usually self-driven, but just need to be pointed in the right direction. When there is a breakdown, they want to be driven and corrected. With this information in mind, the point guard must be an anticipator! The inbound passer must be an anticipator because, without a good inbound pass, the play has no chance of success. On defense, you can play an anticipator at any position on the ball or off the ball where he is guiding and helping his teammates.

Consistency wins games, this is why the team with anticipators will win most of the time. On offense, the anticipator can keep the game simple without mistakes. On defense, their play will take away the opponent's ability to play consistently with their best players.

Conclusion

Each team will have a combination of soft players, dictators, anticipators, and reactors. Coaches need to know each player's type to play them in the positions that fit with their strengths and to know which skills and drills to work on for areas of weaknesses. Next is to think of your coaching philosophy: what are the most important areas of basketball to cover during practice? We will talk about preseason coaching decisions next.

Chapter 3
Coaching Decisions

Once your team is selected, the next most important decisions will have to do with practice planning. (See chapter 4). The practice plans must include what the coach decides are the most important areas of basketball cover. This will give their team a solid foundation and a chance at a consistent winning season.

The following are what I feel are the ten most important areas to be coached in the order that I value them. I recommend they be installed in the first three weeks. Before spending hours planning and filling practice with halfcourt offense, cover the ten most important areas of basketball listed below.

1. Scouting

I like to have my players and team well-scouted before and early in the season. This is covered in chapter 5. Then, as the preseason moves along, I scout my opponent's offense and defense so that I know their weakness and strength. Scouting the opponent is covered in Parts 2 and 4 as well as in chapter 24 of this book.

2. Handling Pressure:

There is more than one kind of pressure. Without the ability to handle pressure, your team can't win close games and pull-off upsets. Players can pass over the pressure before double teams happen, depending on the type of pressure. They can also pass backward or split double teams but attack with the intention of scoring. The topic of handling pressure is covered in Part 4 in chapters 16-23.

3. Delay Game:

It does your team no good to take the lead into the fourth quarter if it folds the last part of the game and you lose the game. This is important because most games are won or lost by a few baskets. In chapters 18 and 19, I share several ideas on how to delay and stall the game.

4. Half-Court Defense:

Half-court defense is placed early in the book because it is so important. The opponent can't beat your team if they can't score. If your offense is sputtering, your defense better be good. Each team's offense and players will present different problems for your defense, so you must have a plan for all situations. I share ideas on half-court defense in chapters 6 through 9 in Part 2.

5. Rebounding:

The old saying that the team that wins the rebound battle will most often win the game is true. This is why rebounding is listed as one of the top 10 priorities. Coaching rebounding is covered in chapter 17 and is mentioned in other parts of the book.

6. Shooting

No matter how good your team's defense is, you must shoot and score to win games. All shooters can be improved and need to be taught what is a good shot depending on skill, range and time of the game. Nearly half of all shots taken in games are forced, out of range and have a low percentage of success. Chapter 17 covers shooting and how to coach shooting.

7. Passing

Good passing teams are hard to beat because they get better and higher percentage shots. Good passing provides assists which builds teamwork and good chemistry. Passing mistakes often happen because of a poor angle or the lack of eye and passing fakes. Try to drill two fakes before any pass. I like the old saying, "Fake a pass to make a pass." Passing skill drills are covered in chapter 17.

8. Out of Bounds Defense and Offense:

With good planning when dealing with out-of-bounds plays, your team can gain a 4-8 point advantage in a game, enough to win many close games. Chapter 23 covers how to turn out-of-bounds situations into an advantage for your team at both ends of the floor.

9. Defensive Pressure:

Often, your team will need to change the tempo of the game by slowing down or speeding up the action. If behind late in a game, Part 2 of the book, chapters 8-11, gives several different ways on how your team can increase the tempo from the full court, midcourt and half court with your defense. Chapters 18 & 19 cover how to slow the action when on offense. Chapters 12 through 14 explain how the offense can speed up the action.

10. Movement and Spacing:

Too often in basketball games, there is a lack of movement and poor spacing. If there is a lot of one-on-one offense, dribbling or two-man play, the remaining offensive players tend to stand around. This makes the offense stagnant and the defensive team's job easier. When on defense, players lose their low wide stance, stand tall and lock their knees. This leads to failure to bluff and retreat. Then the players can't move quickly to give gap help. Chapter 7 covers footwork drills that will improve movement and spacing.

Conclusion

Each coach must make their own list of what they feel is most important so they can have their team ready for the first game and a successful season. The list of ten things doesn't need much practice time, but they should be covered each day. Failure to cover and practice them will end up with a time-out during the game. An unpracticed plan put in place will work against poor teams or if you have better players, but not if you want to upset or beat better teams.

When practice time is spent on the top ten coaching decisions, the players will soon understand the value of these ten areas of basketball and execute them with few mistakes. When a player makes a mistake, have them tell you the mistake and what to do differently next time so they become thinkers and can self-correct.

In life, we make thousands of decisions each day. Just as players make many decisions each second when on the playing floor. Good and bad luck are always factors in a game, but solid practice based on good decisions, produces good luck as "Luck is Preparation for Opportunity." The next big step for the coach is to have their practice plans in place for the first few weeks.

Chapter 4
Practice Planning

A good practice plan is necessary for teams to reach their full potential. After selecting the team, I hand the players an outline list of what they are expected to know after the first three weeks of pre-season practice.

Building a good daily practice plan starts by taking a list of all you want your team to know and putting it on a calendar covering the first three weeks of the practice. An example of "items to know" is listed in an example at the end of this chapter.

The next step is to take each day's list and put the items in the order you plan to teach them, along with the amount of time for that item. For example, you could put fundamental skill work early in the practice, while team offense and defense later in the practice. How you budget your time will depend upon the team's experience. At the end of this chapter, you will see a sample calendar for weeks 1-3, with items listed and time allotted for each item or drill.

The coach needs the first three weeks of practice plans made before the season starts. Daily practice plans can be adjusted each day before the next practice. The plans may vary each year, depending on how many players you have coming back and your player's experience. Don't take anything for granted and cover everything in detail. Due to a holiday break, practice adjustments may be needed during the second week of preseason. At the end of week three, there can be missed practice dates if games are scheduled at that time.

Experience has shown me that it is best to cover a drill for a short period of time, for several days, rather than a few long sessions on a drill for a few days. I like to spend 3-10 minutes time segments on each drill, then move on to the next activity because it keeps players active, mentally and physically.

A coach's practice plan should be detailed and the rotation of players and the coaching points should be clear. Directions and expectations need to be explained but keep talking to a minimum. The drills need to be a breakdown of your offense and defense. For a good idea of the fundamental skills and drills, see Chapter 3.

Drills need to be snappy, with each player getting lots of reps and no players standing around. If things aren't going well with a drill, don't spend extra time with it; move on and fix the problem before the drill is repeated the next day. If the players are the problem when doing a drill, they may need to run some lines so they know you will not stand for a poorly run drill.

Each assistant coach needs to have a copy of the practice plan and they must make sure the team moves on to the next drill so that the time plan is followed. Make sure that the assistant coach understands what you want with each drill. The players must see your assistants as your equals and that they are valued coaches to be respected.

Practice plan adjustments will come later when the season starts and will be based on your players' performance in games. You can use stats and film evaluation to show areas where improvement is needed (Chapter 5) and prepare for teams you have scouted and will play soon (Chapter 24).

THINGS TO KNOW AFTER PRESEASON

DEFENSE DRILLS; (bluff and retreat, charges, long slides, loose balls, close outs, rebounding, chesting cutters, double teams)

OFFENSE DRILLS; (passing, dribbling, shooting, getting open, post moves, screening)

FAST BREAK; (# break, secondary break vs man and zone)

OFFENSE MAN; (orange, motion, Utah, money, blob, slob)

OFFENSE ZONE; (top zone, up & down town, stack, horns, money, blob)

PRESS BREAKER; (full court vs man and zone, half court and traps)

DEFENSE; (base 1-2-2 zone, corner-wing traps man-z, triangle+2, double zone, blob, slob)

DEFENSE HALF COURT TRAP; (claw)

FULL COURT PRESS; (man center field)

DELAY; (Vegas or black-6)

OUT OF BOUNDS; (Blob, Slob, jump ball)

Example of First Three Week's Practice Plan

Week 1 Nov 12-16 2hr+ Practice

40 min Toughness and Skills

2 min	Lane touches 2x 30 sec	Daily
3min	Short slides (bluffs, charge, loose ball)	Daily
3min	Duck walks /+talk	Daily
7 min.	Pressure passing (receiver calls grade)	Daily
3 min	Dribbling	Daily
4 min	Form Shooting (wall/8 feet)	Daily
8 Min	Defensive/Offensive Rebounding	Daily
10 Min	2 Bulls in ring + Miken	Daily

15 min Defense

15 min	12 Tight	M, T & TH
15 min	Corner Traps	TH & F
15 min	Claw & Man	CF W & F

65min Offense

6 min	Shooting (20. 15' shots record)	Daily
34 min	Man Offense - Orange+Motion	M,T, &TH
34 min	Zone Offense – Top Zone + Horns	W & F
15 min	(5 on 0 learn lanes of # break) 8 minutes	M
	Throwing long to 2&3 men 7 minutes	M
15 min	5 vs 3 off free throws	T, W
15 min	Press Breaker	Th
15 min	5vs3 (with press & breaker	F
10 min	2nd Break vs Man	M,T,& Th
10 min	2nd Break vs Zone	W & F

10 min Closing Practice.

5 min	Sideline Plays (SLOB	T, TH
2 min	Miken + Long Slides (record)	M,W, F
3 min	Free Throws –record	Daily

Post practice meeting

Week 2 Nov 20-24

40 min Toughness and Skills

1 min	Lane touches (60 second record)	Daily
3 min.	Defensive slides	Daily
3 min	Duck walks	Daily
4 min	Charges, loose ball	
	Chest cutters, Snake pit	Different each day
10 min	4 min dribbling, 6 min Shooting	Daily
8 Min	Rebounding	Daily
10 min.	2 Bulls in ring + Miken	Daily

25 min Defense

15 min	12 tight	M & F
10 min	Man Z + Triangle + 2	W & Th
10 min	Paw-Tight-Corner Trap	M, T & F
15 min	Mam CF	T, W & T

50 min Offense

4 min.	Shooting 15' 20 shots (record)	Daily
8 min	# Break (0 & 3 vs 5) + Secondary	Daily
30 min.	Man Offense (Red + Motion)	M, W &F
30 min.	Zone Offense (Up & Down Town, Stack Horns, TZ, Money)	T & Th
8 min	Delay	M & F
8 min	SLOB & BLOB	T & Th
8 min	Press Breaker	W

10 min Closing

5 min	Post Moves/Guard Moves	Daily
2 min	Miken + Long Slides (record)	Daily
3 min	10 Free Throws –record	Daily

Post practice meeting

Week 3 Nov 27-30

40 min Toughness and Skills

3 min	Defensive slides	Daily
2 min	Duck walks	Daily
9 min	Charges + Closeouts	Daily
10 min	4 min dribbling, 6 Shooting	Daily
6 min	Rebounding	Daily
10 min.	2 Bulls in ring, Miken	
	Two ball dribbling	Daily

25 min Defense

10 min	12 tight	M, W & F
10 min.	Jump Ball + BLOB defense	T & T
10 min	Man Z	M, W & F
10 min	Triangle-2	T & Th
10 min	Paw	M W & F
10 min	Corner & Wing Trap	T & Th
10 min	Man Centerfield	Daily

50 min Offense

4 min.	Shooting 15' 20 shots (record)	Daily
8 min.	# Break (0 & 3 vs 5) + Secondary	Daily
30 min	Man Offense (Red + Motion	M & W
30 min	Zone Offense (Town, Stack, Horns, Money)	
8 min	Delay	T & TH
8 min	SLOB & BLOB	T & TH
8 min	Press Breaker	W
6 min	Screens (setting and using)	M & F
30 min	Controlled Scrimage	F

10 min Closing

2 min	Miken + Long Slides (record)	Daily
5 min.	Post moves + Guard Moves	Daily
3 min.	Free Throws –record	Daily

Post practice meeting

SAMPLE OF DAY ONE-WEEK ONE-PRACTICE PLAN

(from week one's master plan (2hrs & 5 min.)

40 Minutes	Skills and Toughness
2 min	Lane touches 2 X 30 (second record the best)
3 min	Short slides (including bluffs, charges & loose balls)
3 min	Duck walks 3 X (down the gym while talking)
7 min	Pressure passing (receiver calls grade A to F on each pass)
3 min	Dribbling (stop/go, crossovers, between legs, inside out(using right and left hand
4 min	Form shooting (at the wall and basket from 6' out
8 min	Rebounding (offensive and defensive)
10 min	2 Bulls in the ring + Miken drills
15 minutes	Defense
15 min	Tight 12 defense (position roles & rotations)
60 Minutes	Offense
6 min	Shooting. (record 20, 15 foot shots & makes
34 min	Man offense (motion-circle and orange) A. 8 minutes; 0 on 5 fast break and lanes B. 7 minutes; Throwing long to 2 and 3 players
5 min	Intro 2nd break vs man defense
5 min	Closing Practice
2 min	1 min of Miken makes long slides. (record both)
3 min	10 free throws. (record makes)
5 Minutes	Short team meeting

Post-Practice Team Meeting

The team meeting should include practice grades, reviewing what went well and what to change with practice, next practice time, announcements, and prayer. The "end of practice grade" is a player's verbal guess A- F based on their own evaluation of their practice performance. This can often include several grades, such as an A for effort and defense, a B for rebounding and team chemistry, and a D for passing and shooting, or overall grades of B and passing and defense must improve.

After the first three weeks, you can use good scouting reports to make adjustments to your practice plans. So, scouting is what we will talk about next.

Chapter 5
Scouting Your Team

Only with a good scouting report can you make adjustments to your practice plan. The scouting report will be about your players and team early in the year. Stats from last year, summer league games, fall league games, individual player workouts and open gyms will tell you where your team needs the most help.

Four Ways To Scout Your Team

Coach Evaluation Forms and Player Survey

At the end of the regular season, each player and the head coach are given a detailed report card that grades all areas of basketball for each player. For example, see the player evaluation form at the end of this chapter. Each player also gets a copy of their season stats. Each area of the stats is highlighted with a red, green and yellow marker. Red means needs improvement, green means good, and yellow means ok.

Also, each player fills out a team survey early in the season. A team survey example is shown at the end of this chapter. The player survey will either confirm what the coach knows or it can open their eyes to things they might not have seen that they need to be aware of and address. I would also advise repeating the survey at the end of the season to see if the players have different opinions. If several player's teammates see a weakness or strength in another teammate, the coach needs to have a one on one and share this with the player.

A coach can study the players' stats, the evaluation form, and the team survey form, which will tell a lot about a player.

Eye Test

The last chance to gather initial stat information about your team is the eye test, which should be done during open gyms before the season starts. The eye test is done by watching players on and off the ball on offense and defense, noting what stands out. Notice what you see in athleticism, small signs of physicalness all over the floor, body language, talking and overall game flow. These observations will confirm or open your eyes to what previous gameplay stats and any film show you about a player.

The eye test is used mainly out of season or during preseason; however, it is also a good idea for ongoing practice. In practice, the coach should yell out positive feedback if the eye test shows something good. If the eye test shows something that needs to be corrected, then practice is stopped and a correction is made, or the individual player will be pulled aside for a one-on-one talk.

However, it is easy, during an eye test, to notice something that stands out but gives you a false truth. For example, if a player gets a steal or blocks a shot, that player is thought of as a good defender. However, stats and films will show that often, these movements are counter-productive over the long hall. The shot blocker can be faked out of position, giving up points, or making fouls. The person who makes a long 3-point shot gets everyone excited, but he is more apt to shoot more and more, even when he is missing shots. That hurts the team's offensive PPP and chemistry. That is why it is important to use surveys and evaluations as well as practice films.

Film

With all the media resources and technology available, it is easy to film players and teams. Early in the season, film your practice. After you have watched the film several times, have a ten to fifteen-minute meeting with your team. At the film meeting, you can point out things that need to be corrected. I will often film a shooting drill for 1-2 minutes with my phone and then pull a player struggling with their shot aside for a quick peek. Then, he can jump back into the drill and try to correct the problem.

Film watching will improve players' performance. You can tell a player over and over that they are soft and do a poor job of screening out when the opponent shoots. If the player disagrees, the stats will show them the number of rebounds gained and the film will show them poor screenouts. With this information, the player will believe what you say and be extra proud of their improvement.

The film should be used all year, in and out of season, to improve players and teams. It takes practice to watch the film and see all the things that are happening off the ball. With film-watching practice, you will learn that you must back up and watch each play several times to truly know what your players are doing. The film will show why a play worked or why it didn't and help you break the play down for your team.

Other's evaluations

I also like other people's opinions and evaluations from previous or current coaches, teachers, friends and teammates to inform my plans. Stats alone don't always tell a true story, as a wing player may have poor stats if he is playing out of position as a point guard or post. If a player's shots come off a dribble, he may have a low percentage, but the same shot of a pass will produce a higher percentage. If the player has poor teammates, he may try too hard and look bad. On the School/Equipment/Health portion of the Coach's Evaluation, asking teachers, even family, if the player has a low grade on a few of these evaluation parts is helpful.

How to use the player information

Most teams use eight main players in a tough game; each position has a different role. Scouting and evaluations are used to decide the player's role on the team so that the team will have success on offense and defense.

Scouting your players and team is a year-round process. Stats will help your team and the players understand their weaknesses. With coaching, they can improve as you play to their strengths. All of this will help the team PPP and the chances to win. I hand out stats to players after each game. The good things I highlight with a green marker and things that need improvement I highlight in red.

It takes both stats and film to keep coaches from overlooking players who do not stand out but make everyone on the floor better. This type of player can get some long rebounds or loose balls. They take charge and deflect the ball away from an opponent's pass. However, the ball then goes into the hands of a teammate, who then takes credit for the steal. These players turn down shots and pass the ball to open players who score. This player may only play 3 minutes each half or a total of 6 minutes, but they could get two loose balls, take one charge, give out two assists, get a rebound and score no points. The stats don't stand out, as everyone looks at points scored 0, but the team may have out-scored the opponent by 7 points during the 6 minutes that the player was on the floor. This is a team-first player and he just makes the team and teammates better. Stats, surveys, evaluations and film help you not to miss the team-first players who are great additions to your team's gameplay.

The preseason is over once you have worked on fundamental skills and your team material. Then it's game time and you will need scouting reports on your opponents. For more information on scouting your opponent, please see Chapter 23.

Coach Evaluation Form

Player_____

Team_____

1=Excellent. 2=Good. 3=Average. 4=Weak. 5=Poor.

DEFENSIVE REBOUNDING

_____1. You find someone to screen off the boards.

_____2. You fight for the inside position.

_____3. You get physical.

_____4. You chin and protect your rebounds.

_____5. You make good, fast, strong outlet passes.

Defensive Rebounding Grade_____

OFFENSIVE REBOUNDING

_____1. You crash the boards on all shots.

_____2. You fight for the inside position.

_____3. You give your 2nd effort.

Offensive Rebound Grade_____

PASSING

_____1. You get physical with V-cuts to get open for a pass.

_____2. You protect the ball and face the hoop.

_____3. You keep your head up and see the floor for open teammates.

_____4. You pass with two hands and fake before making passes.

_____5. You make easy passes with a good angle without forcing passes.

Passing Grade_____

DRIVING

_____1. You fake a pass or shot before driving.

_____2. Your drives are straight toward the hoop.

_____3. You dribble 2-3 times getting to the hoop, not 4-6 dribbles.

_____4. You finish your shots off a drive.

_____5. You don't waste your dribble.

_____6. You pull up to shoot the midrange shot rather than driving into pressure.

_____7. You dribble with your head up

Dribbling Grade_____

SHOOTING

_____1. You always shoot a high % shots that you expect to go in.

_____2. You shoot squared-up shots while in rhythm.

_____3. You shoot with good form, backspin and at a 45% angle.

_____4. You can shoot a high % on 3's.

_____5. You shoot a high % on free throws.

Shooting Grade_____

DEFENSE

_____1. You stay in a low and wide stance

_____2. You give gap help when one passes the ball.

_____3. You talk when on defense.

_____4. You look for opportunities to take charge.

_____5. You play physically when on defense.

_____6. You read the eyes of the person with the ball.

_____7. You get tips, deflections and steals.

_____8. You are an aggressive anticipator on defense.

_____9. You know your opponent and their strengths.

_____10. You give weakside defensive help.

_____11. You chest all cutters, so they can't cut your face.

Defensive Grade_____

STRENGTH

_____1. You're strong for your size.

_____2. You do other sports or work out daily.

_____3. You play when hurt or sick.

_____4. You lift weights.

Strength Grade_____

MENTAL

_____1. You stay positive.

_____2. You stay confident.

_____3. You know and follow the scouting report.

_____4. You read and watch lots of basketball.

_____5. You know your team's offense and defensive plans.

_____6. You try to build up teammates and help team chemistry.

Mental Grade_____

PRACTICE

_____1. You keep focused on all that your coach says.

_____2. You are dressed and try to be the first player on the floor.

_____3. You give 100% for the entire practice.

_____4. Your teammates see you as a very hard worker.

_____5. You look for times to help teammates.

Practice Grade_____

SCHOOL/HEALTH/EQUIPMENT

_____1. You take good care of your body with sleep and good food.

_____2. You try your best to get good grades.

_____3. You treat everyone with respect. (players, coaches, teachers, parents).

_____4. You are organized, take good care of the equipment and uniforms.

School/Health/ Equipment Grade _____

Player/Team Survey

This information is to be treated as "confidential." (Don't include yourself)

Three player who always take good shots

A. _____

B. _____

C. _____

Three best shooters

A. _____

B. _____

C. _____

Three best rebounders

A. _____

B. _____

C. _____

Three best drivers

A. _____

B. _____

C. _____

Three best passers

A. _____

B. _____

C. _____

Three best defensive players

    A. _____

    B. _____

    C. _____

Three weakest offensive players

    A. _____

    B. _____

    C. _____

Four players you least like to play with

    A. _____

    B. _____

    C. _____

    D. _____

Four players you like to play with

    A. _____

    B. _____

    C. _____

    D. _____

Three selfish players

    A. _____

    B. _____

    C. _____

Three best hustlers

    A._____

    B._____

    C._____

Three toughest most physical players

    A._____

    B._____

    C._____

4 potential problem players. (attitude, social, grades)

    A._____

    B._____

    C._____

    D._____

What do you see as the strength of this team

    A._____

    B._____

    C._____

    D._____

What do you see as the weakness of this team

    A._____

    B._____

    C._____

    D._____

PART 2:
DEFENSE SKILLS, DRILLS, AND STRATEGIES

Chapter 6
Defensive Philosophy

You may have heard "Defense Wins Championships," which I find to be true when the defense is well taught and played. Having a defensive philosophy will make it easy to see mistakes, hold players accountable, teach discipline, and dictate the action. You need your basketball defensive philosophy to stay organized and so your team can play consistently with clear defensive roles.

Common Defense Problems

In creating my KISS defense philosophy, I made important observations of common problems indefensive play from watching games, game films, playing and coaching. The following are several things I see over and over.

Most teams run their offense to the right side of the floor. Drives with the right hand are from or toward the right side of the floor. I also observed that many floater-type shots are with the right hand from the right side of the floor or down the middle of the key going right. Most fouls on drives are when the driver goes to his right. All of these can be explained by the fact that most players are right-handed.

Also, it's rare to see a team take a defensive charge and it is common for the defense to play with no communication with teammates. I have also observed that most passes around a defense's perimeter are made with little resistance. Cutters move freely through the defense without receiving a forearm chuck and the defender's face is cut. Passes off the dribble by a moving player are weak and off-target. One-handed passes will have no fake and are suspected of failure as is jumping to pass.

Many drives are straight to the hoop and are met with little gap help or the gap help is late, which can result in a reaching foul. The ball pressure is often soft because the defender plays 5-7 feet off the ball for fear of getting beat on a drive. Post defenders usually play behind the post and let the offensive post get a direct pass. Defensive screen-outs on shots are poor as the defenders turn and watch the ball or they move under the basket. Offensive players coming off good screens get good shots and defenders are weak against all kinds of screens.

Late closeouts on the ball give up uncontested, high-percentage shots, as the defender is stuck 6-8 feet from the ball in "no-man's-land." If the offense receives little pressure, it is more successful and will gain confidence.

A strong defensive philosophy will develop physical and mental toughness and enable players to overcome all the observations listed above. This will produce extra possessions and shots for your team due to steals, violations, turnovers, charges, and defensive rebounding.

KISS Defensive Philosophy

The goal of my defensive philosophy is only to give up one shot on each possession and that shot will be a low-percentage shot, under pressure, from outside the key or three-point line and from the left side of the floor. I like to force the shooter to be moving and not squared up because forced shots are usually taken by a poor shooter or the 3-5th best shooters on the team.

The defense gives up no dribble penetration due to gap help, the dribblers are pushed left and under pressure and forced to use their left hand. There will be no direct line pass into the post or the middle of the defense; if that happens, the ball is double-teamed. All closeouts are early and aggressive on the right side of the shooter's body and shooting hand, forcing action going to the left with the left hand. Due to the close-out angle that is early and aggressive, the rotations aren't late, so no players are standing around and the defense is dictating the action.

With this defensive philosophy in place, all the practice drills must prepare the defenders to enforce the defensive action plan and prevent all defensive breakdowns. Good defensive drills train the players to anticipate and not react. The KISS defensive philosophy is always dictating the action to the left side of the floor. This is the opposite of what the offensive players and teams want, so there will be a lot of resistance. For this reason, nearly half of your practice time should be spent on defense. For information on defensive drills, see Chapter 7.

When your philosophy is set and the drills are in place, ensure your defense is flexible enough to play several ways. A sound strategy will need to be flexible because each team on your schedule will present different defensive challenges.

Flexible Defensive Actions

1. PACK BACK:

The pack back defensive action will clog the key as the defenders sag back and play with one foot in the key. There will not be extended pressure, so the opponent will be able to make several perimeter passes and be open for three point shots. This might be used if the opponent is tall and has no outside shooters.

2. FORCING THE ACTION:

To force the defensive action, defenders move several feet from the basket toward the three-point line, deny passes and pressure the ball. This will make the game faster and will force the offense to move off the three-point line. Passes will be harder to complete, so the opponent will try more dribble penetration. This defense is good if you're behind, the opponent has poor ball handlers or the opponent has good outside shooters.

3. TRAPS:

The defense will trap or double team at different spots on the floor, such as the point or wing and the corner. The trap can be used on weak players to force turnovers. Or it can be used on good players so they will pass and no longer are a scoring threat. Traps are explained more in chapter 11.

4. MIXING THE ACTION:

When playing a mixed action defense, some defenders are to be aggressive, overplay, deny and use strong closeouts on the opponent's good players. Meanwhile, the other part of the defense is passive because the opponent's weak or non-shooters are located in their area.

5. GIMMICKS:

I would recommend using gimmick defenses against all teams who are favored to beat your team. Most teams are unprepared against different gimmick defenses, this is why they will work if practiced a lot. Gimmick plans B, C and D are explained in chapter 8.

The Difference Maker

Each coach should have a preferred "difference maker" that makes their defensive philosophy a success. When you're trying to beat a top team with a solid defense, it is nice if your difference maker is a great shot blocker or inside defender. A lockdown defensive guard will have a big effect on the outcome of the game, but your team will usually lack these types of players.

In the 1930s-40s, most teams tried to make the difference maker a hard man-to-man defense; in the 1950s and 60s, the zone defenses were used as a difference maker. That was followed by different types of match-up zones. Most man-to-man defenses had their defense funnel the ball into the middle.

The KISS difference maker isn't a person, but the position of the close out that forces the action toward the left side of the floor, toward the gap-help. The defender's body should be right of the offensive player, by about half a body and at a slight angle. This way, there is no room for a shot and all the action passing and dribbling will be forced to the left side of the floor.

The "difference maker" placed in this overplay to the right of the offensive works because most players are skilled at driving, passing and shooting with their right hand. The closeout will force the opponent to beat you with their left hand. The closeout position with the defender's left hand up, makes it hard for the offense to get off a right-handed shot. The defender can be aggressive and ignore all fakes because he knows what the offense will do with the ball. The offense will attack the defense slower and with less confidence because they are forced to play differently than they practice. The gap helps stop drives and keeps the ball moving toward the left corner, where it is double teamed.

CONCLUSION

The defensive philosophy along with the two difference makers, gives the defenders clear roles that are easy, so players do their roles quicker, without needing time to think first. The defenders will act with aggressive confidence and there will be fewer breakdowns and fouls. The key is to perfect the two difference makers; 1. Pushing the ball left and 2. Give gap help.

Chapter 7
Defensive Skills and Drills

After going to clinics, collecting books, subscribing to magazines and talking with coaches, I found little about one-on-one defensive skills or how to teach drills.

To beat the good teams, individual defensive techniques must be mastered in every day drills. This is because players are working on their offense when playing on the driveway hoop or at the gym.

All defensive skills are important, but the defense selected must have short rotations of 10-12 feet so they can close out quickly on shooters or get to a gap help position. When players have good one on one defensive skills, team skills, know their roles and follow the scouting report, they will have success.

Defensive Drill Coaching tips

The following are a few coaching tips that will improve your defensive drills. Make the practice drills harder than game play, so the defender develops the toughness to succeed. In games, the offense will often gain a player advantage. So, put the defense at a disadvantage in drills by adding 1 or 2 extra offensive players.

Keep practice moving at a fast pace, with lots of reps for each player and no standing around. Most drills should involve full-court transition, so players know their role when going from defense to offense quickly with the numbered fast break (see chapter 14), from offense to a defensive press (chapters 11 & 12) or getting back to halfcourt defense. As the players master the drills, you can do some of them every other day or spend less time on them.

KEY DEFENSIVE DRILLS

TALKING

When on defense, talking is an underrated skill. Talkers who have been taught what to say are like having a coach on the floor, which can be intimidating to an opponent. Talking builds teamwork, excitement, and morale and gives guidance to teammates.

When first teaching defensive talking, have the player yell out what they are doing, such as "gap-help" or "post-deny." Always remind the defense to talk before you start a drill. Stop the drill when you don't hear a lot of talking. Have the non-talking defenders do a set of thirty-second cross-court line touches or ten pushups, then return to the drill again. Teams are only on defense for twenty seconds or less on most possessions, so players don't have to talk very long.

STANCE

The defender is ready to move quickly with a low, wide stance. Their base is strong and balanced and they can be physical with post players and cutters while taking up more floor space.

In practice, place players in a low, wide stance with their backs upward, toes and knees pointed outward, arms out wide, and their tails down low. Have them slowly take small steps down the gym floor. While doing this "duck walk" down the floor a couple times, have the players repeat positive sayings such as: "Stay low, defense wins, I love defense, I will get all the loose balls." etc.

SHORT DEFENSIVE SLIDES

When the defender has to move, they should jab with the lead toe and slide by pushing off with their back foot, but not cross their feet.

Put players in a good stance and have them slide three to five feet. Have them change direction on the coach's finger point and whistle, left, right, or back. The coach should mix in putting their hand behind their head and leaning forward. This is a key for the players to fall back on their butts like taking charge. This short slide is used in the bluff and retreat action when giving gap-help. The drill puts players in position to get loose balls, take a charge and move quickly into the gap help position.

CHARGES

Taking a charge isn't a natural basketball move and must be practiced in order for a player to understand how and when to take one. Taking charge is a good weapon to stop-gap drives, denying a cutter or blocking a moving player when he is driving into a trap.

The defender must be low, in a defensive stance, with their chin tucked down on their chest and with a forearm placed across their chest. Just before or at the beginning of contact, from the low position, the defender rocks back on his heels and falls on his butt. They slide backward while yelling very loudly. The forearm takes the hit and the falling body is only two feet from the floor with the chin tucked so the head doesn't hit the floor. The yell is to let the officials know that you have just been run over, so call the charge foul. The charge forces a turnover, causes a foul, is a great momentum changer and goes a long way toward firing up your team.

During practice in the first week or so, put down a mat for the players to fall on until they learn how to stay low, fall, and catch themselves with their hands. Start by pairing off the players. Each player takes ten to twelve charges while their teammate runs over them at half to three-fourths speed. Then, set up live gap-help drive situations. When a player takes a good charge, I would say, "good one" then the player would jump up and ring the bell several times. If the charge was poorly done, I would have the player repeat the charge until he gets a good one. (Chapter 26 explains the bell)

GAP-HELP BLUF & RETREAT

Bluffing is an underused and important defensive skill. The defender who is one pass away and to the left of the ball must move a step toward the ball and repeat bluffs. Then, they will retreat while yelling "gap-help." The footwork is the short movement of a three-to-six feet slide listed above under "Short Defensive Slides."

In practice, set two cones six feet apart or find two lines on the floor that are about six feet apart. Have the defender slide from cone to cone while yelling "gap-help." Do five sets of slides for twenty seconds with a short rest between each set. This will teach footwork, talking and readiness to give gap help. Bluff and retreat should be an ongoing move by defensive players, so they are ready to rotate on defense.

LOOSE BALLS

There will be several loose balls during a game. Loose balls are like getting an offensive rebound, it is a gained position.

Practice for this starts with the "Short Defensive Slide Drill" listed above when the coach points down to the floor. The drill will teach players how to get onto the floor without getting hurt. Next, match up two players and roll a ball between them or throw it up in the air. The two players then battle for the loose ball; the loser who doesn't get the ball must do five pushups.

LONG DEFENSIVE SLIDES-CLOSEOUTS

From the gap-help position, or bluffing and retreating, the defender uses the "Long Slide Action " is used to get into a close out position. When doing a long slide into a closeout, the defender must be in an aggressive up position and to the right of the offensive player by about a half of a body. They should have their left arm up to prevent a shot or to pressure a pass. This will force all passing or driving action toward the left side of the floor where the down right hand tries for a steal or deflection.

To practice long slides, the players pair up. The offensive player with the ball stands on the three point line. The defender stands ten-to-fifteen feet away doing bluff and retreat actions. The offensive player throws the ball about six-to eight feet in the air. This keys the defender to do the long slide footwork into the close out position. This action puts the defender in a close out position on the offensive player's right side just as he catches the ball that he has just tossed into the air. The offensive player tries to drive right, but is pushed left for two dribbles.

The defender should practice four sets of five long closeouts and then switch positions. As the defenders get better at closeouts, the toss into the air should be cut down to four to six feet so the defender must close out quicker to prevent a drive right.

Put the players along and outside the free throw area to practice long slides. On the whistle, the player uses the proper footwork starting with a toe point, long crossover, and slide hop. The player then repeats this footwork while moving back and forth across the key. They always touch the floor just outside the key with their foot.

This drill should be done for thirty seconds several times during practice. The players should be getting twenty-two to twenty-five touches outside of the key, with their outside foot, in thirty seconds. It is good to record the number of touches outside the key when doing the sixty seconds of slides. This long slide drill will teach the footwork needed to make long closeouts of twelve to fifteen feet or when getting into a gap-help position.

ELBOW SWING

An elbow swing is done from a defensive stance with feet moving. If the player swings their elbow fast to the right, it will open their right hip as they take a short jab step or toe point to the right. This is followed by a long crossover hop and a defensive slide or shuffle. This action will move the defender fifteen to twenty feet from their starting spot.

After this, the defender slings their left elbow, which opens the left hip and they repeat the long slide, footwork going to the left. The player moves down the floor, moving backward and left and right at a forty-five-degree angle. The elbow swing is done for two trips, down the length of the gym floor.

Next, coach the elbow swing and proper talk. Line the players across the court in a gap-help position. After saying: "gap-help" on the whistle, the players sling their right elbow back as they jap their right toe and do the "Long Defensive Slide." This slide should cover about twelve to fifteen feet; while doing this, the player should say: "Closeout." On the next whistle, they repeat this action going left as they sling their left elbow and say: "Gap Help." This action is repeated for several sets of 30 seconds. Most gap help in defense comes from the left side of the floor toward the ball.

POST DEFENSE

The post defender must never let the ball get into the low-post area with a direct pass. This means that the defender is always in a three-fourths deny position when the ball is two passes away and a full front position when the ball is one pass away.

To practice this, two defensive players pair up with two offensive post players on the blocks. The coach calls out: "top, wing, corner or away," and the defender goes to the proper defensive position using good footwork. They should also be yelling out what they are doing while reacting to the ball position the coach calls out. The coach is in a position to see and make corrections as needed after each called position of the ball. The coach starts slow with their calls so they can correct errors, and then they can make calls faster.

DEFENSIVE REBOUNDING

Defensive rebounding is all about getting physical and screening out on shots. The type of screen I like to teach all players when guarding a quick player is the step-through. On the step through, the defender faces the offensive player and waits until the offensive player cuts toward the hoop. Then, the defender steps forward and across their own body with their opposite foot (the step-through). At the same time, they slam their opposite forearm into the chest of the cutting offensive player. This pushes them away from the hoop. Next, the defender puts their butt into the offensive player to seal them off. The bigger players should use the reverse pivot into the offensive player type of screen out because the action is the same action used on an offensive screen and roll.

To teach defensive rebounding, I show the players two different types of defensive screen-outs and then pair them up. Set one is done at a walking speed. The players do a set of seven screen-outs against each other. Set two is at fifty percent effort. Set three at seventy-five percent speed and round four is done at full speed effort.

Another good drill is to put a ball on the floor six to eight feet from the paired offensive and defensive players. When the coach blows their whistle, the defenders yell "shot" and screen out the offensive player for four seconds while the offensive player tries to get the ball. Failure of the defender to keep the offensive player from touching the ball will cost the defensive player five pushups.

CHESTING OR DENTING THE CUTTER:

An offensive player will often cut to the basket after making a pass in hopes of a give-and-go play. A player may cut across the floor toward the ball to get a pass or a player may move to get a better position during the game. The rule I teach without exception is when the offensive player you're guarding makes a cut, never let the player cut your face!

The defender must always be a step above the cutter and toward the ball so they are cut off when the cutter tries to move toward the ball. The ball-side arm of the defender flashes to deny the pass position and the off-side forearm is slammed into the cutter's chest. The defender may draw a charge by stepping above the cutter and blocking movement toward the ball. The cutter is forced to go behind the defender toward the baseline while being slammed with the defender's forearm.

To coach this, have players pair up: one has the ball and they pass to a player on their left or right side. Then they try to cut to the hoop for a return pass, like a give-and-go play. The defender slides toward the ball on the pass and denies the cutter from cutting their face. Or you can have players pair up on one side of the floor and the offensive player tries to cut across the key toward the ball. The defender chests the cutter, as mentioned above and forces the cutter under the hoop or out toward the top of the key by riding him with a forearm. An offense player is never allowed a direct cut toward the ball, across the defender's face.

DOUBLE TEAM

Double teams on the ball are usually near a sideline, mid-court line or in a corner. The double team defenders must not make a reach in foul or let the offensive player split the double team. If an offensive player escapes a double team, make sure it is a dribble down a sideline toward the corner, but never toward the middle of the floor.

To work on this with the team, review where and how everyone is to angle their body. Remind them how to set the trap and how to handle any escape from a trap. Then, practice defense and traps from different locations on the floor.

BULL IN THE RING

If, for some reason, there isn't time to do all the defensive drills, do the bull in the ring drill, as it covers most of the defensive drills listed in this chapter.

To start this drill, place eight to ten players in a circle one big step out from the center jump ball circle and give one of these players a ball. Place two defenders inside of the circle, one on the ball and the other defender in the middle of the circle. The goal is for the offense to pass the ball to teammates as fast as possible with good fakes so that their passes are never deflected, stolen or thrown away. The passer must skip one receiving person when passing the ball. They can't pass to a player standing beside them. If their pass is deflected or stolen, the passer must drop and do five pushups.

The two defenders rotate on each pass, from pressuring the passer, to covering the middle of the circle, on each completed pass, the defenders must quickly trade roles. If the ball is ever tipped or thrown out of the circle, it is treated as a loose ball; everyone goes for it. The offensive passers try to keep the ball moving for fifty seconds. The length of that time the two bulls are in the ring, rotating, from closeout on the ball to being in the middle of the ring. I run this drill for fifty seconds and that leaves ten seconds to get two new bulls into the ring and the last two bulls in the circle. When first learning this drill, do two sets of thirty-second seconds, then do two sets of 50 seconds.

Conclusion

When working on all these defensive drills in practice, the coach must make sure the players perform at one hundred percent without fouling. Players must understand that there are two kinds of fouls: soft and hard.

Soft fouls include trying to block shots and reaching in fouls. Fouls will get your team beat, so soft fouls should be called out and followed with five pushups.

Hard fouls include taking a charge, performing a double team, giving gap-help, denying a cutter or screening out when defensive rebounding. Hard fouls will provide team success and should be rewarded.

Without these drills, players will do things their way and with a halfhearted effort, which will carry over into all parts of their defensive play. Doing these drills 4-5 times a week, the players will be able to perform at a level that makes the team philosophy listed in Chapter 6 successful.

Most of the defensive skills listed and explained above only take a few minutes each and they can be done every day in about forty minutes of your practice time. These drills should always be done before you work on team defense. Keep in mind that "Bull in the Ring" is the best defensive drill you can run in practice, so do it daily. Defense is half of the game, so you need to spend about half of your practice time on defensive drills and team defense.

DEFENSIVE SURREVY   NAME_____

Grades; A= great, B= good, C= avg., D=poor, F=poor

1.____ My closeouts are quick and aggressive.
2.____ My closeouts stop shots and force drives left.
3.____ I bluff and retreat or dance on defense.
4.____ On all shots I screen out the person nearest me.
5.____ I don't try to block shots, but stay on the ground.
6.____ I talk a lot on defense.
7.____ I'm aggressive on defense and bang players and play physical.
8.____ I know where to be on defense at all times.
9.____ I rotate early and often to far when the ball is passed.
10.____ I anticipate the next play not react to it.
11.____ I give 100% to stop all scoring in my area.
12.____ I talk a lot when on defense.
13.____ I step up and stop all gap drives near me
14.____ I try hard on defense because that's what wins games.
15.____ I will take charges.
16.____ I know and do my job when away from the ball.
17.____ I stay low in a good defensive stance.
18.____ I sprint to my defensive position.
19.____ I like to play physical.
20.____ I chin my rebounds and protect the ball with elbows.
____ My overall defensive grade.
***What if anything will you do different this year on defense and why??

CHAPTER 8
1-2-2 ZONE PLAYER ROLE

Over the last 15 years, the 1-2-2 Zone has become my favorite defense because it can be taught very quickly, size isn't a significant factor, and it is flexible. Another big key is that the gap help is always close by, within 6-12 feet. The following are the roles of each player's position in the 1-2-2 Zone defense.

POINT DEFENDER-2 player (Top of the zone)

The #2 player in our offense plays the right wing; this offensive player is our best outside offensive threat, capable of driving or taking long shots. They play the point or top position of the 1-2-2 defense. On all shots, the 2 defender (also called the top defender) bumps the nearest offensive player and then leaks out early, on a fast break sprint. The leak out by 2 is a sprint down the right side of the floor. Top defender doesn't screen out on shots and just bumps the nearest offensive player. They will be the first player down the floor on offense.

The run out by the top defender forces the other team's point guard to get back on defense. This defender is now in no position to press or pressure our point guard. It keeps them from crashing the offensive boards.

The job of the top defender on top of the zone depends on the scouting report. If the opponent's point guard is weak, top defender tries to push the ball out of the middle of the floor toward the left side of the floor. If pressure forces the ball to be picked up near midcourt, the opponent must bring players up toward midcourt for a pass. Now the ball isn't a threat to score and is two or three passes, or four or more dribbles, from a good shot.

If the offensive point guard has a poor outside shot, the top defender can play on the foul line, which gives the defense a more 3-2 look. The defense also plays in this location if the opponent has a good high post player. If the top defender is playing in this sag back position, they must learn to read the person with the ball. Then the defender can tell if a shot, dribble or pass will be coming next.

On all passes to the wing side of the floor, the point defender drops to the elbow on the ball side of the floor and keeps any pass from entering the high post or elbow area. They must also be ready to give gap help, if a drive comes their way, as they dance with a bluff and retreat movement.

Anytime the top defender is pressuring the ball, it is overplayed on the offensive player's right side. This way, the dribbler is pushed toward the left side of the floor using their left hand. The top defender must know the scouting report and, if their coach wants them to, pressure the ball or sag back so that the defense has a 3-2 look.

WING DEFENDERS-#1 & #3 MEN

The point guard, our player 1, plays defense on the left wing because most of our offensive action is pushed down the right side of the floor on the fast break, toward player 2, who has run out early on the fast break. Our offensive point guard plays left wing defender and is able to use their right hand on the fast break. They can attack fast, down the right side of the floor, on the break from a rebound, steal or inbounds pass after a made basket.

The right wing, defensive position is played by offensive player 3. They play the left wing on offense because their role is to run down the left side of the floor on the fast break. The right wing defender can get down the floor fast when on offense, without running across the floor.

When the opponent has the ball in the zone defense, both wings stand at a 45-degree angle, facing toward the sideline. From this position, the wings can see more of the playing floor. From the 45-degree angle, the wings are using the bluff and retreat action, from the elbow and toward the offensive wing player on their side of the floor. Meanwhile, they are watching the player with the ball for clues so they can get an early jump to their next rotation spot. The wing defenders are now ready to provide gap help if the point guard drives past the point defender toward them.

If the offensive point guard passes to the wing away from them, they drop several feet down their side of the key toward the hoop. If the ball is passed into the corner away from the wing defender, they drop to the inside rebound position on the backside block. The defense is now in a 2-3 zone position.

A pass from the point to the wing offensive player on a defender's side of the floor, the defender closes out very aggressively, on the high right-hand shoulder. This is so there is no room for a shot or a drive right. Any pass attempt into a post will be under a lot of pressure. The best option is to dribble and pass toward the left side of the floor or back toward the midcourt. The wing defenders can close out on the offensive wing with an aggressive high shoulder action because they will have gap help on a drive going left.

If a pass is made into the corner, on a wing's side of the floor, they drop toward the ball side block and prevent any pass into the low post. From this position, they are ready to trap if that is the game plan. If a pass is made from the corner back to their wing area, they will use proper, long, and fast footwork for a close-out on the wing's right hand. All actions by the point and wing defenders will force the ball to the left side of the floor and out of the offensive player's strong right hand.

POST DEFENDER 4 & 5 MEN

When the ball is on top of the key with the offensive point guard, the post defenders face the sideline at a 45-degree angle, just above the block. The post defender (4 and 5) must place their forearm on the chest of the offensive post player. This arm bar prevents a flash to the high post or an attempt to screen or move across the key.

If the ball is passed to the wing on the post defender's side, the post defender (4 and 5) steps in front of the offensive low post by swinging their bottom leg in front of the post player. The defender is now in a 100% full front position, on the offensive post.

From a full front on the offensive low post, the defender must close out on an offensive corner player if there is a pass there. The corner closeout is made by the right post (4 or 5), with their butt pointed toward the baseline wall. Their baseline foot is on the out-of-bounds baseline, so there is never a baseline drive. The left post (4 or 5) forces a drive down the baseline where it is trapped behind the backboard.

If there is a wing pass away from the offside defensive post, the defender (4 or 5) drops two steps into the key under the basket. If there is a corner pass away from them, they slide across the key putting their baseline leg and arm in a ¾ denial position around the offensive low post with their butt pointed toward out of bounds.

If there is ever a completed post pass, the offensive post with the ball can't turn baseline for a shot or drive. The ball side wing, who has dropped down, will double team the post with the ball if they turn up toward the foul line.

The two post defenders (4 and 5) must cover the entire baseline from corner to corner. If the post defenders are getting beaten with corner shots and drives, you must trap the corner passes so the opponent won't pass the ball there.

STRENGTHS OF THE 1-2-2 ZONE

The 1-2-2-floor set has several strengths; it is flexible and has easy, short shifts that can be taught very quickly. The defense prevents one-on-one basketball plays by the offense. Players use the same relative rotations and movements as the ball is moved.

It will take more than 1 or 2 passes to get a shot, 3+ passes for a good shot. The Zone is ready to pressure the offensive point guard and the wings, who are often the best shooters.

Most three-point shots are from the top or wing area, so you limit the three-point shots taken from those areas. The defense will reduce the number of team and individual fouls committed.

The top three defenders are usually the quickest players and they have help if they try for a steal and miss the ball. The defense is strong against the post attack because there is pressure on the outside passers and the post is fronted at all times.

Players are in a position to fill their fastbreak lanes on a steal, loose balls, rebounds or any fast break situation. This is because they play defense on the same side of the floor as their fast break, running lanes. The Zone keeps the two best rebounders near the basket.

Each zone formation has a lot to offer; the 2-3 zone is particularly strong at protecting the basket and securing rebounds. The 1-3-1 zone plugs the middle of the key and stops drives into that area. The 1-2-2 Zone defense has strengths, but it requires adaptations and adjustments to change the game's pace or counter the opponent's strengths.

WEAKNESS OF THE 1-2-2 ZONE

Some coaches don't like the 1-2-2 Zone defense because it doesn't conserve energy when played aggressively. When played aggressively, depth or a good bench is needed. Additionally, the defense flexes, adjusts, and moves frequently as the ball moves, requiring player movement and teamwork from all five defenders. The five players must move in unity and stay in their roles. If one defensive player fails at his individual responsibility, there will be a hole in the defense. This defense takes smart, well-conditioned, quick players. Also, the middle of the key, high post and corners are vulnerable without defensive adjustments and traps.

TRAPPING ACTION;

For 1-2-2 zones to be successful, you must use traps. Traps are used to stop good players, to steal the ball, and force a lesser player to make plays. The most common way the traps are defeated but not scored on is when a cross-court pass is made. The trapping defenders must force a lob, skip pass, or cross-court and make sure the pass is caught off the volleyball court. We have a rule that, on all skip-lob passes out of a trap, the defense jumps back into a 1-2-2 Zone defense. By dropping back into our tight 1-2-2 zone, it keeps the defense from getting burned, so they can live to trap on another play.

CORNER TRAPS

A corner trap occurs when the offense makes a pass into the corner, with the ball-side post player (4 or 5) and the ball-side wing player (1 or 3) trapping the ball in the corner. The top defender (2) moves over and denies a pass from the corner to the ball side offensive wing. If there is a ball-side post player, they are fronted by the offside post defender. This leaves two offensive players on the weak or far side of the floor to be guarded by one defender. This defender is outnumbered 2 to 1, so they must split the difference between the two offensive players. They must shade toward the most dangerous while reading the passer for a clue as to where the ball will be passed. If the trap is broken a few times by the same skip pass, the outnumbered, backside defender must cheat and be ready for a steal next time. This corner trap must be used if the defense is getting beaten from the corner! For more on this trap action, see the diagrams at the end of this chapter.

WING TRAP ACTION

The wing trap starts when the offensive point guard passes the ball to an offensive wing. The top defender (2) follows the pass and traps the player with the ball, assisted by the ball-side wing defender (1 or 3). The offside defensive wing defender (1 or 3) moves up and denies any pass back to the point guard at the top of the key. The ball-side post defender (4 or 5) moves out to deny any pass to the ball-side corner. The backside post defender (4 or 5) will split the difference between the remaining two offensive players, while shading toward the biggest threat.

If the wing trap is broken with a skip pass across the floor and off the volleyball court, all five defenders rotate back into the tight 1-2-2 Zone while the ball is in the air from the pass. If the offense breaks the same skip pass 2-3 times, the backside defender who is outnumbered will be ready to cheat and steal the pass next time, just as in the corner trap. For more information on this trap action, refer to the diagrams at the end of this chapter.

TRAPPING CONCLUSION

I like to trap either the corner, wing or both when playing weak teams. Trapping the last 35 seconds of the quarter gives us the ball back, allowing us to work on our delayed offense and take the last shot of the quarter. Getting the ball back with the trap and running the delay offense the last 35 seconds of the quarter gets your team the last shot of the quarter.

Late in the season or the second time through the league, it's easy to think the traps won't work, as the opponent knows that they will be trapped. However, your team has been trapping all season, so they have improved, and the opponent's preparation is with their subs, who can't match your team's execution.

Many teams dislike the half-court trap because when it is broken, often a score is given up. Most coaches who feel this way spend little time on trapping during their practice sessions and haven't scouted their opponent, so they can't adjust their trap accordingly. I like to trap after a score; I call it "Playing With The House's Money." Nothing can fire up a team and build team confidence more than using traps to beat a good team.

KISS BASKETBALL

12 Tight Defense

(12-tight)
A

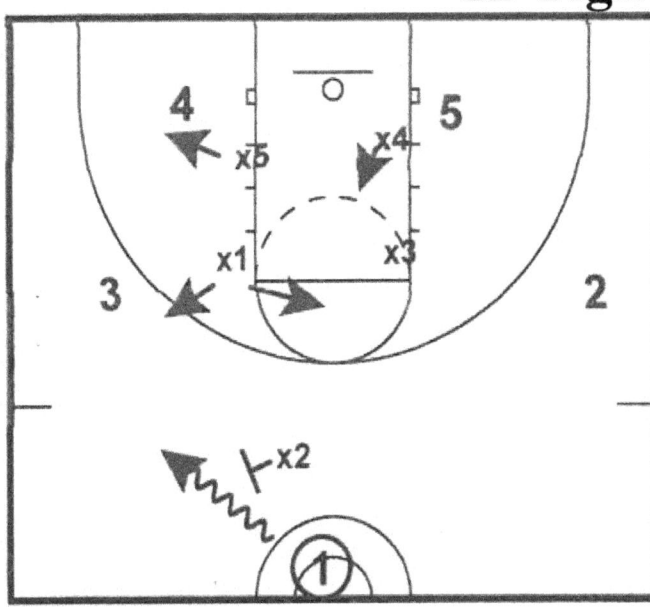

X2 The top defender, picks up the ball and over plays, pushing the ball out of the middle of the floor. The other four defenders bluff and retreat from a 45* angle and take away all passes into the middle of the defense, forcing a wing pass.

(12-tight)
A

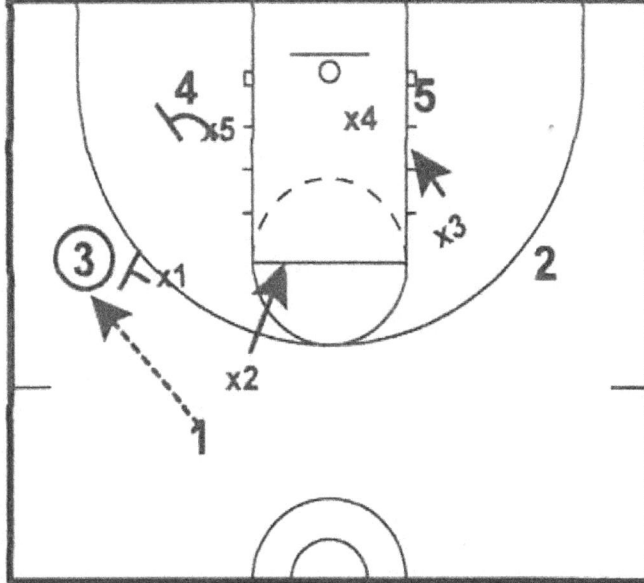

On the pass to 3 defender X1 plays an aggressive close out in 3's high shoulder, pushing the ball toward the left. X5 does a full front on 04, X5 and X2 are yelling gap help!!

(12-tight)
A

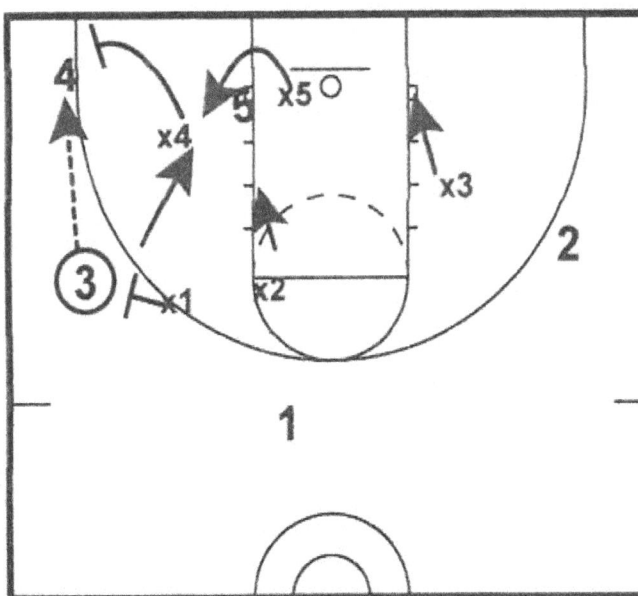

Pass to the corner. X4 does an aggressive close out on 04, protecting the baseline. X1 drops toward the post and gives gap help. X5 wraps around the low post from the baseline side, X3 drops down to backside block.

(12-tight)
A

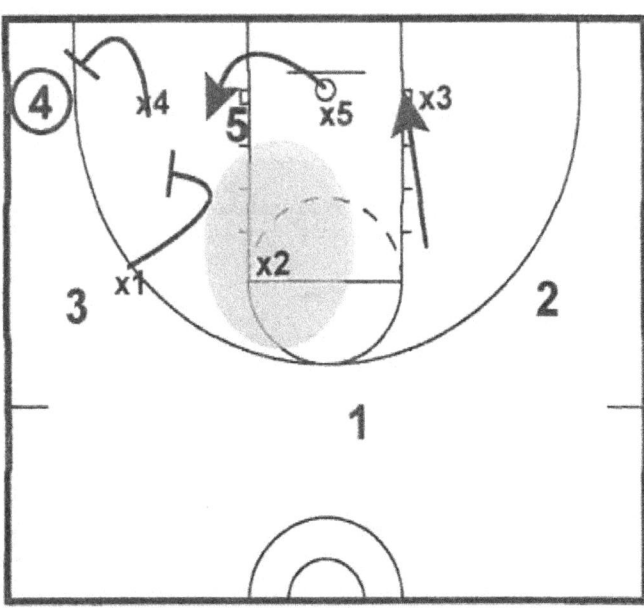

On the corner pass X4 covers the ball. X1 drops with the proper footwork to give and yell gap help. X5 does a 3/4 rap around denial on 5, X2 covers the elbow key area. X3 gets all back side rebounds.

KISS BASKETBALL

12 Tight into corner trap & wing trap

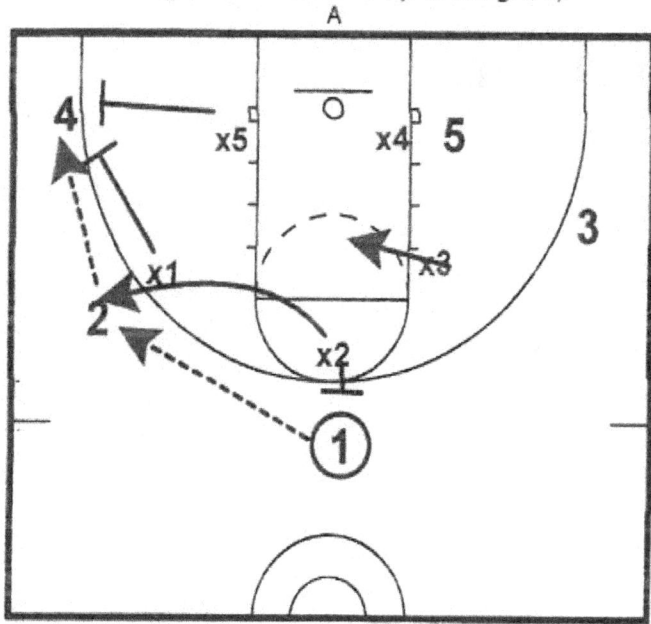

CORNER TRAP 12 tight prevents any pass inside of the three point line but leaves any player in the corner open. x5 and x1 trap the corner

12 Tight into corner trap & wing trap

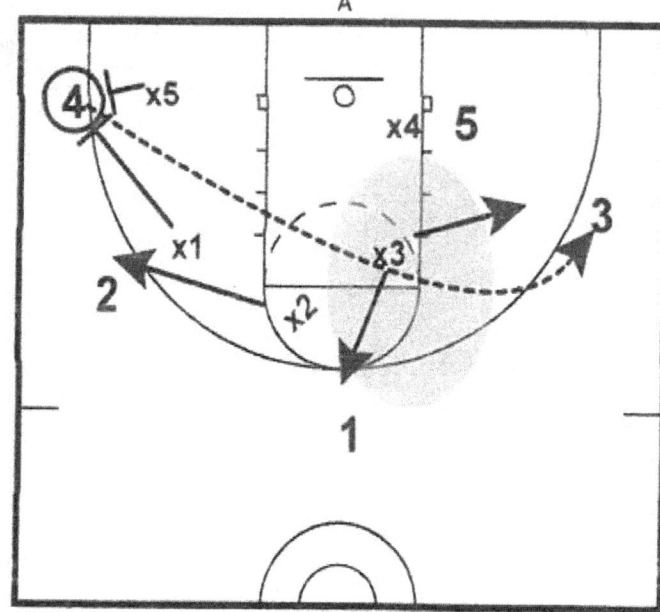

CORNER TRAP The corner pass is trapped by x5 and wing x1, the ball side wing is taken by x2. The back side defender x3 reads player 4's eyes as he covers 1 & 3, looking to steal a skip pass. A completed skip pass off the volleyball court and we return to 12 tight defense.

12 Tight into corner trap & wing trap

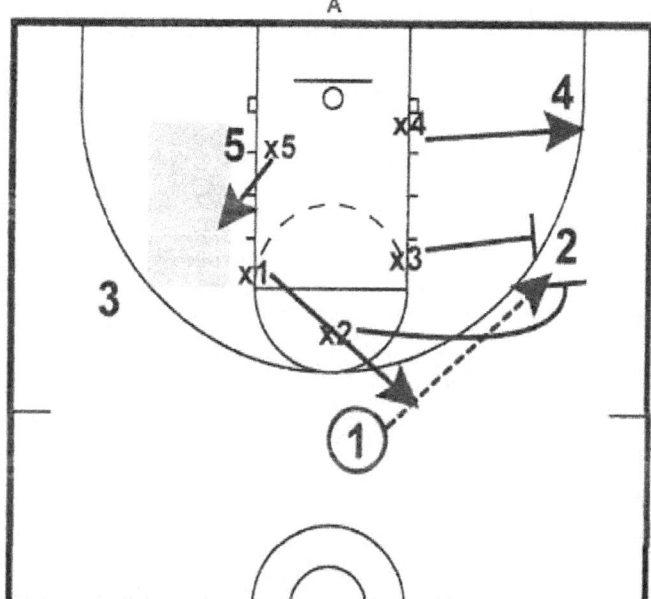

WING TRAP When the pass is made to 2 on the wing, x3 and x2 double team the ball. x4 denies a pass to the corner. x1 denies a return pass to the point guard. X5 must cover two men on the back side.

12 Tight into corner trap & wing trap

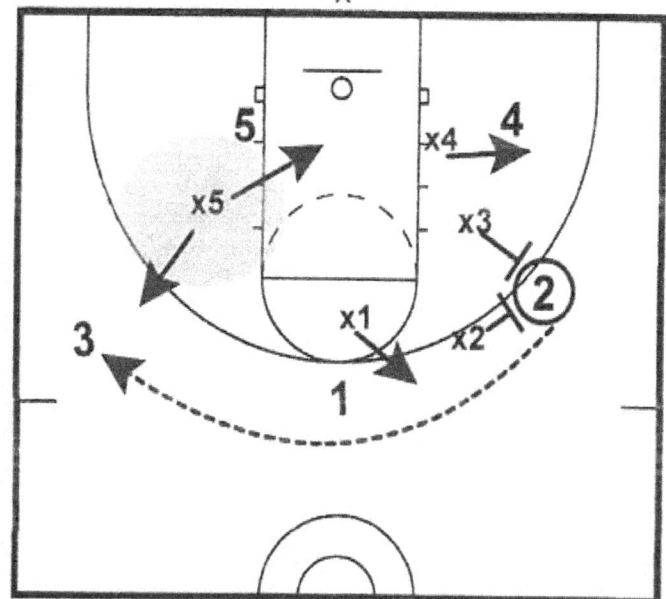

WING TRAP x3 and x2 trap the wing, X1 and x4 are denying a ball side pass. x5 must play between 5 and 3, read the passers eyes and gamble on his cross court pass. On all completed skip passes the team returns to tight 12.

CHAPTER 9
DEFENSIVE PLAN "B-C-D"

There are several things to consider when picking a team defense. The defense must fit with your team's physical ability, size, quickness, experience, schedule, and practice time. Next, I like using an uncommon defense and teach it using adjustments and rotations from our tight 12 defense.

I chose the 1-2-2 Zone defense because players are already set to cover the main outside shooting areas, including the point, wings, and corners. But sometimes it takes more than just a good team to beat them; this is where plans B, C, and D are used. Plans B, C, and D are easy to learn, they require little teaching time, and they are played under the same defensive rules and philosophy.

Plan B: "Triangle and 2 Defense."

The triangle and 2 defense are used when playing against a very good team that has two exceptional scorers. In this case, we want to force the weaker scorers, players 3, 4, or 5, to beat us outside of 17 feet. This way, the defense jams up the basket area to stop inside scoring or drives.

The two weakest defenders play one-on-one on the opponent's two best offensive players. They play in a 100% denial position, face guarding their opponent with their butt pointed to the ball, this position is key. They need to face-guard their offensive man, and if screened, they have to get back on their man; there is no switching. If their offensive player gets the ball, they are to follow the rules of in-your-face, so there is no shot and all dribbles are pushed to the left. They will always have help from a zone player on drives across the 3 point line and if they get screened.

The bottom two defenders of the triangle have their regular 1-2-2 zone rotation rules. (see chapter 7) At the top of the triangle is our best defender who stays between the foul line and the three-point line, 17 feet from the hoop. They also need to stay in line with the ball and the basket. If one of the three weaker offensive players has the ball near the three-point line, the defender steps toward the three-point line and puts his arm into the shooter's face. This forces the third-to-fifth-best scorer to shoot a three-point shot or a deep two-point shot over a defensive arm.

If one of the opponent's best two players gets the ball, the top player of the triangle zone defense steps out and double-teams any drive. If one of the defenders, who is one of the two best offensive players, gets screened or rubbed off his man, the top zone defender covers him until the defender can get back on his man and says, "I got him."

The strength of this defense lies in its ability to neutralize the two best offensive players by employing denial and double teams, thereby forcing the other three weaker scorers to carry the scoring load. The defense has a good rebound triangle, so the offense will only get one shot. The defense will destroy the offensive flow and game plans. The two players being played man-to-man will often force poor shots if they get the ball, as they will receive few touches or good looks at the basket.

Plan C "Man-Z"

If the opponent has four very good shooters and one weak outside shooter, or a point guard who sets up teammates and doesn't look to score much, then Plan C, also known as "Man-Z," is a good defense to use. I like this defense because the rules and adjustments are easy and fast to learn.

The four players on the four shooters will face guard in a 100% denial position, butt to the ball, doing everything possible to prevent their offensive player from getting open for a pass or cutting toward the ball. If an offensive player should get a pass, the defender performs a hard close-out on the right side to take away any shot. They force all dribbles to the left; they will get help from the Z-Man, who will step up above the foul line to double the ball on dribbles that cross the 3-point line. The four, man-to-man defenders will switch all screens and will yell at the Z-Man defender to let them know where the Z-ed, offensive player is located.

The Z man defender could be any player, but it is best if they are smart, good on defense, and have some size. They don't have to screen anyone out on shots and are free to crash the boards. Their defensive position is always slightly above the foul line, positioned between the ball and the basket. They must always be ready to double the ball if it is ever dribbled past the three-point line.

The Z-ed offensive player will miss a few shots and stop shooting as they will feel pressure not to shoot. The Z-ed offensive player needs to be a low-percentage shooter who has limited range and shooting isn't his normal role. If they score 10-12 points and your defense is shutting down the four good shooters, the mission is accomplished.

Plan D: "Double Z"

The Double Z defense is a gimmick defense, designed to stop the three best shooters on your opponent's team. The three weakest defenders, man up on the three best shooters and play in a 100% denial position face to face, without watching the ball. They must play physical, as the offensive players will try to cut their faces and move toward the ball. If this happens, they must chest the cutter and look to take a charge. The three man-to-man defenders follow all our defensive rules. If their man gets the ball, they must close out in an up position, pressuring the ball to go left with help coming from one of the two Z players.

The top Z defender plays near the foul line and stays between the ball and the basket. They must stop all dribble penetration, from the point or wing area, if the ball crosses the three-point line. If a good shooter is positioned below the foul line or in the corner with the ball, the bottom zone defender must move to the three-point line to provide help. The top Z defender must drop down to protect the area around the basket.

The two Z defenders will only go out 15-17 feet and put up their hands to contest the 4th and 5th best opponent scorers. We will give up an 18-20 foot shot to them.

One thing that makes the 1-2-2 Zone, Triangle, and Double Z defenses so effective is that the opponent is very likely not prepared for this type of defense. Your defense will force the opponent to beat you with their two weaker scorers. The opponent's offense will be out of sync and the players will be uncomfortable. It is essential to trust your defensive plan. If the opponent scores a few baskets from their weakest players, don't panic; over time, the percentages will even out.

KISS BASKETBALL

Plan B: E Triangle Defense +2 Defense

TRIANGLE AND 2
A

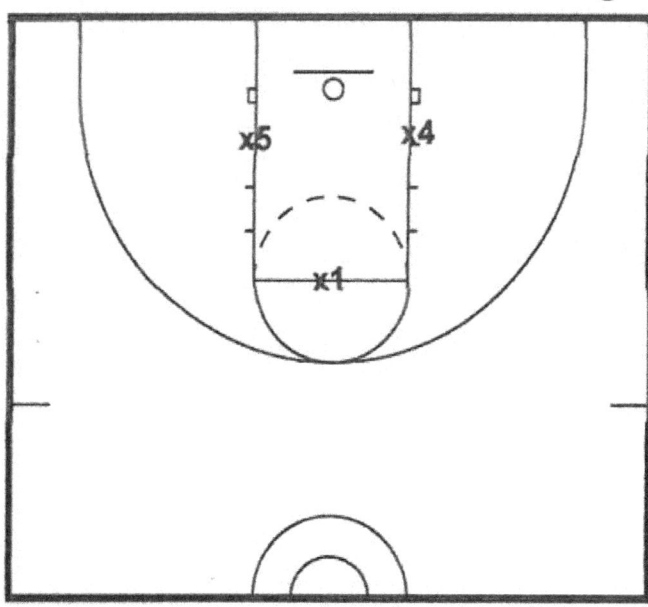

Players X1, X4, X5 set up in a triangle defense and their rotations are the same as in the tight 12 defense.

TRIANGLE AND 2
A

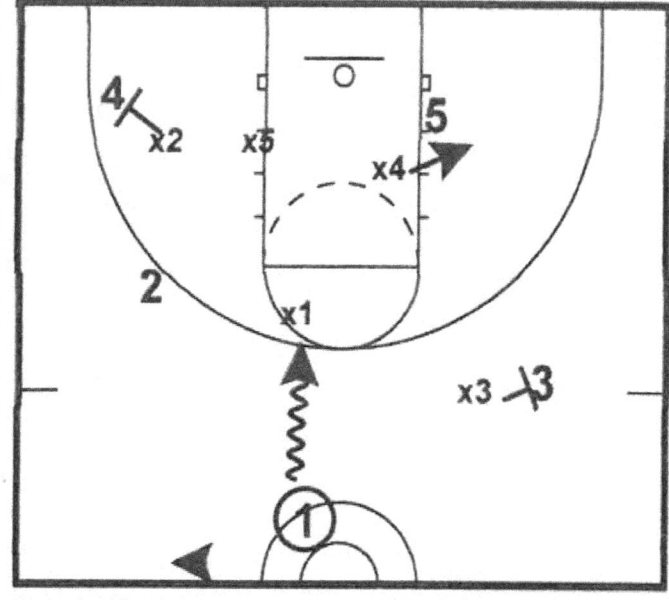

X2 and X3 over play and deny the two best offensive players forcing the ball left. X1 steps out to double team 2 or 4 if they dribble cross the three point line and are above the foul line. X1 must also cover any open player above the foul line.

TRIANGLE AND 2
A

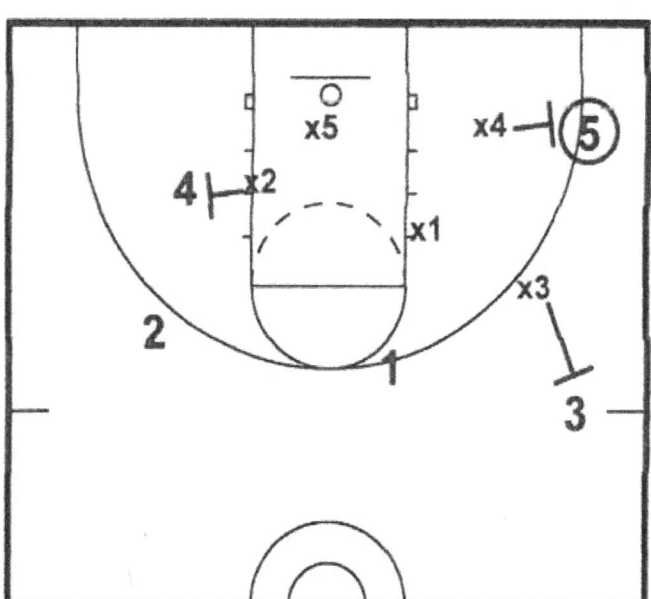

X4 rotates to the corner to defend the ball and X1 gives gap help. X3 and X4 deny with their butts toward the ball to deny ball cuts, they don't look at he ball.

TRIANGLE AND 2
A

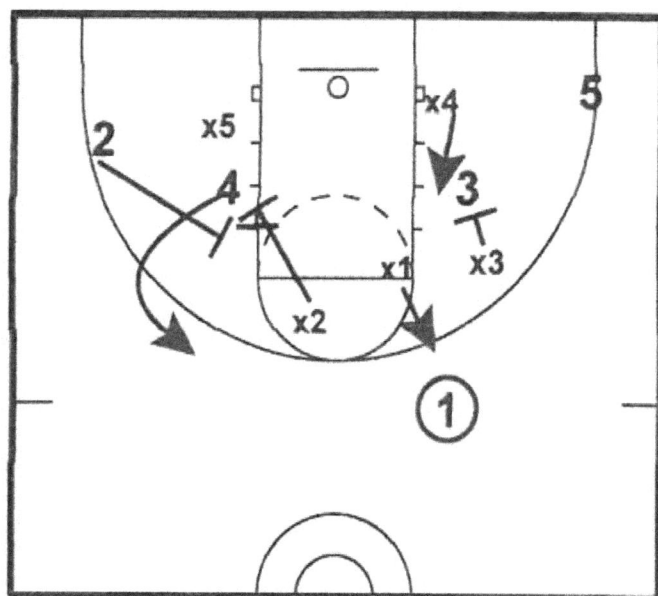

X5, X4 cover any lop pass on a post up as the defenders X2 and X3 will have their backs to the ball. If X2 or X4 get screened they fight to get back on their man, no switching.

KISS BASKETBALL

Plan C: Z Man Defense

Z-MAN DEFENSE
A

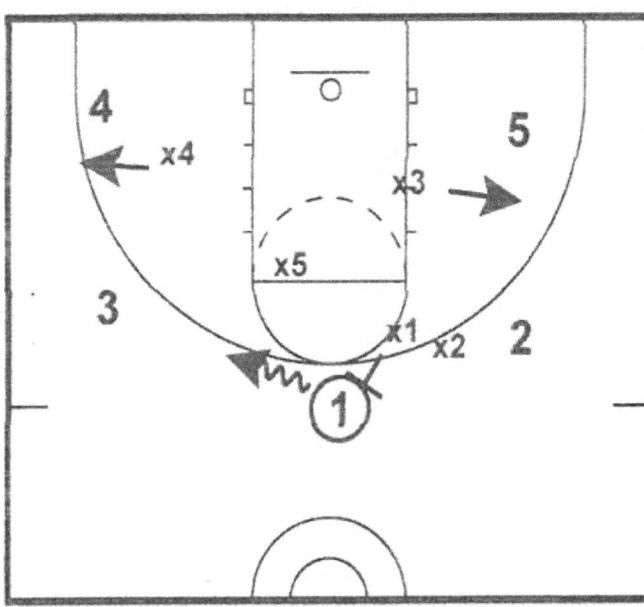

Players X1, X2, X3, and X4 over play and deny their man the ball. If they get the ball they close out hard on the right hand leaving no room for a shot and making all dribbling go left with the left hand.

Z-MAN DEFENSE
A

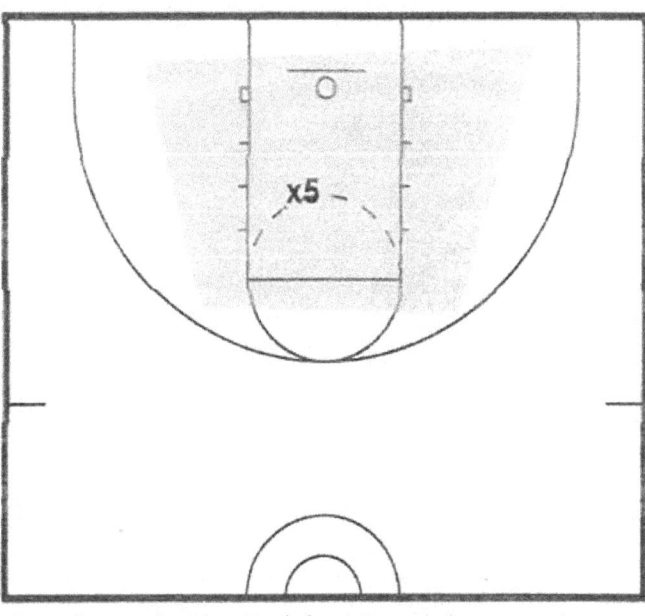

The yellow is the Z-MANs defensive area, there must be no scoring in this area.

Z-MAN DEFENSE
A

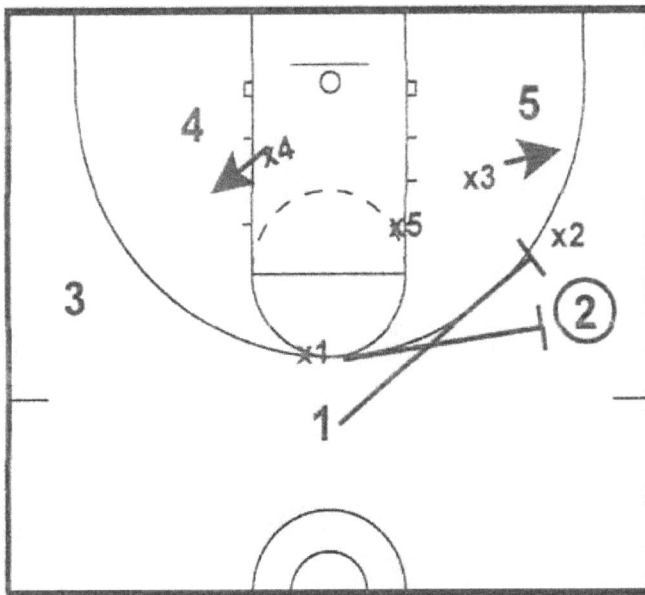

Ball screens are to switched aggressively with lots of talk. X5 is ready to help if the ball gets out of the double team and drives toward the hoop and X4 is two passes away sagging and ready to yell of 3 goes behind the Z-MAN to the hoop.

Z-MAN DEFENSE
A

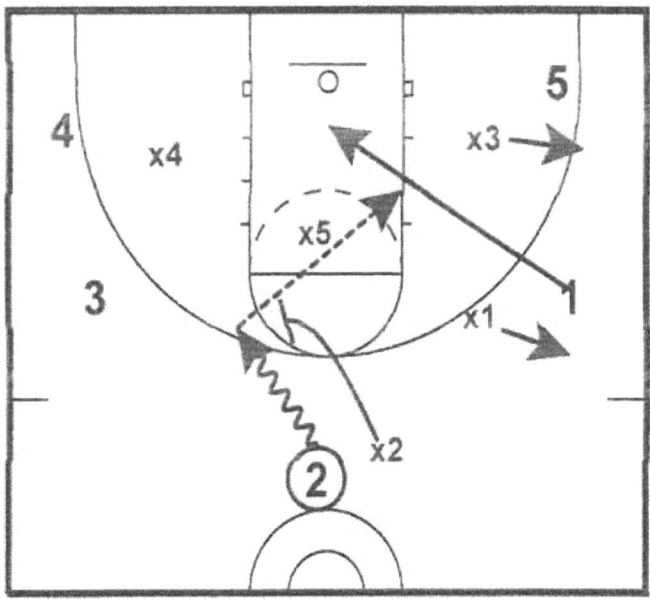

The Z-MAN must cover all backdoor cut, X4 and X3 could also help as they are two passes from the ball.

KISS BASKETBALL

Plan D: Double Z Defense

DOUBLE Z

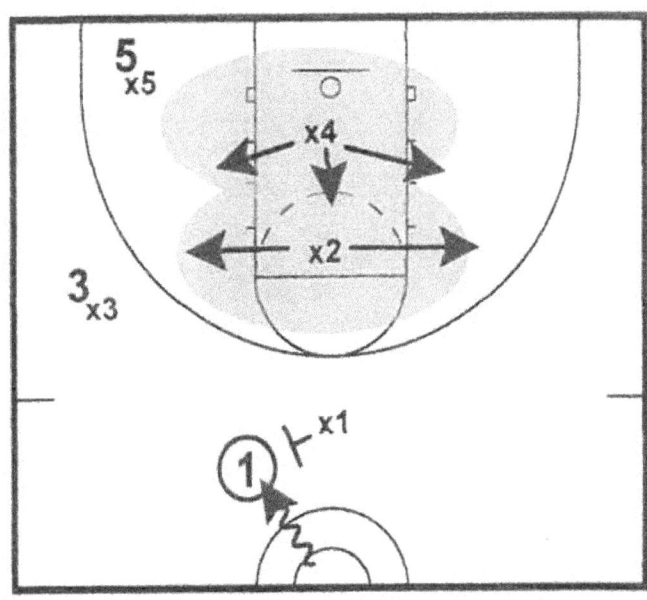

X1, X3, X5 man up on the three best offensive players and 100% deny them a pass. If their man gets the ball they close out tough and over play forcing only a dribble to the left. X2 zones the area above the foul line and x4 protects the basket area

DOUBLE Z

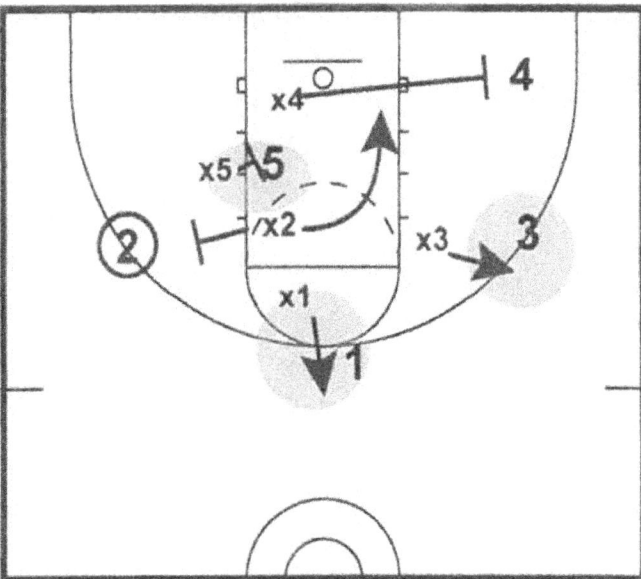

X2 goes out 17 feet to cover any unguarded offensive player above the foul line and X4 protect the hoop. X4 goes out 17 feet to cover any unguarded offensive player below the foul line and X2 drops under the hoop.

DOUBLE Z

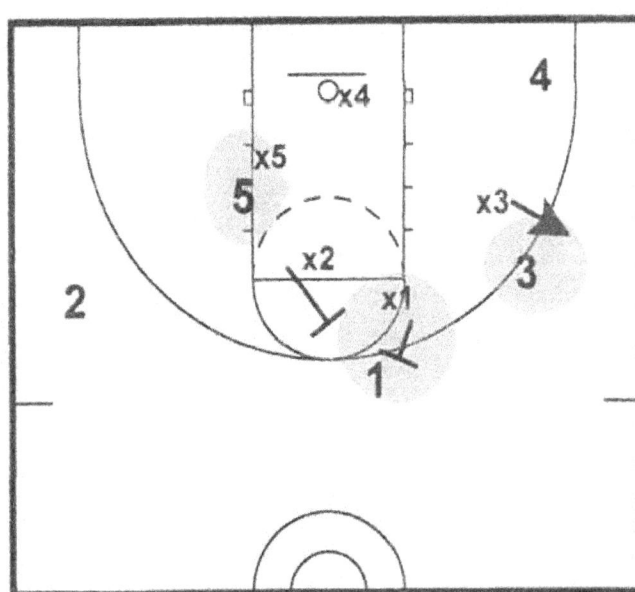

The three man defender, play tough, over play, deny and switch all screens, while X2 and X4 double the ball if it crosses the three point line in their area.

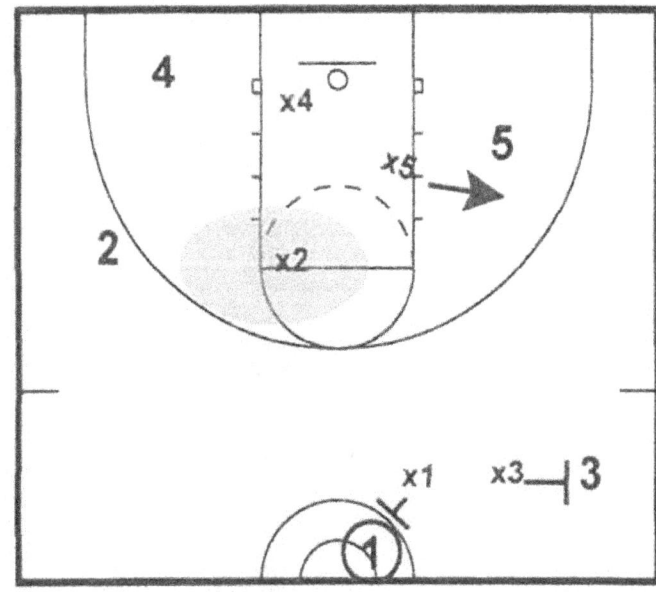

x1, x3, & x5 should pick up their men at mid court and deny them the ball. The goal is to force the 4th and 5th best players to carry the scoring and from outside of 17 feet

CHAPTER 10
PAW THE Half-COURT TRAP

Over the last 20 years, I have transitioned to using the half-court trap. I named the half-court trap PAW after our school's mascot, a Husky dog. From the sideline, I formed a 'PAW' with my hand, high in the air, so the team would know when I wanted them to get into the half-court trapping position on the floor.

The following are several reasons I like the half-court trap-PAW. Steals made from the half-court trap have fewer turnovers and quicker scores, as there is an open backcourt free of defenders. When in the Paw trap, there is less court for the defense to cover and less quickness or energy is needed. The offense must cross half court within 10 seconds, which adds pressure due to the risk of a time violation. If the PAW trap is broken and the ball is passed out of the trap, the offense will often be rushed and turn the ball over or miss an easy shot because of the fast pace, or a less skilled player may take the shot.

You can mix up which side of the floor you trap. For example, you may trap only the side of your opponent's best player, so if the trap is broken, the skip pass is to a weak or non-shooting player. Also, it's easy to drop back into PAW from your offense, regardless of whether you made or missed your shot. It is a team defense that yields instant rewards when successful, so it builds pride among the players and fans love it.

GETTING INTO PAW

When the defense is setting up the 1-2-2 Paw halfcourt zone trap, all five defenders sprint back to the half-court line. The top defender stops at the top of the center jump circle, 10 feet into the backcourt. The other four defenders cross midcourt and match up with the nearest offensive player across halfcourt. It is key that these four players match up man-to-man and overplay the offense in a ¾ denial position; this way, there can't be a completed pass across the half-court line to the person they are guarding. Most often, there will be two offensive players left in the backcourt: the rebounder/inbound passer and the person with the ball. The frontcourt man-to-man defenders will outnumber the offense 4 to 3, so it should be easy to deny or steal a pass across the half-court line.

When the ball does start across the half-court line, it must be on the dribble, not a pass. As the ball crosses half-court, the four man-to-man defenders leave the person they are guarding and jump into their zone trap spots. This move from man denial into the zone trapping position must be well-timed. If the man-defenders move too soon or too late, offensive players will be left open for a press-breaking pass in the middle of the floor. This leaves the defense outnumbered near the basket.

TOP DEFENDER IN PAW

The 10-second count is on, so the ball must be advanced across the half-court line. When there are two offensive players in the backcourt, they may pass the ball back and forth to each other. This is so the top defender starts on the jump circle in the backcourt. He must not overcommit to either person in the backcourt, but instead slide 5-6 feet toward the ball. If there is only one person in the backcourt with the ball, the top defender may apply more pressure to push the ball toward a sideline.

The ball-side wing and point defender double-team the ball just as it dribbles across the half-court line. The wing and point who trap the ball have two goals. First, they must keep the ball from splitting the double team and being dribbled onto the volleyball court or getting onto the middle of the floor. Second, there can be no fouling when trapping.

If the dribbler beats the trap, it must be down the sideline and the the wing defender on the ball will push the dribbler to the corner where it will be trapped. At this time, the defender's roles are the same as when playing our corner trap out of the 1-2-2 Zone. (chapter 9) The point defender now guards the ball side wing, so that a pass can't be made out of the corner trap.

BALL SIDE WING DEFENDER IN PAW

The ball-side wing defender is guarding man-to-man in a denial position on anyone in their ball-side area, so the ball must be dribbled, not passed, across half-court. The ball-side wing defender must time his movement out of man-to-man denial, up into the zone trap with the point defender. This way, they both reach the ball at the same time. The two defenders try to apply pressure, without fouling, so that the dribbler will pick up the ball. The wing defender can't leave his man too early, especially when making a midcourt trap, or the dribbler won't dribble across half court with the ball.

If there are two offensive players on the ball side wing's area in the backcourt, they must guard the one closest to midcourt in denial until they rotate into the zone trap. If the dribbler beats the wing trap dribbling down the sideline toward the corner the wing defender on the ball will push the dribbler to the corner.

OFF-SIDE WING DEFENDER IN PAW

As the ball is dribbled across half court, the offside wing leaves the person they were denying, in a man-to-man position and goes to the middle of the floor between the center jump circle and the top of the key. From this position, they 100% deny anyone in the area. If there are two players in this area of the floor, he takes the player closest to the ball. The defender must not allow a completed pass into this area. The pass out of a trap to the middle of the floor is one of the main areas the trapped will look to complete a pass.

BALL SIDE POST DEFENDER

When the ball is in the backcourt, the ball-side post defender plays man defense in a 100% denial position, several feet above the person they are guarding. If there are two offensive players in this area, they call for help and go to deny the offensive player closest to the ball or the mid-court area. The ball-side post defender watches the ball-side wing defender. When the defensive wing leaves his position to trap the ball mid-court, the post defender rotates up to deny the pass to the offensive player that the wing player has just left. This is the most common pressure, breaking pass. The post defender must rotate early so that he can get above the offensive wing player by 4-5 feet, thereby denying or stealing the pass. This position, between the ball and 5 feet above the receiver, allows for a steal of the pass without fouling the receiver. The ball-side post player can make this rotation quickly if they start 8-10 feet above the post area person they are playing man-to-man denial on.

OFF-SIDE POST DEFENDER

The offside post defender plays above their man when the ball is in the backcourt and allows no deep pass from the backcourt. They play in this denying position to invite a long lob pass that they can steal. At all times, they must be ready to chest any cutter breaking up toward mid-court for a pass. When the ball is being double-teamed near mid-court, this defender will be left with two players to guard on the backside of the floor. The offside post must guard the offensive player who is the biggest danger to score.

Conclusion

The four defenders that get back across half court must match up man-to-man and overplay in a denial position so that their man can't get a pass from the backcourt. This is key to Paw's success, as the ball can't be passed across the half-court line, and the defense must force the ball to be dribbled across half-court toward a sideline. The only open pass from a double-teamed must be a forced, cross-court, lobbed skipped pass, to an offensive player off the volleyball court. Lob passes are slow and in the air for a long time, making them easy to intercept.

When trapping, don't accept players making fouls. If a player makes a foul when going for a steal of a pass, it's usually because they rotated late and weren't above the receiver.

It's okay to gamble on cross-court passes when going for a steal. On completed cross-court passes, we drop back into the 1-2-2 Zone while the ball is in the air and yell 'tight 12-tight 12.' If we are behind on the scoreboard, we stay in the trap on all passes.

Make sure your players have handouts and drawings of how and what they are expected to do, while filling their role in Paw. Drawings are located at the end of this chapter. Before practicing PAW, review roles and ask lots of questions. When there is success in practice, give lots of praise.

You will soon find that you can't trap when certain players are on the floor, because they are often the same players who are out of position during both practice and games. It is key for your players to see film, as they will make improvements faster from watching it than from being told or shown their mistakes.

Because timing and player positions are so crucial, the Paw trap will require a significant amount of practice time. After 61 years of using Paw, I have found that often the offense is content to break the press and will not attack the hoop, allowing your team to press for free. Most coaches will abandon the use of a half-court trap immediately if it results in a basket, so don't rush to make this decision. The players will adjust as they are well-trained.

Paw defense is hard work, quickness and smarts will overcome the lack of size. Gimmick defenses and the Paw trap are the main reasons my teams have had 55 winning in 61 seasons, produced many upsets, and made it into postseason games.

KISS BASKETBALL

Paw: the Half Court Trap Defense

1/2 court trap PAW
A

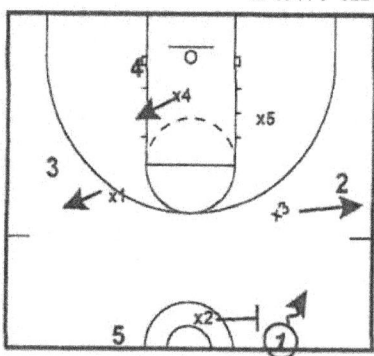

The top defender picks up the ball in back court and herds it toward either sideline, making the weakest player dribble across half court if possible.

1/2 court trap PAW
A

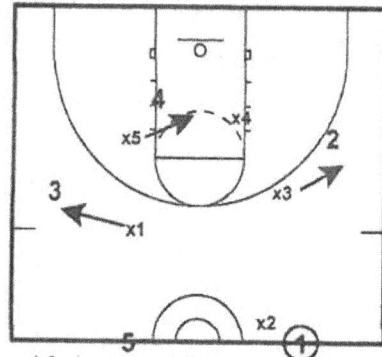

All other front court defenders must match up on the nearest man, over play and deny any pass from back court to front court.

1/2 court trap PAW
A

Force the ball to be dribbled across the half court line. NOT PASSED!!!!! As all receivers are over played and denyed

1/2 court trap PAW
A

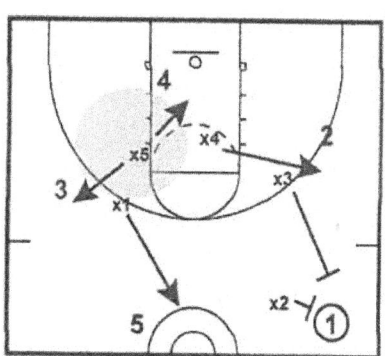

As the ball crosses half court on the dribble, the defenders leave their man & rotate to their zone trap/deny spots on the ball side of the floor.

1/2 court trap PAW
A

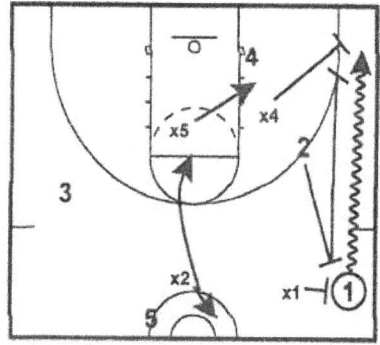

If the dribbler escapes the mid court trap, force him down the sideline and trap in the corner, other defenders rotate toward the basket.

1/2 court trap PAW
A

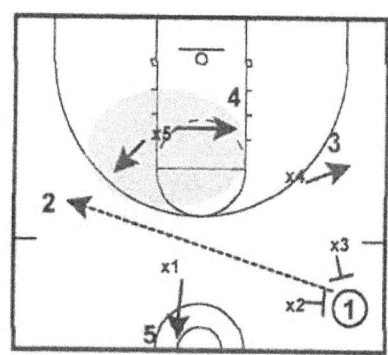

Only possible open pass from the trap should be cross court. The backside defender, will have two offensive players to guard, he must read the passers eyes and gamble for a steal.

CHAPTER 11
FULL COURT MAN CENTER FIELD

I love to press when on defense, but good teams will easily destroy a full-court or back-court press. So, I like the "Two and Out" philosophy or you may want to play "One and Out." If the opponent completes two passes against the full-court press in the backcourt, the press is over and your team gets back to the half-court defense. The exception is when you are playing an average or poor team or a team without good guards.

I love using a full-court press when you can exploit a one-player advantage (5 vs. 4) safely while saving energy. The 5 vs. 4 or one-player advantage for a full-court press occurs when you score or turn over the ball with a dead ball turnover violation. The opponent must take the ball out of bounds and they will have one less offensive player on the playing floor.

The following is the backcourt, man-to-man, center field players' press roles, when playing the two-pass and out rule. Four players play man-to-man defense. They must play aggressively while 100% denying their man from getting an inbounds pass. The 5th defender plays the center field position and doubles the first pass from their defensive position. The goal is to force the first pass or inbounds pass to be made into the backcourt with a lob pass that the center fielder can steal.

Distance: 15 feet from the passer

First, we explain how to guard an offensive player within 15 feet of the passer. The defender points their butt toward the ball in a low wide guarding position. They have physical contact with their offensive man in the position we call "Bellying Up." One arm is on the offensive player's chest in an armbar position, and the arm closest to the inbound passer is in the pass denial position. The defender is in a belly-to-belly and eye-to-eye position with their man. This defensive position will last only 5 seconds or less. The defender doesn't look at the passer or the ball; they must read the eyes of the person they are guarding. If the offensive player makes any movement, the defender moves forward a step or two and drives their offensive player back two steps. This pushes the opponent off balance toward mid-court and away from the passer by using the arm bar on the opponent's chest. This aggressive action on the slightest movement by the offensive player will push the offensive player backwards, destroy timing, and hinder any movement toward the ball or the ability to set a screen. Failure to play this belly-up position and to push the offensive player two steps and the offensive player will be the aggressor and dictate the action by breaking to get open or setting a screen.

At no time is the offensive player allowed to cut the face of the defender and break toward the out-of-bounds ball passer. The offensive player can only break away from the ball or passer by moving toward the backcourt or by moving parallel to the ball or passer. All screens must be switched in an aggressive double-team manner. The defenders must force a lob pass over the offensive player's head, but never give up a direct line ball pass inbounds.

Distance: 20 to 60 feet from the passer

When guarding an offensive player down the floor, the defender's butt is pointed toward the middle of the floor so they can see the passer and their man. The defender sets up in a ¾ denial position, several feet (6-20 feet) ahead of the offensive player and toward the ball. The greater the distance the offensive player is from the ball passed inbound, the greater the distance the defender is off their man, toward the ball. The deep offensive players (20-60 feet away) must not be allowed to cut the defender's face and move forward to receive a pass. If the offensive player attempts to cut the defender's face while moving forward toward the ball, the defender must deliver an arm bar slam to the cutter's chest and prevent a cut toward the ball. The defender must force a long pass that they can steal. The defense is now playing aggressively, employing denial, a 4 vs. 4 man-to-man strategy. The one-defender advantage, or the fifth person, is the center fielder.

Playing the center field position:

The center fielder starts about 15-20 ft from the passer near the head of the key. While watching the passer's eyes, they slide in the direction the passer is looking. They steal any lob pass over the head of a defender who has their butt toward the ball and are within 15 feet of the passer. Anytime an inbounds pass is made, he must yell "Ball, Ball" so that all defenders with their backs to the ball can adjust their position and see the ball. The center field defender's job is to steal a lob pass to any offensive player within 15 feet of the passer. If an inbound pass is completed, he must double-team the ball on that first pass. This will force the second pass, 15-20 feet from the passer, to a player in the backcourt.

Second Pass Cover

If the first or inbound pass is completed, there are several options for covering the second pass if your team is playing the two-and-out rule. Take away the strongest ball handler and force a pass out of the double team to the most distance offensive player, or the weakest dribbler/ ball handler who is in the backcourt. On the second pass, go for a steal. If it's a missed attempt, then it's been two passes, and the two-and-out rule is in effect. The team must sprint back to their half-court defense, the press is over. This retreat is necessary because the defense is out of position, has lost the one-player advantage, and is now outnumbered 5 to 4 due to having two players trapped.

If you're getting steals on the first or second pass, it's easy to let your pride get in the way and not follow the "Two and Out" rule. However, good teams in your league will hurt you if you stay in the press for the 3rd or 4th pass. Good teams may force you to play the "One and Out" rule.

In Practice

To prepare for this press defense, spend 15 minutes each practice night on the "Man CF Press" drills shown at the end of this chapter. Drills will teach players how to play belly to belly in a deny position while reading their man's eyes. The defenders will learn how to defend against any movement, chest cutters, and switch screens. The deep defenders must learn how to deny and steal long passes. The center fielder must be drilled on how to move with the passer's eyes, steal lob passes and double team the first pass. They must also be trained to yell "Ball" when the inbounds pass is made. You must drill on where you want the second pass to go so that you have a great chance for a steal. The center fielder must be quick, lead and talk.

Examples in Play

The time spent working on applying defensive pressure will be rewarded when your offense must face a pressing team. The following are examples where defensive pressure saved the day for my teams in past years. One year, we played the #2 team in the state twice in league play. The first time we were down 12 late in the second half. We utilized the man-to-man press in the backcourt and wing/corner traps out of our half-court 1-2-2 zone to pull out the win. The second time, we were down 15 with a little over 4 minutes left in the 4th quarter. We pulled out a 5-point win by using our press and three-point shooting until we could get ahead and use our delay game.

In 60 years of coaching, the biggest comeback any of my teams have ever made was in a sub-state game. It was a game we needed to win for a trip to the State Tournament. We trailed 37-13 with 3:30 left in the third period, when we pressured with our defense and got on a hot streak. We overcame a 24-point deficit in the last 11 minutes of the game and pulled out the win 45-43 with a last-second shot and a trip to the State Tournament.

Winning big games against ranked teams takes a prepared team that has been drilled on traps and solid defense, so they can overcome a scoreboard deficit and a delayed offense at the end of the game when behind.

KISS BASKETBALL

MAN CF DRILLS
A

MAN CF DRILLS: Defenders practice keeping an offensive player playing below 20' from cutting their face, for 5 seconds by being physical.

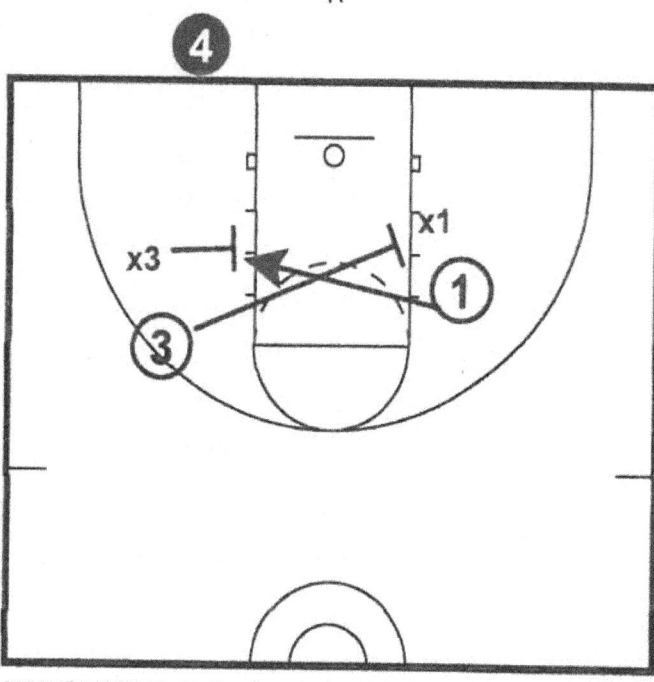

MAN CF DRILLS
A

MAN CF DRILLS: Defenders below 20 feet work on switching all screens.

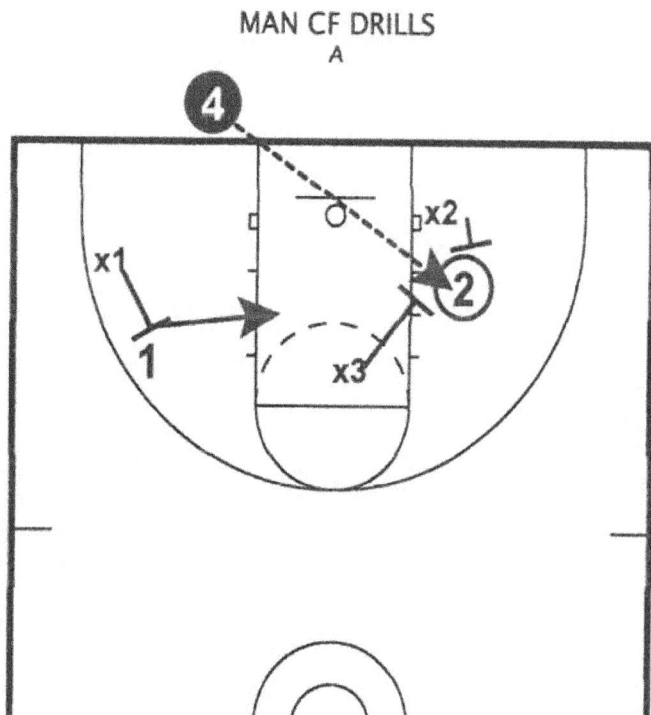

MAN CF DRILLS: The center fielder practices double teaming the ball, while the off defender looks to steal the second pass.

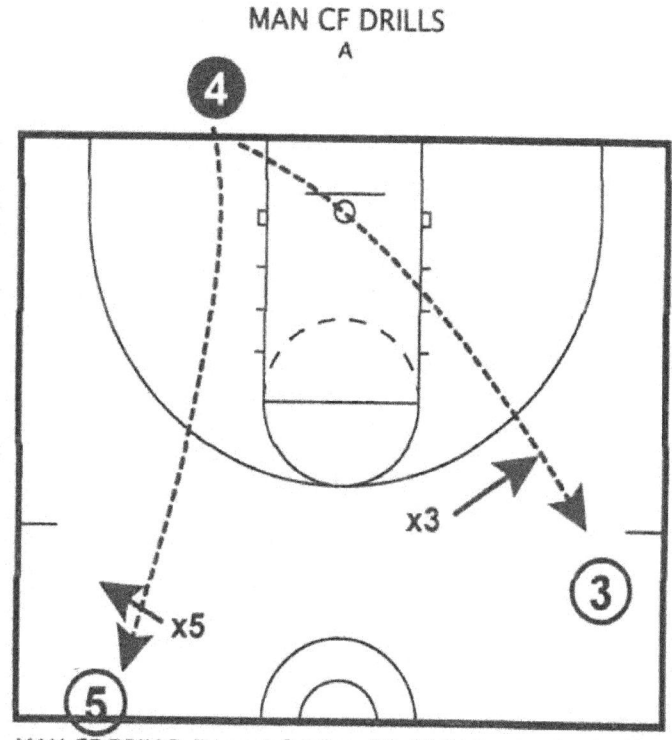

MAN CF DRILLS; Deep defenders 20-60 feet away from the ball, work on seeing the ball and their man, stopping face cuts and stealing long passes

KISS BASKETBALL

MAN CENTERFIELD PRESS A

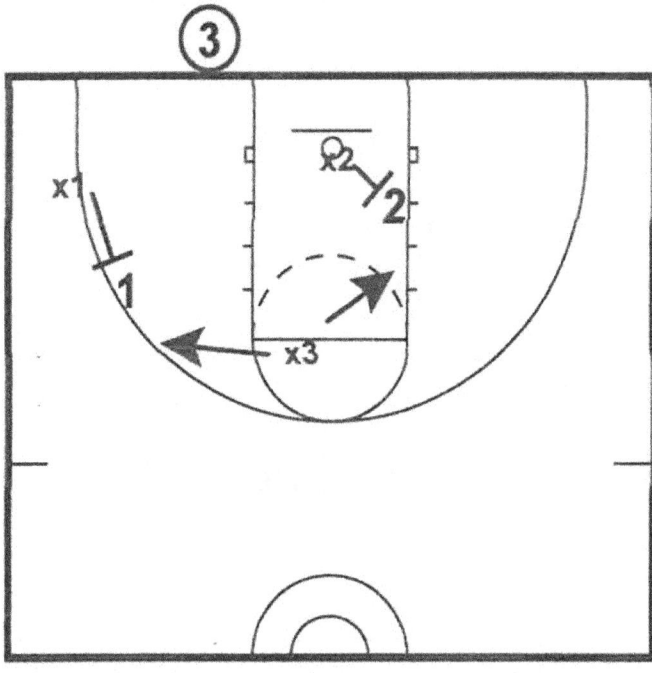

MAN CF; X1 and X3 physically deny their man the ball with their back to the ball for 5 seconds, allowing no face cuts. X3 moves left & right where ever O3 looks.

MAN CENTERFIELD PRESS A

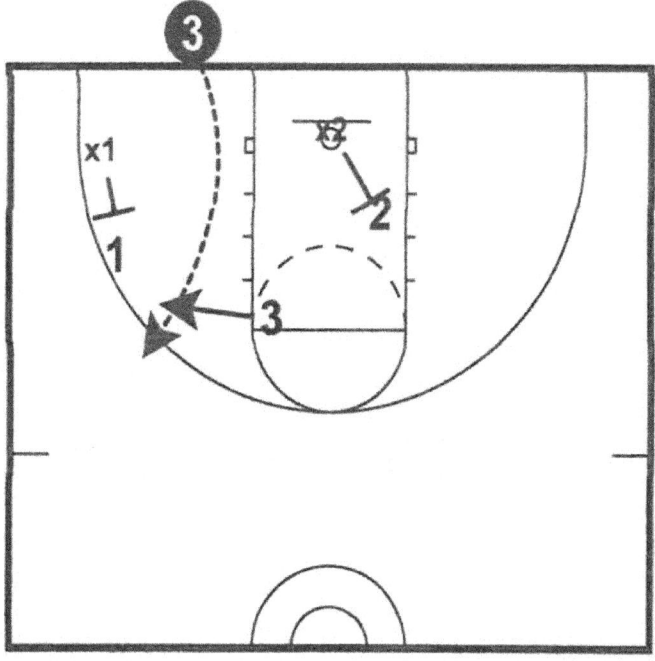

MAN CF; X1 & X2 are denied so O3 tries a lob pass to O1. X3 is moving that direction because O3 is looking at O1, X3 steals the lob pass.

MAN CENTERFIELD PRESS A

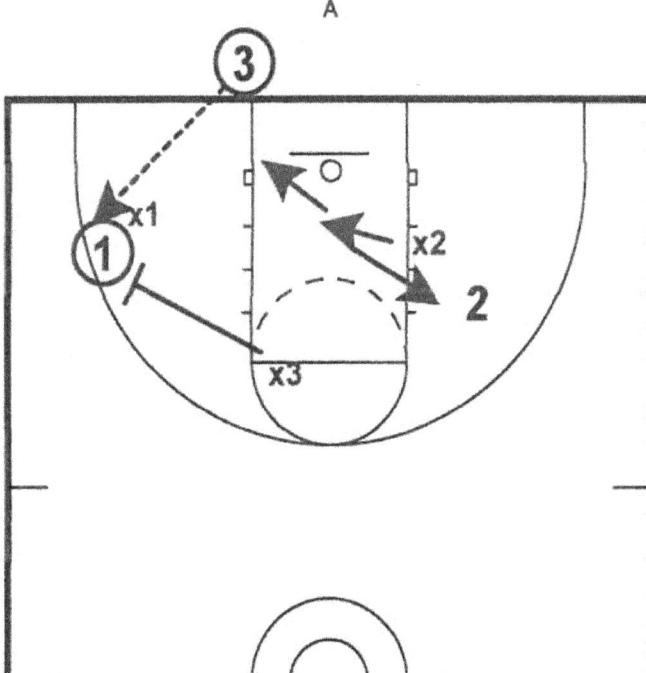

MAN CF; If O1 gets free for a passs. If the team is in 1 & Out defense the defenders retreat to their half court defense. If in 2 & Out defense, X1 & X3 trap the ball and X2 tries to steal a pass to O3 or O2

MAN CENTERFIELD PRESS A

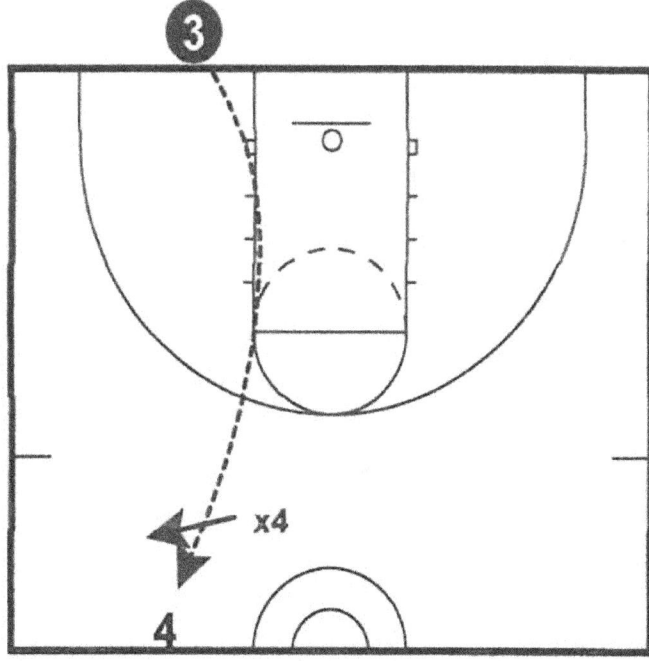

MAN CF; If a player is guarding a player 30-60 fee down the floor X4, they stay between the ball and their person O4 so they can steal a long pass.

Part 3
Player Roles and Fast Break

CHAPTER 12
NUMBERED BREAK

Most coaches talk about their players as numbers, for example, their point guard is the one man, but they don't always have each player numbered 1-5. This is an important place for the KISS plan to come into play with the" NUMBERED BREAK;" all five players have a number to dictate their role, lane, and floor position on offense and defense in back court to front court.

WHY HAVE FLOOR POSITION BY NUMBERS

Having players with numbered positions when on the floor will keep your team organized. The floor set-up for positions and roles should be the same for made shots, missed shots, free throws, fast break, or press breaker.

During timeouts, I have players sit in numerical order (1 to 5) so I can see who is in the game in each position. The other players stand behind the coach. If there is a 30-second timeout, the five players who are in the game stand in the order in front of their chairs. By always sitting or standing in order, the players are executing discipline, and their eyes are on me.

Player 2, you need to run wider when running your lane. This is a message to all players who play the number 2 position. Positioned the floor and set running lanes, keeping the team organized and disciplined. It is easier for the coach to identify players who are out of their lane, have poor position on the floor, or are late or slow, which saves coaching time. Players can play mentally free as they will know their location, and their roles are always the same.

The position of each player on a fast break, after made or missed shots, when free-throws are shot, and to break full court pressure, the players' roles are always the same.

PLAYERS NUMBER BY POSITION

The following are each numbered player and their position:

point guard = # 1

right wing = # 2

left wing = # 3

first post down the floor = # 4

last post down the floor = # 5.

It is beneficial for each player to learn more than one position/number.

PLAYER ROLES

Player #2

This player plays on top of our defense and runs down the right side of the floor 4-6 feet from the sideline, after leaving his defensive position on shots. When the opponent takes a shot, 2 bumps the nearest opponent, who is usually the point guard. They have no screen-out rebound responsibility. They just sprint wide, going down the right side of the floor to the baseline, before coming back toward midcourt looking for a pass. While sprinting their lane, two is looking over his left shoulder for a pass. Player 2 can get to his offensive running lane easily, from the top defensive position in our 1-2-2 zone defense.

This early sprint out takes an offensive rebounder off the boards, as a defender must follow player 2 down the floor. This deep defender, who goes back with 2, is often the opponent's point guard, who is the quickest and fastest player. Failure to get a defender back will allow the offense to get a fast break layup by 2. If we drag the opponent's point guard deep, out of the backcourt, they can't be used in a full-court press or pressure on the ball as we come out of backcourt.

Player 2 is the first option when passing the ball down court. Player #2 sprints to the end line at the offensive end of the floor, and V cuts back toward midcourt while looking for a pass from Player #5, who is out of bounds or on a made basket. If not, they look for a pass from 1-3 or 4, who are in the backcourt, getting a defensive rebound or steal. If 2 receives a pass coming out of the backcourt, they rip the ball as they pivot to face their basket, while reading the floor and the defense at the same time. Wing 2 is evaluating whether #4 is open for a layup or a skip pass, or if #3 is open for a good shot.

Player 2, our best offensive player, must look to score, especially in one-on-one situations where no teammate is open for a better shot. The 2 player is free to drive or shoot any good open shot, within his range.

If player 2 misses a shot, 3 crashes the backside board, and 4 comes toward the front rim to rebound, from down the middle of the floor. If the 2 player has no drive or shot, he must dribble toward the corner and look for 4 player who is coming down the middle of the floor or is in a post-up position on the block. As the 2 looks at 4, he must read how 4 is defended. If the 4 is guarded on the topside or from behind, he must make a post pass to 4.

If 4 is covered on the bottom side, 2 passes to #1, who is now at the foul line extended near the three-point line on 2's side of the floor. Player 4 must physically seal his defender, and 1 must be a willing passer.

Player #3

The 3 player plays on the left side of our 1-2-2 Zone defense and screens out on all the opponent's shots and then runs wide down the left sideline looking over his right shoulder for a pass. Player 3 will be late getting down the floor, slower than 2 by 30-50 feet, because he must screen out and try for a rebound before taking off on his run down the left sideline. By the time 2 gets down the floor on the break, 3 will be at about mid-court near the sideline. Player 3 is the second option for a pass down the court by players 1, 4, or 5, whoever has the ball. Player 3's role is the same as 2, but on the left side of the floor. If either 2 or 3 gets a defensive rebound, they pass ahead if there is an open player; if not, they dribble down their sideline toward the corner.

Player #4

The 4 player is often the fastest post player. They screen out on the opponent's shot if they get the defensive rebound. Their first look is deep at the 2 and 3 men running their routes down the sidelines, if they are covered 4 outlets to the 1 man or bringing the ball down court. If a teammate gets the rebound, 4 runs rim to rim down the middle of the floor while looking over the ball side shoulder for a pass.

On a made basket, 4 starts on a rim-to-rim run while looking over their right shoulder at 5, who is taking the ball out of bounds. If no pass has been made by the time they reach the head of the key 4 must pivot and come back toward the ball for an inbounds pass. If they don't get a pass from 5, he must set a back screen on the defender guarding player 1. Player 1 will be open for a pass from 5 when coming off the back screen toward the ball, if there is no switch by x4. If 1 gets the inbound pass, 4 then runs rim to rim. If there is a switch and player 1 is covered on the back screen, player 4 pivots and seals on x1 before rolling back toward the ball two steps. Player 4 is now looking for a bounce pass from player 5.

Player # 1

Player 1 screens out on shots. If a teammate gets the rebound, he goes to the foul line extended, ball side, with his back to the sideline. On a made shot, 1 goes to the right sideline, foul line extended, to the same position as on a rebounded shot. Player 1 watches player 5, while looking for a pass. If covered, player #1 must wait for a back screen from player 4. Player 1 always cuts off the back screen by 4 toward the ball. If there is no pass, they must continue moving across the backcourt toward the opponent's basket, to the middle of the floor, then head down the middle of the floor, running rim to rim.

If player 1 gets the ball after coming off the back screen by player 4, he must jump stop, pivot, and look up court for a possible pass ahead to player 2, 3, or 4. Player 1 must always fake a pass before passing or heading down the floor with a dribble. If player 4 receives the inbounds pass from 5, he scans the floor for a pass to #1, who is moving down the middle, or to 2 and 3, who are cutting back toward mid-court.

Players 1, 2, 3, and 4 must attack the basket to score whenever they are in a one-on-one break situation. If player 1 or any other player ever makes a pass ahead to a wing (2 or 3), player 1 runs to the ball side of the floor to a wing extended position and must be ready to run the secondary break.

Player #5

Player 5 screens out on all shots. If he gets a rebound, he outlet passes to player 1 on the ball side, sideline, foul line extended, after looking deep at 2, 3, and 4 for a possible long pass. If a basket is made, the player takes the ball out of the net and, while taking two big steps, gets to the right side, away from the backboard and out of bounds, and looks deep to players 2, 3 & 4 who are breaking down the floor. If all three of these players are covered 5 looks for 1. When the ball is inbounded by 5, he jumps inbounds away from the ball and is a trailer.

The trailer looks for a possible pressure-relieving backwards pass. If player 5 gets a backward pass from 1 or 4, he takes 3 dribbles away from the passer, jump stops, and looks for a pass ahead to the wing or pass backwards to the new trailer: 1 or 4. If player 5 has no possible pass when out of bounds, he must call a timeout, or he can also throw the ball off the legs of the defender on the ball. This pass must be thrown so it will go out of bounds off the defenders and doesn't come back and hit them while standing out of bounds.

(If the ball is being dribbled down the floor by player 1 or 4, the ball side wing comes up for a pass, and the offside wing goes deep for a pass.)

READS BY # 5 WHEN PASSING

Player 5's four passing reads on a made out-of-bounds pass or a rebound are in this order.

1st read - deep and long right for 2

2nd read - mid court left sideline for 3

3rd read - player 4 down the middle of the floor.

4th read - player 1 on the right sideline, 15 feet away.

Conclusion

When teaching the numbered break, each player is given a number from 1 to 5 that fits their size and skill. They are also given a handout that explains the role of that number, along with a diagram that shows the numbers' running lanes. (like the one at the end of this chapter)

The number you give each player should match their skill level, strengths, and adjust for their weaknesses. For example, a left-handed guard might be given 3 so he can play the left side of the floor and use mainly his left hand. Tall posts are given the numbers 4 or 5 as they need to get rebounds. A player who is very good at dribbling with both hands and passing would be a good number 1, as he will face pressure when dribbling and passing.

Some players should learn two numbered positions, the 2 and 3 have somewhat similar roles, but just on different sides of the floor. The 4 and 5 need to know both numbers as they are interchangeable. Players should learn one number well before taking on a second number because each number has responsibilities on both offense and defense.

PASSING OPTIONS
A

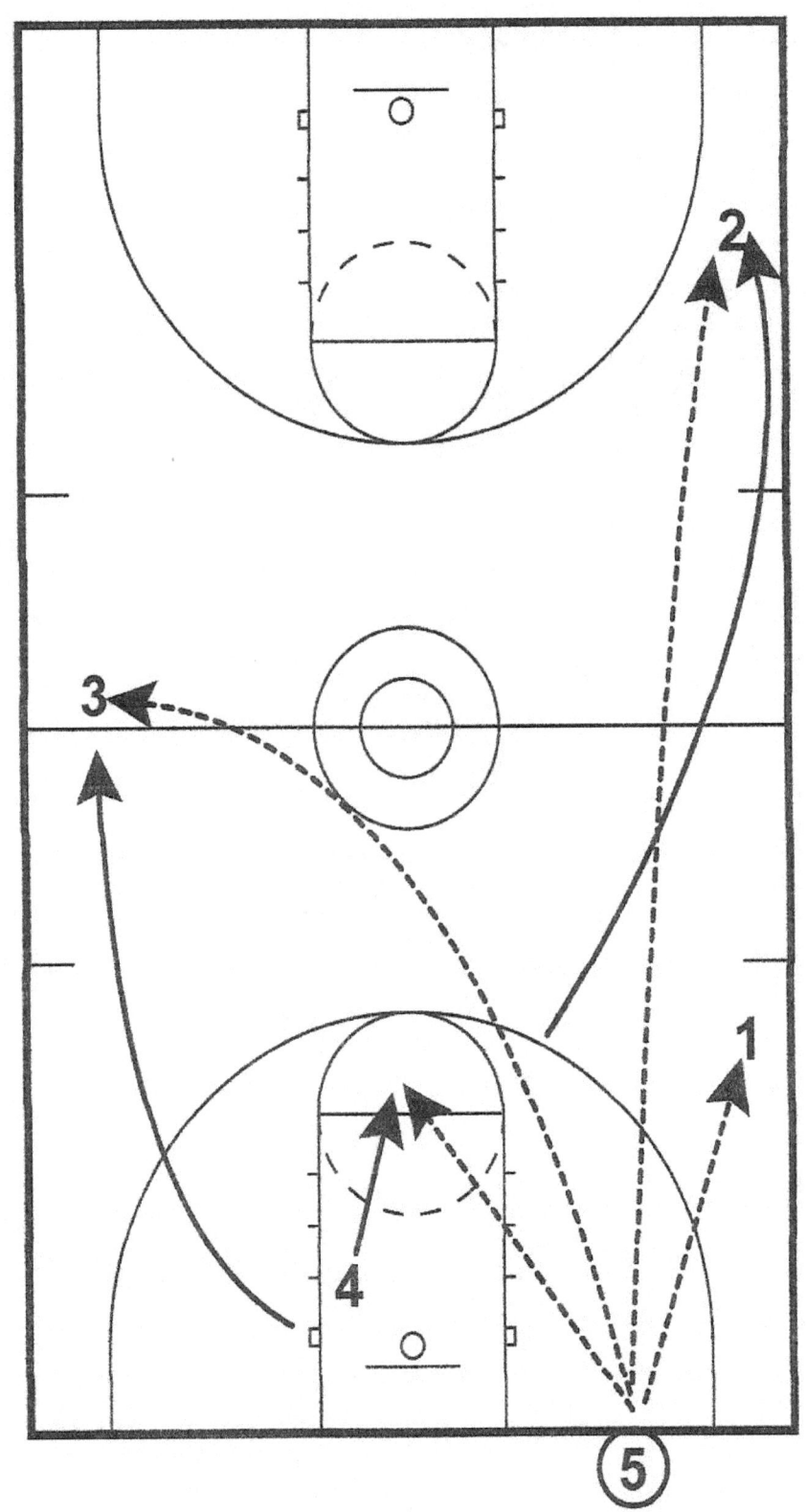

SSER #5 READS WHILE RUNNING OUT OF BOUNDS; 1ST CHOICE DEEP PASS TO 2 OR 3 IF OPEN

KISS BASKETBALL

Numbered Break Roles
A

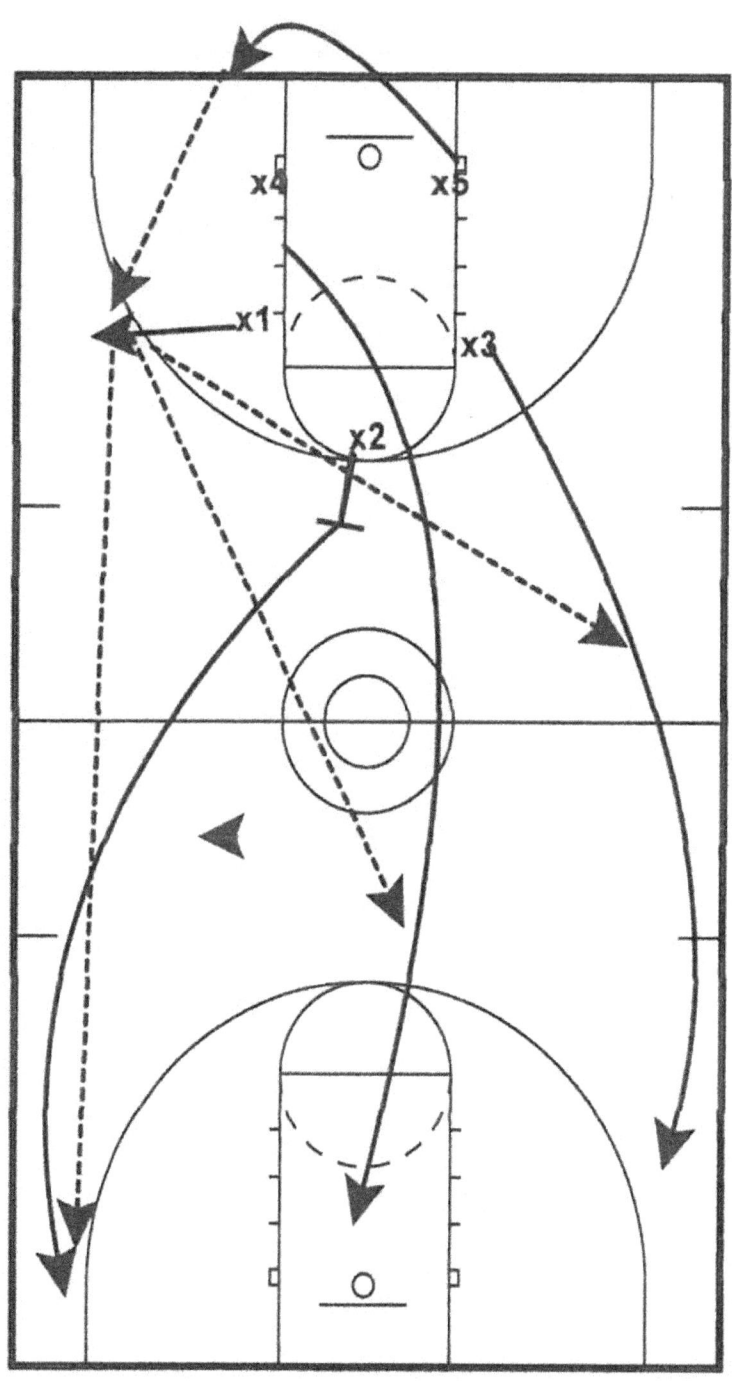

On any shot or made basket, 2 bumps the offensive player on top and sprints down the floor on the right side looking for a pass. 3 screens out and runs down the left side. 4 screens out and runs rim to rim. 5 screens out and takes the ball out of bounds and passes long to 2,3 or 4 if they are open. 1 screens out and goes to the ball side, foul line extended looking for a pass from 5, if he gets the ball he looks to pass ahead as he dribbles down the floor.

Chapter 13
EACHING RUNNING ROLES

Once all players have a numbered position (1-5), they must learn their running roles on the floor with progressive drills (for numbered positions, see chapter 12). The running drills need to build up to a point where the players can fill their lanes when running and, without mistakes, while under pressure. The progressive running drills will be mastered fast and make moving on to the secondary break or sprint break easy.

Start teaching running roles with 5 offensive players vs 0 defenders, then progress to 5 offensive players vs 3 defenders. After this, you can teach running from made or missed free throws and against backcourt pressure. Last of all, you can teach 5 vs 5 and the secondary fast break.

5 vs 0 Running Drill

A group of five offensive players, numbered 1 to 5, is positioned at one end of the floor. The coach then throws the ball up on the backboard. The rebound is passed to player 1, and all 5 players break down the floor using their numbered lanes. This group of 5 players will make five trips up and down the floor, nonstop, with each player shooting a layup in the order of player 1 to player 5.

On the layup shot, players 3, 4, and 5 crash the boards and put any missed layups back into the hoop. Player 2 always heads back down the floor on their right-side running lane after sprinting to the top of the key for a possible long rebound. Player 1 goes to mid court for defensive protection, then to the right-side foul line extended for an inbounds pass from 5 after the made shot . On shots, players 3, 4, and 5 always crash the boards. Meanwhile, player 2 moves to the top of the key, and player 1 moves toward mid-court for defense, which prevents any fast break by the opponents.

After a score or made basket, player 5 makes an inbound pass to any open player. The team then goes the other direction for a layup. Player 5 can make the long baseball pass to 2 or 3 running down the sideline and 4 going down the middle of the floor, or to 2 on the right sideline, foul line extended.

Whenever player 1 receives an outlet pass from 5, he should only make two dribbles before passing ahead to an open player. He must learn to use one dribble to gain speed and, on the second dribble, keep his head up, looking ahead, reading the floor, and the defense. Player 1 must pass the ball before 1 he reaches half court.

When the ball reaches the offensive end of the floor and the shot is taken, the 2 and 3 men cross the key, ending up on the opposite side of the floor. 3 looks to rebound and put back a missed shot. Then 3 continues back up the opposite, left side of the floor. The 2 men goes to the top of the key and then down the right side. On a made shot the 2 man is now on the right lane and the 3 man is in his left lane, as the ball is inbounded to start back up the floor.

These 5 trips will be completed at a dead sprint, and the 5 players should finish their 5 trips in under 30 seconds while shooting in order 1 through 5. Then the second group of 5 players 1 through 5, runs the 5 vs 0 drill, taking their 5 layup trips, at this time, the first group of 5 have a 30-second rest, any player who misses a layup or who doesn't go to their correct spots on the offensive shot, must do 5 pushups while their group is resting.

The second time, the two groups of 5 players take 5 trips up and down the floor, each player takes a 10' to 15' foot jump shot. On made or missed shots, players 1-5 assume the same roles as during the first five trips: players 1 & 2 get back, and 3-5 crash the boards to score any missed shot. Player 5 always takes the ball out of bounds. Only allow 5 to touch the ball when the basket is made. The other four players should be sprinting in their lanes.

The third time the groups take their 5 trips, they shoot at 15 feet or from the 3-point line. These three trips of different shots (layup, 15-foot jumper and three-pointer) for each team's five players, will take a total of 3 minutes for both groups. If the players struggle with their roles, repeat these three trips.

Later, player 2 is taught to run from the head of the key to the ball side three-point line. If players 3-5 get the rebound, they are ready for a kick-out three-point shot if they don't have a put-back shot. Doing this drill 2 times will take 6 minutes, and it is a good warm-up drill while reinforcing players' numbered lanes and roles.

3 vs 5 Running Drill

The next part of the drill is to put 3 defenders at each end of the floor within 25 feet of the baseline. The group of players 1 through 5 will attack the 3 defenders. The offensive must read the defense and get a good shot from any players 1 through 5. When the offense makes shots, they must inbound the ball while the three defenders force the offense to break the backcourt pressure with a pass ahead to a wing 2 or 3 coming back toward half court. Once the ball gets past half court, the five offensive players attack the three defenders at the other end of the floor.

On any missed shots in this continuous 5 vs 3 drill, the offense tries to get a rebound with players 3-4 and 5 until they score. If a defender gets a rebound, they roll the ball out of bounds, and the offense must then get it back in bounds under pressure and go back down the floor. If the offensive team scores, player 5 inbounds the ball, and the offense is attacking the other end of the floor. After six trips up and down the floor, the coach stops play, corrects problems, and then flips the teams.

This 5 vs 3 drill teaches the offensive players to run their lanes, execute against pressure, crash the boards with players 3, 4, and 5, and players 2 and 1 getting back for offensive balance. The five offensive players learn to make good decisions before passing, driving and shooting. They also read the three defenders, when moving at pace, but under control. The three defenders are learning to scramble, when outnumbered and to screen out on shots. The three defenders are expected to talk and predetermine who is the weakest offensive player and force him to shoot while never giving up a layup.

Team A and B Running Drill: 5 vs 5

The next step involves creating two teams, A & B, each with five players. Then, one player from Team B will take one free throw. Team A lines up with their 2 and 3 men deep at the other end of the floor near the left and right corners. 1 cuts off the shooter from the left side, and the 4 & 5 players are in the bottom rebound spots, along the free throw lane. Player's 4 and 5 must step into the lane and up toward the shooter while screening out.

The five players on team B can do whatever they want, make or miss, on the free throw. The offense must break down the floor on a miss shot rebound or after inbounding a made shot. The key is not to practice turnovers but learn when there is no break and then set up the halfcourt offense. After teams A and B have had several turns, the teams should be able to break defensive pressure and get the ball quickly down the floor for a good shot when playing against five defenders.

In games when the opponent is shooting a free throw, we always line up with our 2 and 3 deep, down the floor in the corner, on their side of the floor. If the ball comes toward one of them, they break toward midcourt for a pass. The opposite wing stays deep; we call this yo-yoing. This way, our best scores are ready deep down the floor, ready to attack, and it forces the opponent to put two defenders back deep.

Secondary Break

The next step is to teach the secondary break against a man-to-man defense when the fast break is stopped and no good shot is possible. At this point, the ball should be in a corner with an offensive wing (2 or 3). The point guard (1) will be at the foul line extended 15 feet from the ball. The trailing post (5) will fill the spot 15 feet from the point guard near the top of the same side of the key, and the first post (4) will be at the low post on the ball side of the key, near the hoop. Player 4 tries to seal his defender for a pass from the corner wing. If the ball side wing (2 or 3) can't get the ball into the post, (4) the ball is reversed from the corner to the point guard (1), if the point guard (1) can't make a low post he will pass to 5 or skip the ball to 3 who has moved up toward the left side, of the key top. as 4 works his way across the key looking for a pass.

The ball is reversed out of the corner from player to player with passes or with skip passes. Each player with the ball first looks to see if they can make a pass into the low post, where they are fighting for a sealed position and for a possible basket attack. If no pass is made to the low post (4), he will end up in the short corner, across the key, from where he started.

When the ball gets to the offside wing, after being reversed, from the corner wing, the point guard (1) and trail post (5) set a double stagger screen for the wing coming out of the corner. If the cutting wing is open, there is a pass, followed by a shot or drive from near the foul line near the elbow. The post (5) seals his screen. If the post defender switches to cover the wing coming off the double stagger, then the post rolls to the hoop for a pass. The goal is to get our best offensive wing players open with the ball so they can look for a shot, drive or a pass to the point guard cutting off the ball side posts down screen.

If the ball is reversed or skipped to the offside wing, near the top of the key area, the short corner post can come up and run a screen and roll on the open side of the floor.

As the team advances in skill and understanding, the coach can add other options to the secondary break, depending upon his players' strengths and the half-court defense. Small tweaks will be needed if the half-court defense is a zone. The drawings at the end of this chapter will show and explain the secondary break.

If there is a dead ball in the backcourt, your offense may not get down the floor until all five defenders are back and set, but your secondary break will still get you a great shot and keep the game flowing at a fast pace.

Conclusion

In the first few days of teaching running lanes, be patient and correct mistakes, but demand good decisions. Turnovers and poor decisions must have a penalty of running lines, pushups or sub out and run. The players can now get the ball down the floor vs pressure, after a made or missed shot, in an organized manner. The offense will soon be pushing the ball down the floor at pace and scoring out of their break or secondary break. Often, there will be no need to set up and run a half-court offense.

The players will love fast break drills because there is lots of action, everyone gets to touch the ball, take shots, and get rebounds, all of which builds good chemistry and conditioning.

KISS BASKETBALL

SECONDARY BREAK VS MAN DEF.
A

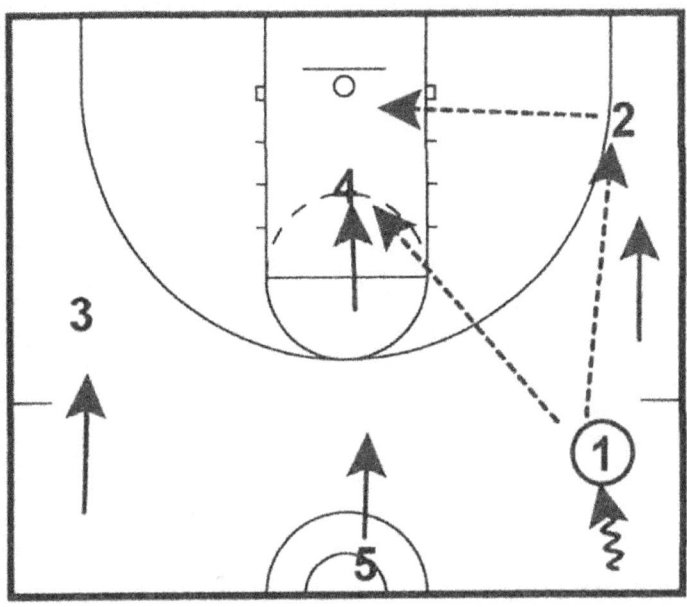

#1 passes ahead to (RR) #4, If he is open, if not he passes ahead to #2 who passes to #4, shoots or drives to the hoop.

SECONDARY BREAK VS MAN DEF.
A

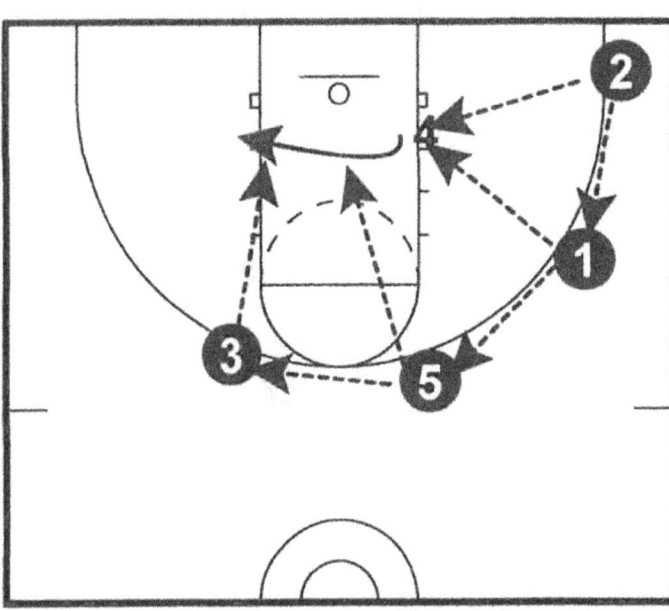

If there is no play for #4 or #2, the ball is reversed to #3 by passes or skip passes. All players look inside at #4 as he moves across the lane ball. The defense is now shifted from right to left.

SECONDARY BREAK VS MAN DEF.
A

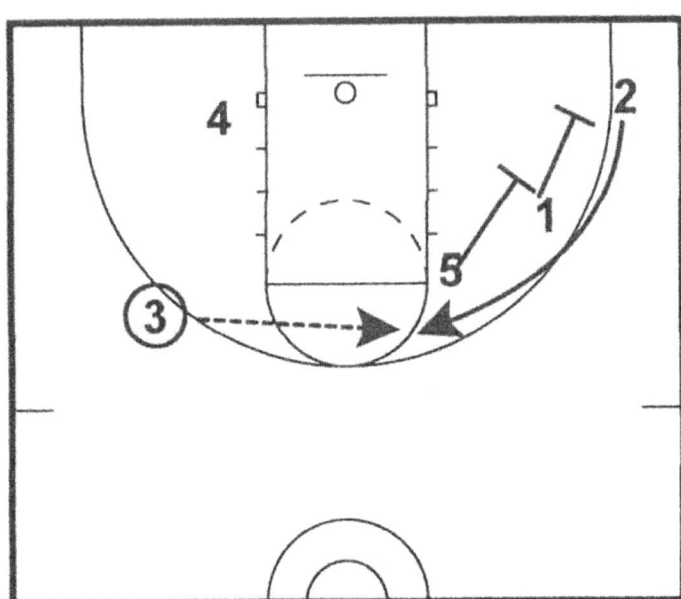

If 3 has no drive or shot, #2 comes off of #1 & #5's double stager screen for a pass from #3. 2 looks for a shot or drive a shot.

SECONDARY BREAK VS MAN DEF.
A

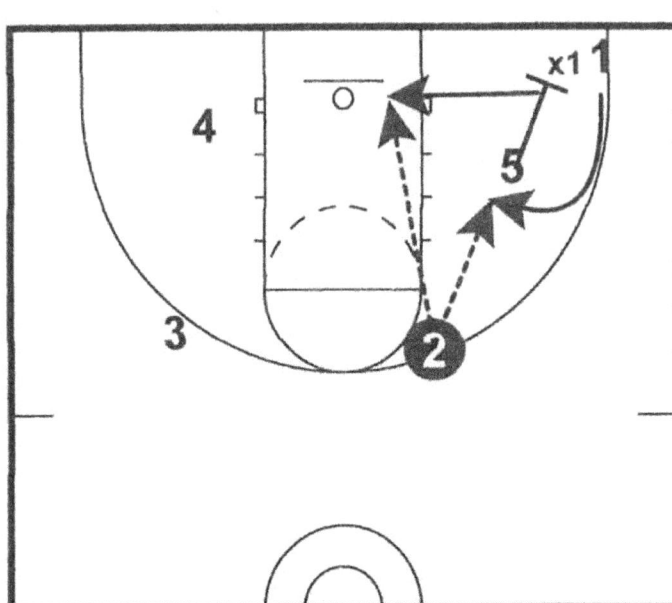

If #2 has no shot or drive his first look is for #1, who is coming off 5's down screen. 1 or 5 will get a pass if open.

KISS BASKETBALL

SECONDARY BREAK VS MAN DEF.
A

SECONDARY BREAK VS MAN DEF.
A

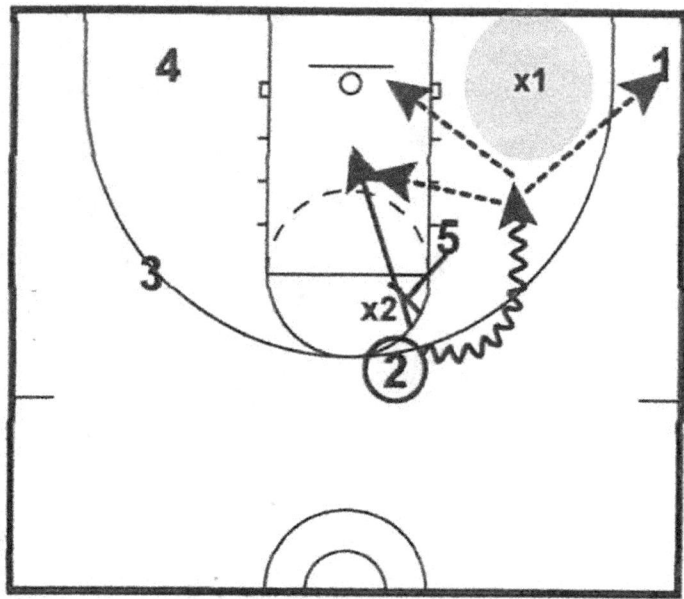 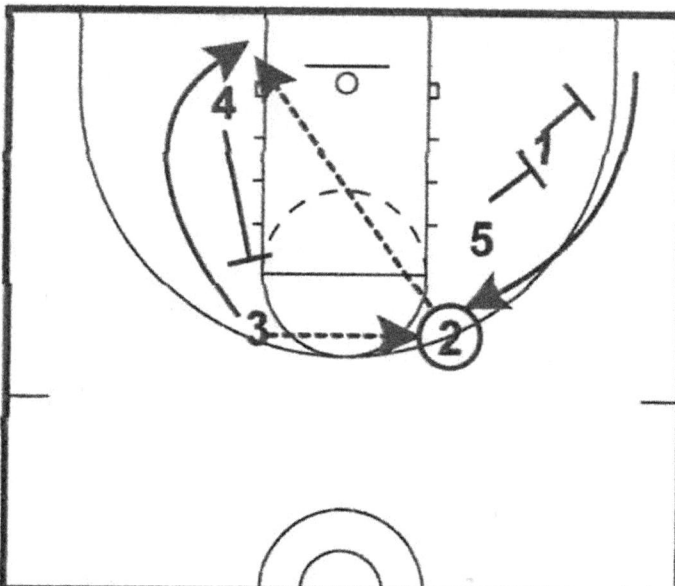

If #2 has no play with 3 or 4 on the left side of the floor, #5 sets a screen for #2 and rolls as #2 drives. #2 may pass to the rolling #5 or get his own shot. If x1 sags off #1 in the corner he will be open for a shot.

#4 can set a back screen for #3 who gets a lob pass from #2 or #4 can break to the foul line for a pass from #2 and #3 can run a back door.

CHAPTER 14
8.5 SPRINT BREAK

In 1985, after coaching at smaller schools for over twenty years, I moved to a school of 1,800 students. At that school, there were many talented basketball players, and during this time, I was fortunate to coach the sprint break.

A high school game consists of four 8-minute quarters, totaling 32 minutes. About half of the game is spent on offense and half on defense (16 minutes each). If you take the 16 minutes on offense, times 60 seconds, you will get 960 seconds of offense. My goal was to take 100 shots during the game. With 100 shots plus 16 turnovers, I totaled 116 possessions. I divided 116 possessions into 960 seconds of offense, and I got around 8.5 seconds. From this, the 8.5 sprint break was born. We needed to get up a shot in 8.5 seconds when on offense and get the ball back in 8.5 seconds when on defense.

8.5-second method

Players can go hard for 8.5 seconds, and 100 shots sounds like a good goal. Goals should be set just out of reach, but not impossible, or the players will give up. The two numbers, 8.5 and 100 shots per game, send a message that running will now be replaced with sprinting, and players need to get moving with a hard, all-out sprint on their first three steps, giving their full effort.

I coached track and cross-country for 25 years. The goal was to make the basketball game a sprint, like the 100 meters in a track meet, requiring the endurance of a cross-country racer. This fast pace would require depth and would negate size, because it is easier to find quick kids between 5'8" and 6' than 6'6 "players.

Co-coaching with the 8.5 seconds method

This method requires one or two assistant coaches, each with their own role. The key is to have an assistant who is loyal, free of pride, and believes in the 8.5 philosophy. In practice and games, one coach might focus on full-court defense, while the other coach emphasizes total offense, including half-court and fast-break strategies. Additionally, you may split the kids up, with each coach taking a team of five. In this system of play, the head coach needs to become more patient, a cheerleader, and a praise giver. All coaches must be on the same page regarding philosophy and roles. This should build coach closeness, as the head coach learns to share responsibilities.

When the pace is fast and you're correcting players who are out and those getting ready to re-enter the game. Your eyes or mind can miss parts of the floor action. It is for this reason that, as a head coach, I prefer to have my assistant handle the bench work. The bench work will include calling the offense, defense, and substitution patterns. This frees the head coach to watch the game, allowing them to provide suggestions to the bench coaches on what the next group of players should do before entering the game. An example might be that the opponent's only good point guard has substituted out, so the next group should do a more aggressive press.

Your team with the 8.5-second method

The 8.5-second method requires 12-15 players for practice and the game. I liked to run two equal teams, each with ten players, and ensure that each player received equal coaching and playing time. Each player must be taught the responsibilities of their designated position. Each player must be convinced to accept a role and perform it at a physically and mentally demanding sprint pace. Additionally, it will take time for all players to adjust to the short playing times of only two minutes or less and being substituted out for a two-minute rest.

The coaches will have to work out a good sub-pattern of position and time. The sub-patterns will depend on your depth. Some players have better skills, while others will improve, and some possess more endurance. The pattern will change as the season progresses. Some players may come out after two minutes, while others may come out after a minute or 90 seconds. It isn't too likely that you will have two equal teams of five players. Over a few practices, players will see the need for rest after 2 minutes or less, because they will run out of energy at the sprint pace.

8.5-second method goals

The coaches must sell the team on the goals needed to make 8.5-second basketball work. The 8.5-second game's pace will cause fatigue for your opponent's players. This will result in fouls and a decline in their overall performance. One of the goals for my team is to get up to 100 shots. Some of these will come from offensive rebounds, defensive steals, fast breaks, and secondary breaks. Other offensive goals are to score 75-80 points per game, have a PPP of .8 or better, get to the foul line 20+ times a game, shoot 65% or better from the foul line, get 30-40% of all missed shots, shoot over 50% from the field and have less than 16 turnovers. Defensively, some key goals are to force 25 or more turnovers, take 2 or fewer charges, give up 55 points or fewer, commit 15 or fewer fouls, and secure 20 or more steals per game.

The 8.5-second fast pace should cause the opponents to cross half court close to 100 times on defense, plus that many times when on offense. The goal is to make the opponent cross half court about 200 times a game on a dead sprint.

Advantages of 8.5 Basketball

In this method, you can dictate tempo and make the opponent play your style. This method is simple to learn, organized, and forces you to use your bench. It enables a less-skilled player to grow into a more advanced role. This method also makes size less of a factor. 8.5-second basketball produces more shots, rebounds, steals, charges, assists, and free throw attempts. For the opponent, it's challenging to prepare for, leading to fatigue and fouls. You will score in runs of 6-8 points very fast, which can make up for a big deficit when behind. Besides all this, the fast pace is fun for fans, players, and coaches.

Disadvantages of 8.5-second basketball

This method requires everyone to go at a full sprint pace, which means decisions must be made fast. Better players will have less playing time. With the speed, there will be some wild plays and turnovers. So, players have to believe in or buy into the method for it to work.

Subbing in an 8.5-second basketball

When playing 8.5 basketball, the first and most significant change, aside from the pace, is the substitution. Sometimes, you will have two equal teams of five players, and each group will sub after 90 to 120 seconds. However, if you only have 8 good players, they will have less rest time.

8 player subbing

If you have only three posts, a post may play for two minutes and then rest for one minute. They will be on the floor 67% of the time. If you only had five guards with three positions, the three best guards would play two minutes, then rest for one minute, just as the post players do. The two weakest guards play the 3 position, playing and resting every 90 seconds. They will be on the floor 50% of the time.

When and How to Sub-out

You must know your players and how long it takes them to recover after a fast 90- to 120-second sprint at full pace. At no time can you let a player stay on the floor too long. If a player stays on the floor too long, their battery runs down, and they may not recover. If one of our players pats the top of their head, that is a sign that they need to come out of the game. We always honor this sign and often let a player put themselves back in when ready

I like to script the positions and playing time on paper for the first half. This paper is placed on a clipboard and kept on the bench. This way, players can substitute themselves. You can use the same player script or mix up your team for the second half. (See the position script sample at the end of this chapter.)

The subs go to the clock 20 seconds early, but if there is no dead ball to stop the clock so the subs can enter the game, I have a player with the ball drive into a defender while heading toward the hoop. This will result in a foul or charge, which will draw a whistle and stop play.

Role of Film and stats in 8.5-second gameplay

Stats and game film are needed to prove coaching points and evaluations. Players love film, and stats help support the 8.5-second method. The game film doesn't lie, and the use of visuals confirms what happens on the floor. When the pace is fast and you're correcting players who are out and getting ready to go back into the game, your eyes or mind can miss parts of the floor action. So, it is helpful for the coach to watch the film a few times before sharing the evaluation with the team. (For more on film and stats, see Chapter 24)

Chapter 15 will explain the keys to making the 8.5-second basketball method/fast break a success. For visuals on the fast break, see the charts below.

Chapter 15
Keys to Sprint Break

When running the 8.5-second sprint-break, many of the roles are similar to the fast-break roles listed in Chapter 13. Everything in this style is about being the aggressor and anticipating, while forcing the pace. The action at first may seem hectic, but with reinforced drills, it is organized and disciplined.

Key # 1 - Automatic Pick Up

Somewhere between 50% and 70% of your shots will be missed, and there are usually 15 or more turnovers when on offense. If the ball isn't regained with an offensive rebound, there must be a plan to get the ball back in 8.5 seconds. The plan is to use automatic pickup to pressure and regain the ball.

When the offense takes a shot, the point guard (1) moves back toward midcourt. The point guard (1) must let no one get behind him while players 2-5 all crash toward the offensive boards. They run to predetermined spots while pushing to get two feet into the key. The left wing (3) goes to the left block area, the first post (4) moves to the right block area, the last post (5) goes to the front of the rim, and the right wing (2) the foul line area.

Sending players to predetermined spots does three good things. First, it gets the players moving toward the boards, which is key to getting offensive rebounds. Second, we are set up to apply full-court pressure if the opponent gets the ball. Third, the opponent is now forced to pick up the tempo, as the 10-second count is in effect.

The following are the responsibilities of each player when they reach their predetermined rebound spots.

Right Wing

He runs to the foul line and looks for a long rebound in his area. If the opponent gets the ball, he must sprint to the opponent's point guard and deny him an outlet pass. If the point guard gets an outlet pass, the 2 player must not let him dribble the ball onto the volleyball court. If player 2's teammate gets the offensive rebound, player 2 is to run to the three-point line on that side of the key for a kick-out pass and three-point shot. Statistics show that a kick-out pass for a 3-point shot will produce a 10-15% higher success rate than a normal three-point shot.

Left Wing

They run to the left block area on all shots. This is easily done from their left-side fast-break position. After 3 gets both feet inside the key, there is an effort to get an offensive board. If they get a rebound and don't have a put-back shot, they pivot outward and pass to player 2, who has moved to the three-point area for a pass and shot. If the opponent gets the rebound, player 3 attacks the rebounder with pressure.

First Post Down The Floor.

This player runs to the right side of the key by the block for the offensive rebound position.

Last Post Down the Floor.

They run to the front of the rim in the key. If they get a rebound, they do the same as player 3: shoot an open layup or kick a pass out to player 2 for a shot. Where they go in automatic pickup defense depends on what kind of press they are using at that time.

In our missed shots, our automatic pickup is a lot like a 2-2-1 zone. However, we try to take the point guard of the opponent out of the play. This is done with player 2, who is playing deny on the point guard. Player 2 may end up out of the formation when guarding the opponent's point guard. The press set now ends up being a 1-2-1 or a diamond formation.

On dead-ball plays, such as free throws, I switch the press to a man-to-man center field or some type of zone. Players 2 through 5 repeat the new press call so that they are familiar with their new roles.

Practicing the Automatic Pick-up

All rebound drills should be done five on five on five. All defensive rebounds should be taken to the other end of the court on a fast break against automatic pickup pressure. You need to spend a considerable amount of time on different presses, traps, rotations, transitioning to rebound positions, and running the sprint-break.

Teams will always experience defensive breakdowns, so practicing how to handle them is necessary. The following are some examples of possible defensive breakdowns. The ball lands on the volleyball court, or the defense is outnumbered in the deep area. If the opponent doesn't get a layup, breakdowns are not all bad. The opponent often dribbles or passes to daylight so quickly that they lose control. If the point guard(1) doesn't have the ball, the wrong player is dribbling, passing, and shooting. A fast pace and a low percentage of correct plays by the wrong players characterize the results. This type of pace forces the opponent to play out of their comfort zone, making it a great time to draw a charge. Most teams use their best players in the backcourt to break the press, so if they give up the ball to break the press, the pass is to a less skilled player struggling to make a play at pace.

It is wise to spend time being outnumbered, such as 2 on 1, 3 on 2, or 4 on 3. Teams will often outnumber you by breaking the press or as part of their regular offense. Time must be spent on bluffing and retreating, forcing the ball to an open non-shooter, taking away a right-handed layup, and looking for charges. There is to be no blocking shots and fouling in practice. If a score is achieved during practice, instruct the defensive team to inbound the ball quickly and look to attack on offense, utilizing the sprint break.

Key # 2 - Throwing Long: baseball pass

Just like in football, good basketball teams throw the long ball. The baseball pass is used to throw long and has the following advantages. It's the fastest way to move the ball. It helps to make an 8.5-second basketball game possible by keeping the tempo and team goals within reach. This type of pass makes a quick score possible. It forces the opponent to retreat, making them less likely to press.

Additionally, the baseball pass forces a quick retreat by the defense, making them less likely to send players to the offensive boards. The baseball pass is also a skill used to help break full-court pressure. It develops the skill of looking at the entire court and reading the defense before passing. The baseball pass should be used on both made and missed shots.

Reading the floor

When the passer is set to throw, they must make four quick reads of the offense and defense. First, read to look long down the right sideline for player 2, who has leaked out early. If player 2 is covered, the second read is for player 3 just across the midcourt line, near the left sideline. Player 3 runs their route after doing a defensive screen out or a defensive rebound. The <u>third read</u> is for player 4, running down the middle of the court rim to rim. Player 4 will end up on the offensive block, on the ball side of the floor if a pass is made to the 2, 3 or 1. The <u>fourth read</u> is for player 1, who is about twenty feet away, on the ball sideline, with the foul line extended.

Baseball Throw Form

The thrower needs to spend a lot of time working on their form, using the correct position of their feet, hips, arm, hand, and follow-through to achieve success. The baseball pass is made with the strong hand and arm. The throwing hand is placed behind the ball. The throwing arm should come from over the top and with the arm near the ear or head of the thrower. A step and follow-through are made toward the target. Their arm will follow through, downward toward the floor, and the off-hand helps to hold the ball in position. Ensure the throw isn't made with a sidearm action.

Baseball throw in play

On a made shot, player 5 grabs the ball out of the net before it hits the floor. As 5 heads out of bounds, they must quickly take two big steps to the right and bring the ball back into a throwing position while reading the four passing options mentioned above.

It is especially important to throw long a lot early in the game. As a coach, you must adjust to a throwing long turnover. If you throw long 12 times and make 6 open layups, the 50% success rate will give you a PPP of 1.0 This is better than what you would get from a halfcourt offense.

#3 Key - Send A Player Out Early

Just as an opponent begins their shot, an 8.5-second team sends a defender or 2 man to the offensive end of the floor. The team must know which predetermined players will run out early. We usually send our best one-on-one player or best three-point shooter, player 2. If your opponent is playing man-to-man, send the person guarding the opponent's point guard. This forces the opponent's quickest player into back court with our cherry picker. Now the opponent's best and quickest defender is moving away from our point guard. Another plan is to pick a different position every few minutes when subbing. You can even let the players pick, as it doesn't really matter. We typically send our player 2, and most of the time, we send out 2 and 3 if we send out two players.

Sending someone out early will speed up the game, stretch or spread the floor, and it hurts the opponent's offensive rebounding. You can take advantage of a thrower's skill, and it forces the other team to send a player or two back on defense. If the opponent sends two defenders deep, it's hard for them to put on a full-court press if they score. If player 2 is covered, make a pass to player 3 and attack two-on-one. If the opponent sends two defenders deep, pass long to Prayer 4 and attack three-on-two. If the opponent gets back and stops all long passes, it's easy to flow into our secondary break.

#4 Key Secondary Break

When you are unable to get a fast break, the offense must flow right into a secondary break. The secondary break must be fast and produce ball and people movement with a good shot within 8.5 seconds.

It is essential to thoroughly assess your team's strengths and conduct a secondary break that leverages the players' strengths. If your point guard is only so-so at scoring, send them through the key and into the corner away from the ball. If the wings are only average at scoring, but your point guard can post up and score inside, send him to the low post and get him the ball.

It may be as simple as reversing the ball from one side of the floor to the other. This ball movement will shift the defense and give you a chance to break down the defense. Four teammates will touch the ball in under a couple of seconds, all with opportunities to shoot, pass, or drive.

As players' one-on-one skills improve, they can create their own scoring opportunities out of the secondary break. If there is no scoring opportunity from the secondary break, transition into a half-court offense. For more help with the secondary break, see the secondary break from Chapter 13.

Subbing instructions

Before a player goes onto the floor to play, there are three things they must know.

1st. What numbered position am I playing, 1, 2, 3, 4, or 5?

2nd. What press are we using on missed and made shots?

3rd. What offense will we use if the break or secondary break doesn't work?

I like to sub in a new group of 5 players every 1.5 to 2 minutes. Before a group of 5 players goes to the clock, they should sit in the first five chairs on the bench in their designated role positions, numbered 1 to 5. The resting players are reviewing the presses they will use on makes and missed shots, as well as the offense they will be running.

When 5 players come out of the game, they sit in the same order (1-5), and the coach will have time to make substitutions, corrections, and get them ready to report to the clock after resting for 1-2 minutes.

PART 4
OFFENSE

CHAPTER 16
OFFENSIVE PHILOSOPHY

The objective of the offense is to score on each possession, but how to reach that objective is another matter. Before coaching, I would spend hours drawing up plays, sure that each play was a new idea that would win games. When I began coaching, I soon found that plays will not work without skills. Winning without good offensive skills is nearly impossible.

It didn't take me long to see that about one-third of the practice, especially early in the season, needs to be spent on offensive fundamental drills. This is true of all offensive skills, including passing, dribbling, shooting, screening, rebounding, pivoting, spacing, fakes, and cutting.

Just as with defense, a basketball coach must have an offensive philosophy based on the team's tempo, style of play, and the ability of the players. No matter if you're a systems coach or a flexible coach, there is no magic formula or offense that will be a sure winner. In my early years, I coached a slow-tempo offensive game because that was what my past coaches used when I was playing. I coached control basketball for 20 years because I was at a school that had limited numbers, size, and gym space. Over the past 40 years, I have enjoyed different school resources and coaching fast basketball.

My approach is to have a few plays and use them year after year, making minor adjustments based on the player's skill, size, speed, and overall talents. All of this saves time, and players know the offense plan, so they can play freely with confidence.

There are several parts to my offensive philosophy, such as utilizing my players effectively, looking to run at all opportunities, and unselfish team play. It is also important that players only take high percentage shots and are thoroughly prepared with offensive plans B and C, if plan A fails. My philosophy's goal is to achieve a PPP (points per possession) of .8 or better. The players need to gain a numbers advantage, such as 2 vs 1, 3 vs 2, or 4 vs 3, so they can read the advantage and make good decisions. As a coach, I like a lot of passing over dribbling, high percentage shots, and plays that will get the players to the foul line. And plays with lots of ball movement and screens. All of these elements will be explained further in the next few chapters of Part 3: offensive skills, drills, and strategies.

CHAPTER 17
OFFENSIVE SKILLS and Drills

Offensive skill development takes good planning and drills, which require a lot of practice time. For this reason, skill teaching must have a high priority in practice. Make practice and drills harder than game play. Once the offensive skills get better, in some drills, put the offense at a disadvantage by adding one extra defensive player. Skill development will make gameplay simpler and more successful. The main offensive skills to be mastered are passing, dribbling, rebounding, shooting, spacing, and screening.

Passing Skill

Good passing gets teammates open for shots, builds team chemistry, and produces assists. One key to good passing is playing with your head up so you can see both the defense and your offensive teammates. Teach players to make many fakes before passing; fakes will freeze the defense and put the passer in control. Passes can move the ball faster than dribbling and make it easier to get an advantage on the defense. Passing teams usually have better player movement and are harder to play against.

Passing Drills

Place two players 15 feet apart, give the passer the ball, and place the defender on the ball. Teach the passer to put the ball on their right hip and have them make 1-2 fakes toward the floor. If the defender's arms go down, make a quick pass past the defender's ear and hit the receiver on the chest.

The receiver calls out a grade A-F. A grade is a pass to the chest. A B grade is a pass near the waist or chin of the receiver. C grades are where the ball is catchable but off target. D or F grades are turnovers or passes that force the receiver to move. The receiver returns the ball to the passer, and the drill starts over.

I have the passer start three times with the ball on their right hip, then three passes on the left. If the defender moves their body over to block the pass, the passer makes a fake, then does a cross-over step past the defender and passes with their opposite hand. The passer can make 6 passes in one minute, then the players trade positions. In 6-7 minutes, each of the 3 players will get two turns to make 6 passes. The passer will make an air or bounce pass, whichever is open, after many fakes, while trying to score an A grade. After a few days, you will see a big improvement. Any passing turnover in practice after a week or two results in an automatic drop and five pushups. I teach the defender to get physical, up into the passer, but without fouling.

Dribbling Skill

Today, most players over-dribble. This often causes teammates to stand around. The dribbler penetrates into a double team and then is left with a tough pass or low-percentage shot. Stats show that teams with a losing record dribble more than winning teams. Players must be taught to dribble with a purpose, such as getting a better passing angle. Most dribbling in an offense should be straight-line dribbling when going to the hoop.

Dribbling Drills

I like to start all dribbling drills with a shot fake or a jab away from the intended direction, just to move the defense. Set up your offense so that your best drivers will have some chances to go 1 on 1 and teach players to attack defensive gaps. Make sure your drills require the use of both hands, with your eyes up and dribbling low to the ground.

Combine some dribbling drills that end up with a shot or a passing decision, such as a 2 vs 3 drill. Never let a player return to a drill, walking with the ball in their hand, because in a game, this is a turnover.

Line all the players across the sideline and have them throw the ball in the air and catch the ball as if it were a pass to their left side. This is followed by a shot fake and a jab with the left foot going left, with the ball on the left hip. After the jab step, the player sweeps the ball low to the ground to his right side, along with a crossover step to his right. Then they go two fast dribbles with their right hand, then they crossover dribble to the left hand and repeat crossover two dribbles as they go across the court, where they jump, stop, and pivot.

Next, the drill is repeated, going back across the gym after starting with a toss in the air to their right side, followed by a shot fake, a jab right, and a fake right and then a sweep and cross over, to start dribbling two times with the left hand while changing hands with the cross over move. The second time, the crossover dribble is replaced with behind-the-back dribble after two dribbles. The third trip, a between-the-legs dribble is used. The fourth trip is a speed dribble. Trip 5 is stop and go with a backup dribble. Trip 6 is an inside-out dribble. The last dribble is a speed dribble. The seven trips, across the gym floor and back, take about 20 seconds. Doing this for all 7 types of dribbling takes about 3 minutes total. The coach must remind the players to keep their heads and eyes up.

Rebounding Skills

Most teams make about 40% of their shots, so there are rebounds on about 60% of all shots taken. The winning team usually gets the most total rebounds, because more rebounds mean more shots and opportunities to score. Teaching rebound angles and skills such as position, screening out, and use of the body are necessary.

Rebounding Drills

During practice, I start with players throwing a ball up on the wall, then ripping down the rebound. They land low and wide with the ball under their chin and elbows pointed outward. This is followed by pivots left and right. Ten of these rips take about one minute. After this drill, we do wall taps. Twenty total taps are done, ten on each hand, left and right. This takes less than 2 minutes. The ball is tapped onto the wall so that it hits at about 10 feet from the floor or rim height. This builds leg strength, jump timing, and ball control when tipping.

Next, I show the players two different ways to physically screen off their man by using the reverse pivot or the step-through to box out. The reverse pivot footwork is just like setting a screen and rolling when on offense, so the same footwork is used with defensive rebounding. The step-through is used to screen out a very quick player. The defender steps into the offensive player on the shot. When the offensive player moves to the hoop, the defender steps in the direction of the movement with their foot away from the action, while slamming their forearm into the moving player. Next, have the players pair up. One player pretends to shoot, and he moves at half speed left or right two steps while his partner screens out using the screen-out method they like. After many trials of screening out the pace, the effort is at 3/4s speed, then full speed.

After teaching this, pair players up one-on-one at about 15 feet from the basket. Player A shoots and follows their shot. B screens out, and whether the shot is made or missed, they get the rebound. Player A takes 5 turns, then he trades roles with Player B. Every time the shooter gets a rebound, the defender must drop and do 5 pushups. Three sets of 5 or a total of 15 turns only takes about 5 minutes.

Shooting Skills

Players should focus on shooting 8-10 shots at a height of 10 feet on the wall. If they can do this with the correct form: elbow in, an arc of about 45 degrees and with a good backspin on the ball, then the players can shoot with good form, the next step is for them to make 5 in a row 6 feet from the hoop, then make 5 in a row shots 10 feet from the basket, then move back to the foul line. Watch and make sure their off-hand comes off the ball before the shot is taken, so the ball has good back spin, not spinning wrong from side to side. With good form near the hoop, players can move out toward the three-point line.

For the right to shoot three-pointers in a game, players must make 8 of 20 shots or 40% of their shots from the three-point line. In order to gain the privilege of shooting 3 pointers, a player must stay after practice and take his 20 shots. Each player must understand his range and know what is a good percentage shot for them. Without these guidelines, players will go to the 3-point line the moment they enter the gym and start taking 3-point shots, smiling big when they make one out of five or 20%. Players must understand how their shot percentages impact the team's PPP.

Shooting. Drills

Players pair up and shoot 20 shots from 15 feet out. This is recorded each day and will take four minutes. As the players shoot, the coach walks around and helps with shooting form and compliments the shooters. After a couple of weeks, the shooting drills should be a breakdown part of the offense. On basket drives, players often overpenetrate into tall defenders and can't get off shots, or their shots get blocked. The players also need to practice pull-up jump shots 12 to 8 feet from the basket.

Spacing And Standing Skills

Poor spacing on offense can clog an area of the floor. This makes it possible for one defender to guard two players. It can also prevent the offense from driving or making open passes.

I like our Orange Offense, which is a high 1-4 set. On each pass or ball movement, all five players are moving and replacing. Players are 15 feet from each other. The basket area is free of players, and there are passing triangles. Poor spacing hurts passing, cutting, screening, dribbling, and shooting, so the offensive performance and production are lowered. Chapter 20 explains the high 1-4 Orange offense and has drawings that show spacing and movement.

Spacing And Standing Drills

The best way to teach good spacing is to run an offense that starts with the players spaced 12-15 feet from each other and has movement. This movement and spacing will make playing defense harder. It is also important that everyone gets to touch the ball and be a part of the offense, even if their role is to be a passer and screener. When offense is built around only one or two players, the defense can sag off the weaker offensive players. The coach must keep reminding the players to move to maintain their spacing. Players will soon learn that movement will get them open, and good spacing will give them room to shoot or drive toward the hoop.

Screening Skills

It helps if your team can get a one-player advantage, so you're playing 0 vs 1, 1 vs 2, or 2 vs 3. With a one-player advantage, scoring gets easier. Screening the defense can create an advantage for one player. Screening can cause a switch, and the offense can gain an advantage of size, quickness, or ability.

Screens are ineffective for two reasons. First, the cutter doesn't walk into their defender. Wait for the screen to be set, then v-cut, followed by rubbing shoulders with the screen setter as they cut. Second, the screen setter must set the screen at the proper angle, not move, and then pivot to seal the screen before rolling to the hoop.

Screening Drills

I put the players in groups of four, two on offense and two on defense. During the first few days, I walk the players through how to execute screen actions. As the players perform the screening action, I have the defense switching and not switching. The offensive players must say what they are going to do, for example, the cutters say, "walk into the defender, wait for the screen, v-cut off the screener's shoulder."

After walking and talking for a few days, we went live at full speed. If the screen fails, stop the action, ask the offensive players what went wrong, then have them tell you how they can fix it. You will be using screens all year, so make the players do it correct. Correcting with push-ups will take a few minutes out of practice, but the team will reap rewards for the rest of the season.

Conclusion

Many coaches fill practice time with scrimmaging rather than skill work. Then, teams are running up and down the floor with poor offensive skills, with little correction, as bad habits are used. During most scrimmages, only the point guard and the 2-3 best players get to touch the ball, and the scrimmage soon turns into an open gym rat mess. If you want your team to keep improving while playing their best, work on skills. Skills work can be monotonous, so change up your drills. Players who are winners want to win, so correcting and push-ups or other additional exercises for mistakes should be accepted because players want and need to get better.

CHAPTER 18
DELAY GAME POINTERS

Successful teams win close games. Winning close games changes the outcomes of the season. When playing good teams at the end of the year, the games are close, with a winning margin of 6 points or less. This leaves little margin for error when handling pressure. The key to winning close games and having great seasons is beating pressure. This includes mental pressure of being ahead in the fourth quarter, as well as physical pressure of taking care of the ball.

Since the first grade, kids have enjoyed playing "keep-away." Pressure in basketball is similar to "keep-away." If the offense is calm, has a few rules, and uses its strengths, it will have fun beating pressure. With a clear plan and lots of practice, beating pressure builds confidence.

Getting Ready for Pressure

The first half-court offense I teach is the delay and pre-delay, or milking the clock. Good teams can keep the lead if ahead late in a game.

The first step in getting ready for pressure is to know your opponent. Scouting reports, newspapers, films, and talking to other coaches will help you know the who, where, why, when, and how your opponent will apply pressure. (For more on scouting, see chapter 24.)

Scouting is half the battle; the other half is practicing to attack the opponent's weakness, while using your team skills wisely. If your team has a lot of fourth-quarter success in keeping their lead and winning games even in overtime, people will say your team is lucky, but luck is really preparation for an opportunity.

The following are some variables that you must plan for when installing your delay game. The score, players, time-outs, substitutions, floor position, free-throws, PPP(points per possession), and practice

VARIABLE #1 SCORE WHEN AHEAD

Lead of 10 or more points

If your team is ahead by ten plus points, there is a good chance you will not need to change what you have done in previous quarters. If at any time the lead gets under 10-points I would take a time-out and remind the team: the clock is our friend. Don't stop it with fouls. Move the offense out 5-6 feet from midcourt and "milk the clock." This takes time off the clock and keeps the ball in your possession, while preserving the lead.

Milking the clock

When milking the clock for 25-plus seconds, we make it look like we are trying to score. We set the offense out beyond the three-point line, making several extra passes. We do not take three-point shots, only wide open shots during the last 8 seconds, unless a layup is possible early on the play clock..

We call milking the clock Blue 3, this is when our regular offense moves 3 feet away from the basket toward mid-court. Then we move the ball, while making it look like the offense is looking for a shot, but no shots are taken during most of the clock time, unless it is a very good shot, close to the basket by a good shooter.

Milking the clock helps the players prepare to transition into our delay offense or Blue 6 offense. Blue-3 and Blue-6 are explained more later in this chapter and in Chapter 19.

Lead of 6 or fewer points

At this time, I would go into a full delay, where the only shot taken is a layup that the shooter feels is a sure make. At this point, play for fouls on the opponent; get the opponent's foul number to five for the quarter. This way, all fouls are worth two foul shots. In an all-out delay play, the opponent can't score when you have the ball. The opponent is getting in foul trouble, tired, and anxious to score when they get the ball back, so they take hurried or long shots with low percentages.

When shooting free throws, your team can set its defense before the free throws are shot. If the free throw is missed, there won't be a fast break or an easy basket. You can put your big players back on defense and put your quick guards on the foul line to rebound.

Many coaches say that going into an all-out delay too early will kill your momentum, and you will lose your lead. I agree this could happen, but rarely if you do the following. Work on your delay game each night of practice, making sure each player knows the delay rules.

Delay game rules

The poor foul shooters must be screeners or cutters. If a weak shooter gets the ball, it must be passed before they can be fouled. If at any time a player makes a back cut, they must go to the hoop. The ball always has the right of way when being dribbled at you, so run away from it, screen away, or cut to the hoop; do not stand. If a pass is faked or you do not receive a pass, cut to the hoop or screen awway. If guarded by a slow or poor defender, get the ball. Good foul shooters, passers, and dribblers handle the ball.

9-12 SECOND PLAN

When players catch the ball, they never use up their dribble. Have them hold the ball until they are attacked or doubled-teamed. After 3-4 seconds of passing fakes and jab steps, they dribble for 3-4 seconds away from the defense. Dribbling is followed by a jump stop and pivots, while holding the ball for 3-4 seconds before passing. All of this adds up to "9-12" seconds. This 12-second plan is only to be used by players who can dribble and shoot free throws at a good percentage. The 12-second players must learn to count in their heads and watch the official's hand count so that they don't have a 5-second turnover from holding the ball while being closely guarded. The offensive player can throw the ball off the legs of the defense, causing it to go out of bounds if they are in trouble, or they can call a timeout.

VARIABLE # 2 PLAYERS

Each player has a different mental makeup, skills, confidence, and experience, so the coach must hand-pick the players who can best play the delay game. Some players may be picked for the delay team, for a special or limited role, but all delay players must know their roles well.

VARIABLE # 3 TIME OUTS

Always save 3 or 4 timeouts for the last quarter. Players must always know when to use a "TO" and how many TO's the team has left. On offense, players should use a timeout if they are in danger of committing a turnover. If possible, dribble the ball toward the foul line extended or under the basket before asking for a timeout. This makes it easier to execute our BLOB or SLOB plays, which are game point savers with a good chance of success. (More on this can be found in chapter 22).

Turnovers

There should never be a passing turnover. It could result in a steal and lay-up for the opponent, which can have severe negative psychological effects on your team. If the ball handler is in danger of a 5 second violation or a passing turnover, they must call a timeout. Any teammate can call time out if they see the player with the ball is in trouble.

Make sure the team knows if all timeouts are used so they will not get a "T" foul, which could result in a 0 to 7-point swing in points. If there are no timeouts left, then it is best to hold the ball for a violation, this stops the clock and gives you time to set your defense.

VARIABLE # 4 SUBSTITUTIONS

During the first three quarters, substitutions are made more freely. During the last quarter, when there was a delay, you only played the best five delay players. The only variation may be to shuffle in some players for offense or defense if they have a special skill or quickness.

VARIABLE # 5 FLOOR POSITION

In the delay game, you need to keep the area from the baseline, out to the top of the key, empty of offensive players. This way, there is an open space for cuts, drives, and backdoor moves that are free of defenders. The players should be spaced out 12-15-feet apart, so that one defender can't guard two players or the ball can't be double-teamed. Any open, unguarded player should move under the basket in a defensive free area for a pass. If an offensive player's defender sags into the key, near the basket, that offensive player must go to midcourt, where they get the ball and hold it until the defender comes out of the key.

VARIABLE # 6 PPP (POINTS PER POSSESSION

The PPP should drive everything your team does on both ends of the floor, it drives who takes three point-shots and when it is taken. The same goes for any shot taken during a game. The PPP determines your type of defense and whether you press. The following is an example of how PPP works;

POOR TEAM

Out of 10 possessions, they will turn over the ball two or more times, take 3 forced or low percentage shots, miss, and make 2 baskets out of the remaining possessions. The result is 4 points out of 10 possessions or a PPP of .4.

GOOD TEAM

Out of 10 possessions, they will turn over the ball one time, take 1 forced shot, make 2 out of 5 shots, and shoot free throws on two possessions. The result is 7 points out of 10 possessions or a PPP of .7.

To win games, it takes a PPP of .7 or better in most cases. If you multiply the 10 possessions by 5 or 6 you will get 50-60 possessions for the game, which is the normal number of shots for most games.

When shooting layups in the delay game, your PPP is near 2.0. When there are 5 fouls or more on the opponent, your team is shooting two free throws, which gives your team a PPP of over 1.2 or better if you have good free-throw shooters. A normal offense will have a PPP around .5 to .8, so you double your PPP by playing for the opponent's fouls and a chance to shoot free throws or layups during the game.

The PPP must be taught, and if done along with the discipline to follow game plans, the players will soon be playing to their and the team's strengths.

VARIABLE # 7 FREE THROWS

Don't let your opponent shoot free throws. When your team is on offense, you should do everything possible to get to the foul line. The PPP (POINTS PER POSSESSION) is higher on free throws than when you run your offense. When you're shooting free throws, you can place your players in the position you want for defense.

I like to end each practice with 7-10 minutes doing different free-throw shooting drills that put players under pressure, with a penalty for missing. First, the players pair up and do their ladder and free throw chart, with 10 free throws, which are recorded.

That is followed by what we call Reno, where you run down and back on a miss. It is a free-throw drill, which got its name because it is a gamble. You run if you miss your shot. Or we play swish/bounce on 5 free throw shots. These three things will improve their free-throw shooting percentage because players will feel pressure and be very focused on each practice shot.

VARIABLE # 8 PRACTICE

It is best if the delay offense is part of your regular offense, the following is an example; when we run out motion offense, "BLUE," "BLUE 3" is what we call "Milking the Clock" the only difference is that the offense out 3- 6 feet beyond the three-point line, but the player movement is the same. In "BLUE 6" our delay offense, we set up 6 feet from the midcourt line and look to get fouled or make a layup.

You must spend 6 to 10 minutes each practice night getting ready to beat pressure and getting into the delay offense. I teach delay by giving the team three or four possessions of 5 vs 5 defenders, three or four possessions of 5 vs 6 defenders. As well as three or four possessions of 5 vs 7 defenders, and three or four possessions of 5 vs 8 defenders. If at any time there is a turnover, play is stopped. Then there is discussion on why the turnover happened and how it could have been prevented, 10 push-ups for the mistake follow this.

Practice against extra defenders forces the offense to move players and the ball after many ball fakes. The lack of movement or fakes will result in mistakes and turnovers. The delay players must also practice the use of time-outs when in trouble.

DELAY DURING THE GAME

In the last 35 seconds of the first three quarters, we trap to get the ball back and go into our Blue 6-delay offense. This way, we can get the last shot of the quarter. Ending the quarter with a made basket will deflate your opponent and fire up your team. This will also give you 30 seconds to practice the Blue 6-delay offense three times before the fourth quarter comes up. Then the opponent doesn't get the last shot of the quarter and a possible score, and it gives your team practice on trapping. Then you can practice your quick-hitter play the last 8-10 seconds of the quarter for a quarter-ending shot.

If your team does well with the variables listed above during the last 35 seconds of each quarter, they will have a successful season and achieve an above-average score late in a game.

KISS BASKETBALL

VEGAS-- CLOCK MILKER
A

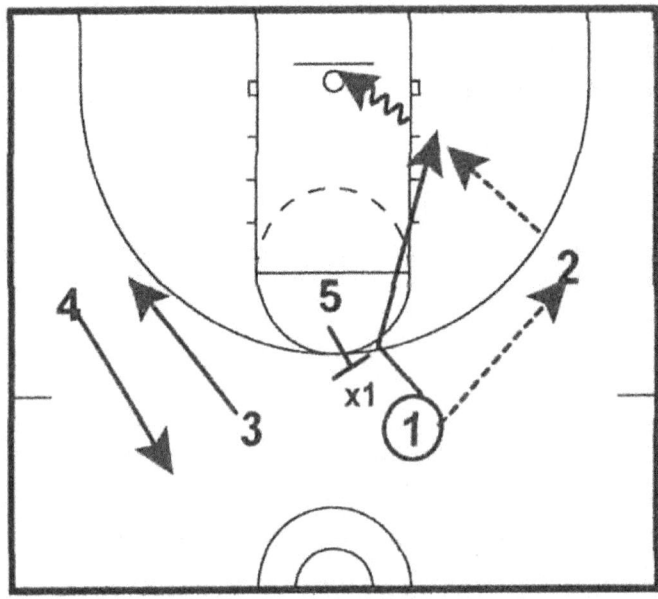

1 passes to the wing 2 and makes a v-cut off of 5's back screen toward the hoop for a lay up. 2 may shoot or drive or to the hoop if there is no pass to 1. 3 and 4 interchange spots.

VEGAS-- CLOCK MILKER
A

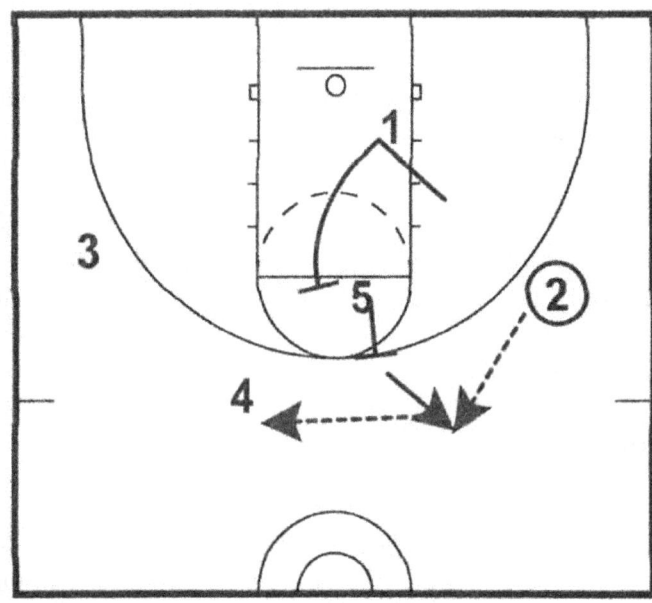

After 1 cuts off of 5's screen, 5 steps out as a guard and gets a pass from 2 and reverses the ball to 4 who has replaced 3 as a guard. Cutter 1 replaces 5 in the high post if there is no pass to him.

VEGAS-- CLOCK MILKER
A

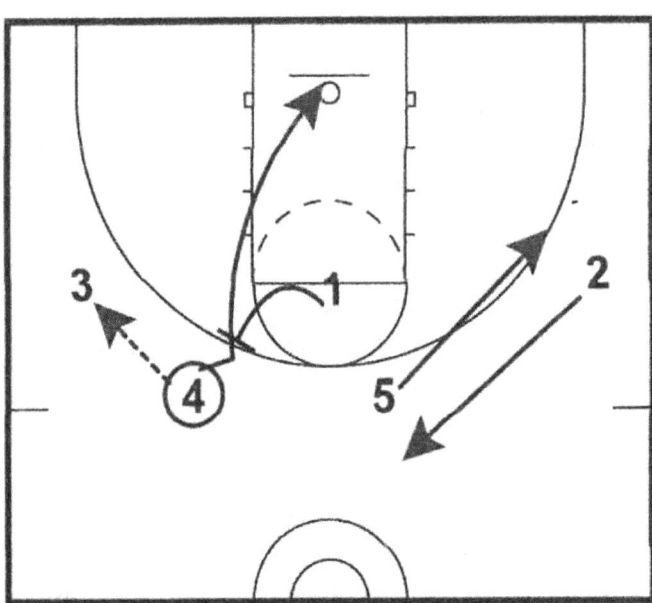

4 passes to the wing 3 and cuts off 1 screen and cuts to the hoop as 5 and 2 inter change and the offense repeats in the left side of the floor.

VEGAS-- CLOCK MILKER
A

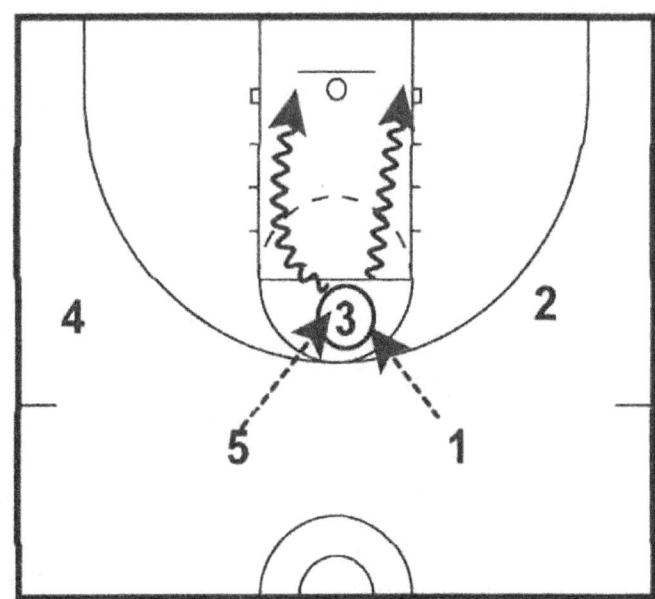

when your best player is in the post or you have a miss match feed the ball to the post player and let him go 1-on-1.

CHAPTER 19
STALL

When the team moves from milking the clock in the Blue 3 delay into the stall, they are ready to set up the Blue-6 offense formation. The players have not only worked on Blue-6 each night in practice, but they have also used Blue-6 during the last 35 seconds of the first three quarters of the game to secure the last shot of the quarter, so they are now ready.

When wanting to stall, we cross half-court and set up a predetermined stall offense. This should feature a lot of player and ball movement, accompanied by numerous back and down screens, as well as cross and slip screens, back cuts, and dives.

Stall formation

Blue 6 is a high 1-2-2 floor set that forms a good stall. If you have a couple of good free-throw shooters and ball handlers, this high 1-2-2 floor setup allows you to control who has the ball and might get fouled. I like to use one or two of our bigger players as the top 3 players. This will draw the other team's key players to midcourt, forcing them to play one-on-one defense without help.

Blue-6

Our motion offense means a total stall, 6 feet from midcourt, with all players above the foul line level and 5 feet from the sideline.

In the 1-2-2 BLUE-6, the three best offensive players handle the ball and take the foul shots. The two lowest-skilled players are mainly screeners or cutters to the hoop for layups. Players must be patient and not shoot unless they are completely sure and have an open layup. The offense must not let its defender sag near the basket to protect the hoop. If a defender sags off an offensive player, that offensive player must come out to midcourt and get the ball. They will hold until the defender leaves the key and comes to midcourt to play defense. Never screen the ball when in the stall game, but use all kinds of screens off the ball.

Practicing Blue-6

The Blue-6 stall requires a lot of off-ball screens so we can get players open while keeping the defense from standing and watching or double-teaming the ball. A lot of practice is used to teach setting different kinds of screens, such as down and back screens. Just as important is the use of slip screens and back cuts.

When setting a screen, the offensive screener must seal the defender with a reverse pivot and roll toward the hoop. This screen is just like screening out when defensive rebounding or executing a screen and roll when on offense. The player coming off the screen must v-cut before cutting off screens just as they do when cutting off a screen when on offense. The use of back screens and slipping screens isn't something defensive players play against often, so they must be used and mixed in with the other screens. These screens are taught when teaching offensive skills, Chapter 17

Practicing stall

Of all time spent during a practice, stalling practice for the last 35 seconds of a quarter is the most important. The skills, mental discipline, and focus will carry over into all other parts of basketball. Fourth-quarter stall work should be done at different times each day, not always as the last thing done. When I do stall early in practice, it produces a sharper practice because players are mentally alert and focused.

SPORTSMANSHIP OF BLUE 6

Milking the clock (Blue 3) or running the Blue-6 stall can be judged as unethical or poor sportsmanship. Some people would say you are holding on to the ball and not shooting. The stall game isn't against the rules; it is just a different strategy. The stall is like a large anaconda, a constrictor snake slowly choking the life out of a larger prey, while being in total control. Most states use a 35-second shot clock, so the stall can only last that long. It is essential to have a few quick-hitters for securing a good shot in the last 6-7 seconds, as the shot clock is winding down.

Starting The Game With Blue-6

When there was no shot clock, I ran the stall, BLUE-6 from the start of the game, if my team was the underdog. Blue-6 helped slow down the game and make it shorter, allowing us to dictate the pace; no shot was taken, even if we stalled for 2-4 minutes. Blue-6 forced the better opponents to play a lot of the game on defense and away from the basket, as we worked for lay-ups or drew fouls.

Today's basketball game has a shot clock, so the ball must be given up within 35 seconds. To utilize most of the game time in a delayed offense like Blue-6, it will effectively cut the game's length in half. It is a great equalizer against a superior opponent. The slow pace means each team will only get 35-40 shots during the game, not the normal 60-80 shots. If the superior team misses or makes a poor number of their first 10-20 shots, they will feel the pressure of being behind and the slow pace. Players will not like not getting many shots, so they will force, hurry, or take bad shots. If the better team is behind, they will be more apt to gamble when on defense, be out of position, and foul or give up a good shot. This slow type of game against a strong team can have a negative effect on both the opponent's offense and defense.

VALUE OF Blue-6

My team always shoots a higher percentage of made free throws when we run our Blue-6 offense than when we run our regular offense. This is because it is the better players who shoot all the free throws. In tight games when we need to manage the clock, we slow the game pace and use Blue-6 frequently. We usually shot and made more free throws in the fourth quarter than in the first three quarters combined.

BLUE 6 DELAY

DELAY BLUE 6
A

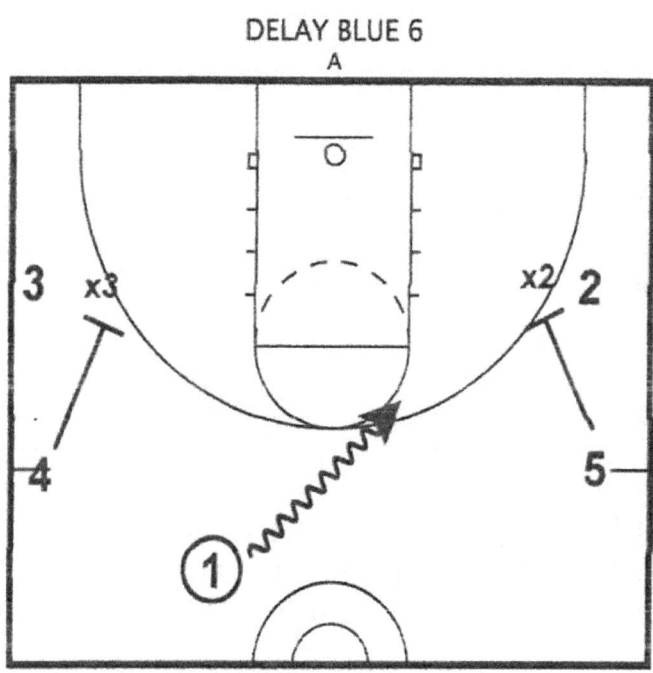

1 holds the ball until he is closely guarded, then after 3 seconds he drives toward the three point line and right side. When 1 starts his drive 4 & 5 down screen or 1 & 2 back screen.

DELAY BLUE 6
A

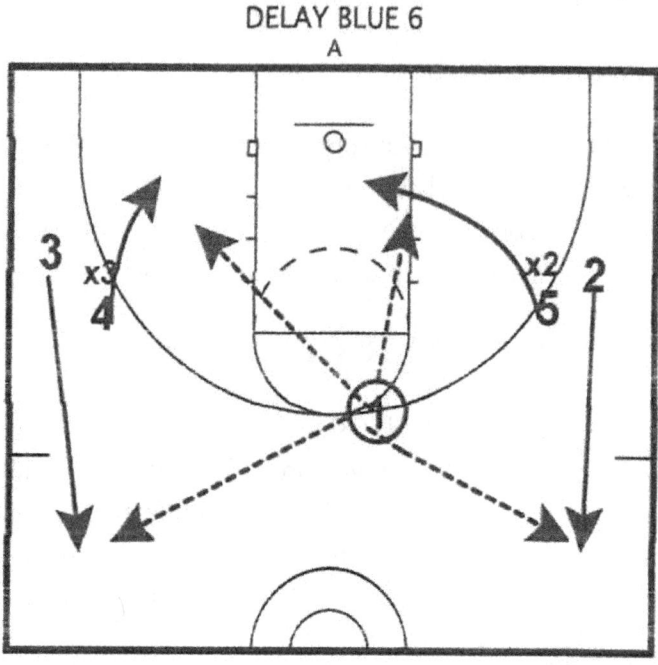

1 lands on a jump stop and passed to 4 or 5 for a lay up if they are open after their screen and roll. If 4 and 5 are covered he passes to 2 or 3.

DELAY BLUE 6
A

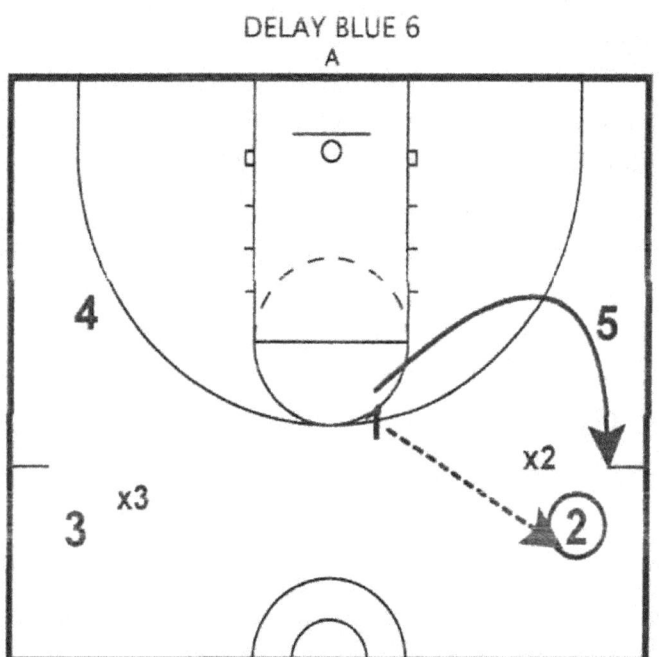

If 1 passes to 2 coming off 5 screen. 2 holds the ball as the passer 1 goes to the side of the floor he passes to.

DELAY BLUE 6
A

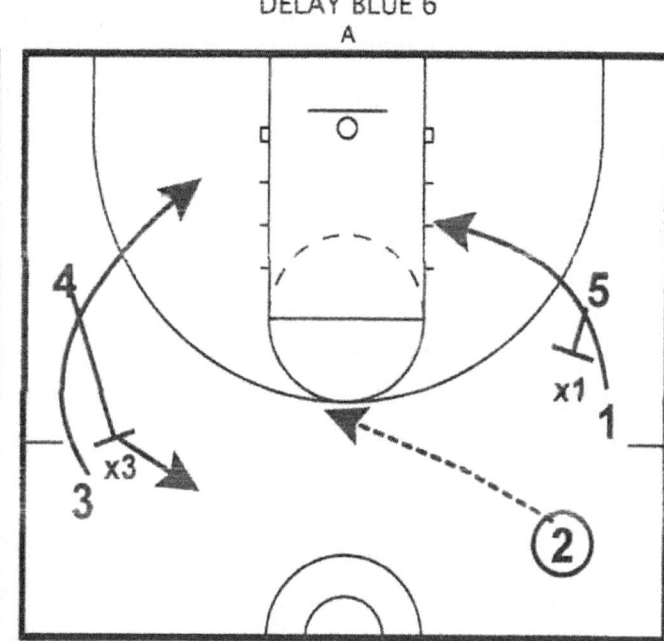

The screens on the sides of the court can be down screens like frame 1 or back screens like frame 4

CHAPTER 20
Half Court MAN OFFENSE

Probing Action

On offense, the players must run a disciplined attack that probes the defense until a high-percentage shot is found. Probing often means a player attacks with a drive, but then backs away, fakes a shot or pass, which gives him a chance to read the opponent. Sending the defense to the other side of the floor is a probe to determine if the defense is playing man-to-man or zone defense.

Probing action may take time early in the game and during a possession, as that is when the defense is at its best. If an offensive team is patient and disciplined, it can affect a defense's physical and mental performance.

Players who know their abilities will be able to probe the defense, knowing whether to attack or back away. The probing action will improve as the game and season progress. With time, the team learns its individual and collective strengths and weaknesses, and your team will be at its best by the end of the season.

Learning how to Probe

This disciplined probing is taught in practice. If a player takes a shot, drive, or pass in practice, they must know whether it is a high or low percentage shot and whether it is a good decision for the team. If the coach isn't completely sure the player's decision was best, the whistle stops play. Then the player needs to explain what would have been a better decision and why.

Probing requires strong leadership from the point guard, who acts like a coach on the floor. It is easy for the point guard to start the offense because he has four passing options spread across the floor. Where the point guard passes, to the wing or post, will determine the action all five players take. (See the drawings at the end of the chapter for the options for probing)

1-4 Floor Set Offense

I only use a few plays out of the 1-4 floor set. This plan comes from my studies of college teams. When I was young, I lived in Corvallis and followed the Oregon State Beavers basketball team. Ralph Miller coached the Beavers, and he ran a high 1-4 offense that became popular in the 1970s. There are several advantages of the 1-4 floor set. It gives a high PPP if run with discipline. Because there are no defenders or offensive players near the basket, that area is free for basket drives. It's hard for the defense to give help on drives to the hoop or on shots because they are spread across the floor. The high 1-4 posts players play at the foul line, 15' from the hoop. They can be of any size, and they can shoot from the free-throw line if the defense sags. Or the post player can out-quick the defense on a drive to the hoop with one dribble. The wings and point guard are on a full run toward the hoop when they cut for a pass. All players can get to the hoop after 1-3 dribbles. All four of the offensive players, including wings and posts, are within shooting distance when they receive the ball. The offense is quick-hitting, easy to learn, and it is easy to locate the problem if there is a breakdown.

Depending on where the first pass goes, all five players are moving on a post or wing pass. This way, the defenders off the ball are always on the move. This offense is good if the opponent plays a very aggressive denial defense. The 1-4 high set is also good vs a zone with small adjustments. Sending an offensive player through the defense to the other side of the floor is a probe to determine if the defense is playing man or zone defense.

Circle Offense

Along with the high 1-4, man offense, I use a circle-motion offense with 5 players out and no post. The circle motion offense has players cutting toward the basket when they get passes. This draws fouls and gives high percentage shots. It is also a very fast cutting and passing offense. The circle offense is ideal for a small team with fast-moving players who excel at passing. This offense requires a lot of energy, as players are constantly moving due to its continuity. The players must read the defense to see if they are sagging, overplaying to deny, or switching all screens, so they can adjust their cuts to the hoop.

The high 1-4 and circle motion are two good offenses because all five players are in the action, and a weak opponent's defender will be exposed. If a player has low offensive skills, use them as a backside rebounder or as a screen setter. Five players out works great when you have more guard-like players who are able to pull larger opponents away from the hoop, beat them off the dribble, or with a basket cut.

Man offense plays

Along with our two main half-court offenses, we have a few quick hitters, such as Utah. Utah is a quick hitter off a screen and roll action, utilizing the two best players against man-to-man defense. MONEY is another quick hitter to get a three-point shot. Money can be used as a continuity or a set play against any kind of defense, man or zone defenses.. Money is a good three-point play, and I only run it for the best three-point shooters on my team. Quick hitters are needed for the last 7-8 seconds, when the shot clock is about to expire.

Drawings of Utah and Money are shown at the end of this chapter.

3 Point Shot rules and expectations

It is essential to record the shots taken during each night of practice, particularly during shooting drills. The field goal percentage should be shared with the shooters so they will know if they have the license to shoot threes during the next game.

My players must earn the right to shoot 3-pointers during a game. If a player can't shoot between 40% and 60% on 3-pointers when not guarded, they aren't allowed to shoot. When your offense is pushed out past the three-point line, the shooter is tired, rushed, and pressured by a defender; their 3-point percentage will drop by 10-15%. Shooting 25% in practice is like shooting 20% or lower in a game.

Shooting 25% or 1 out of 4 on three pointers will give you 3 points in four possessions and a PPP of .75. When you figure in turnovers, which are at 25 to 30 percent in most games, and the number of possessions needed to reach a .75 PPP, the 25% three-point shooting PPP is now .6 or lower. A PPP of .6 won't put your team in the upper third of your league, or make it possible to pull off upsets or win postseason games.

Winning teams usually have a PPP of over 0.8 for the entire game, on all their shots, including 2s and 3s combined. So, if a player isn't shooting over 30% on 3's in games, I'm not in favor of the three-point shot. It doesn't lead to any free throws that have a PPP between 1.0 and 1.6+. Today, it's a big deal for players to shoot and make 3-pointers, which often breaks down ball movement, teamwork, discipline, and team chemistry. The three-point shot isn't for all players, and it is the coach's job to let the players know who has the green light. See Chapter 21 on statistics for a breakdown of PPP and percentages.

KISS BASKETBALL

ORANGE A

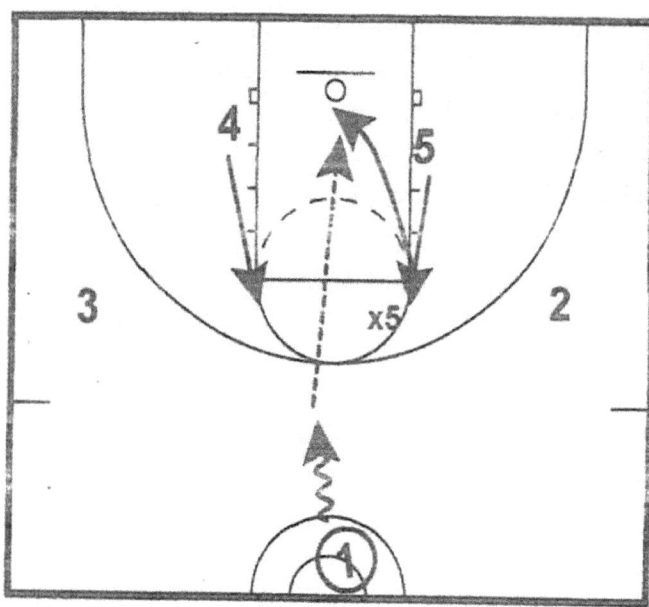

POST PASS**IF THE POST PLAYER IS OVER PLAYED BY THE DEFENSE X5, HE CUTS BACK TO THE BASKET FOR A LOB PASS.

ORANGE A

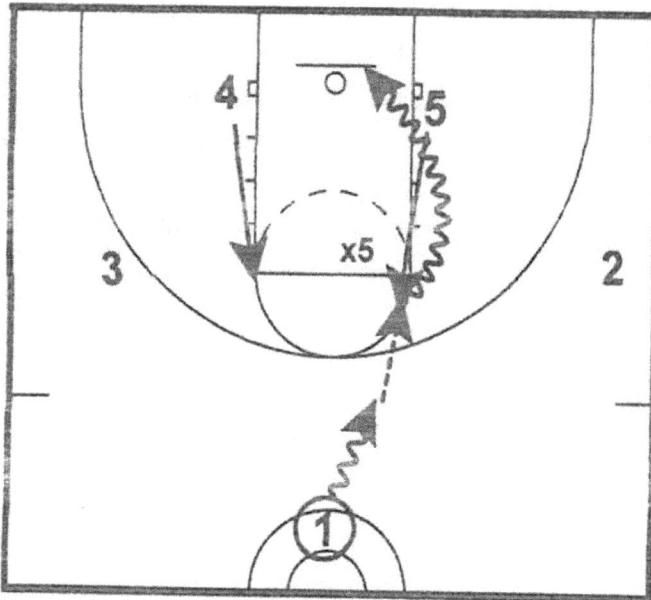

POST PASS** IF THE POST CAN BEAT HIS MAN 1 ON 1, HE SHOULD ATTACK THE HOOP.

ORANGE A

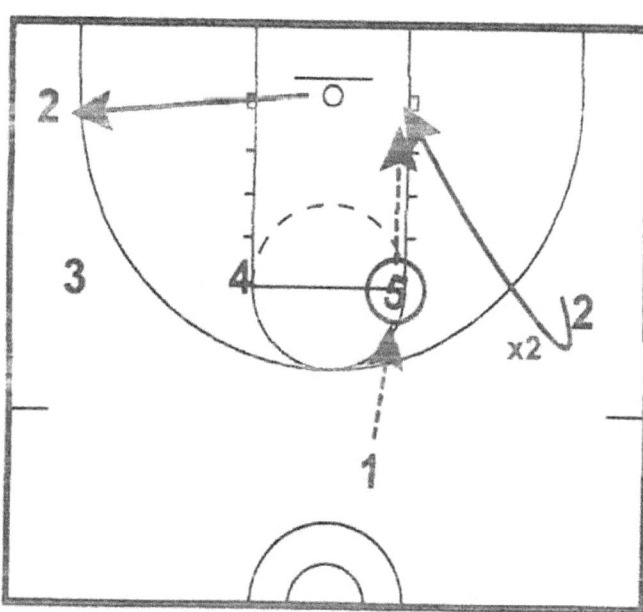

POST PASS**OPTION 1*THE BALL SIDE WING JABS UP AND CUTS TO THE HOOP FOR A LAY UP. IF 2 DOESN'T GET A PASS HE CONTINUES TO THE CORNER.

ORANGE A

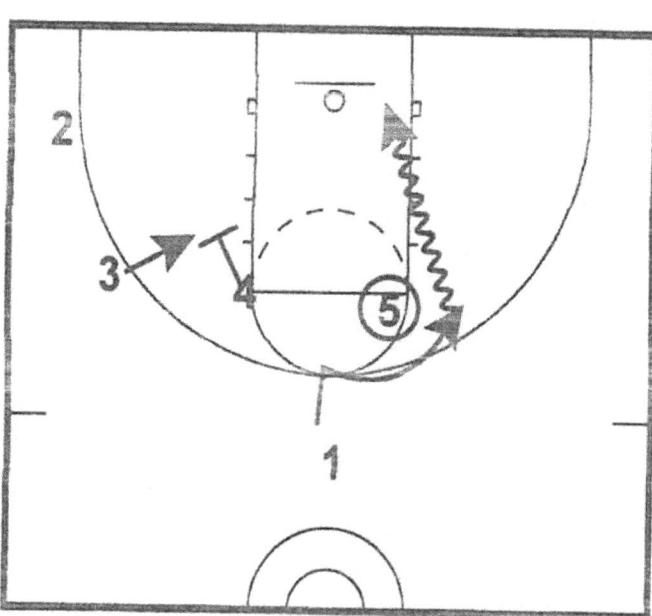

POST PASS**OPTION 2*AS 2 IS MAKING HIS CUT, 1 JABS IN AND CUTS OFF 5 FOR A HAND OFF AND A LAY UP.

KISS BASKETBALL

ORANGE
A

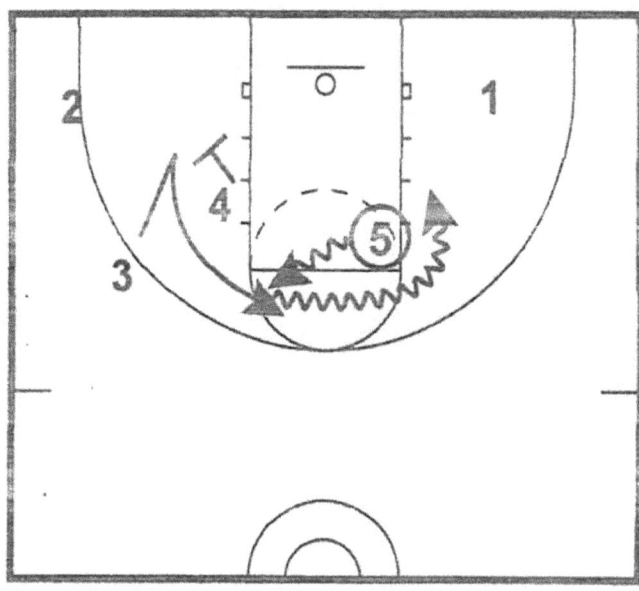

POST PASS**OPTION 3* AS 1 IS MAKING HIS CUT, 3 JABS DOWN AN CUTS OFF OF 4'S SCREEN. 5 TAKES 2 DRIBBLES, JUMP STOPS AND HANDS OFF TO 3 FOR A SHOT OR DRIVE.

ORANGE
A

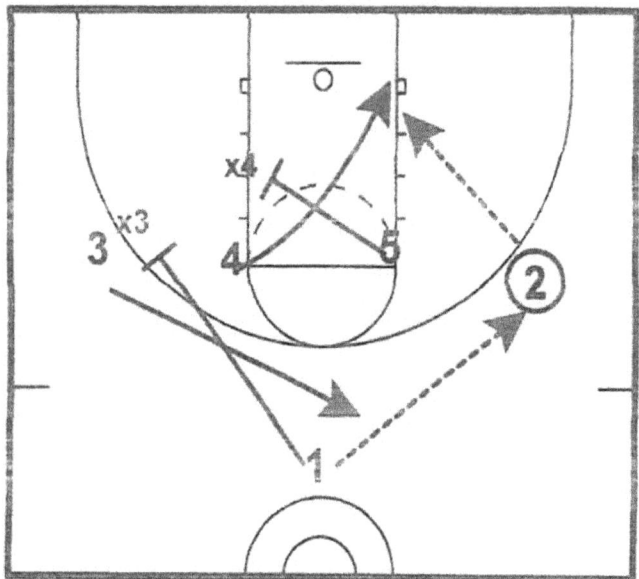

WING PASS**ON THE PASS TO 2,1 AND 3 TRADE PLACES, WHILE 5 SETS A SCREEN ON X4, WHO CUTS TO THE HOOP FOR A PASS.

ORANGE
A

WING PASS**AFTER 5 SETS HIS SCREEN ON X4 HE SEALS AND COMES BACK TO THE BALL. 5 HAS A SHOT OR DRIVE AND CAN PASS TO 4.

ORANGE
A

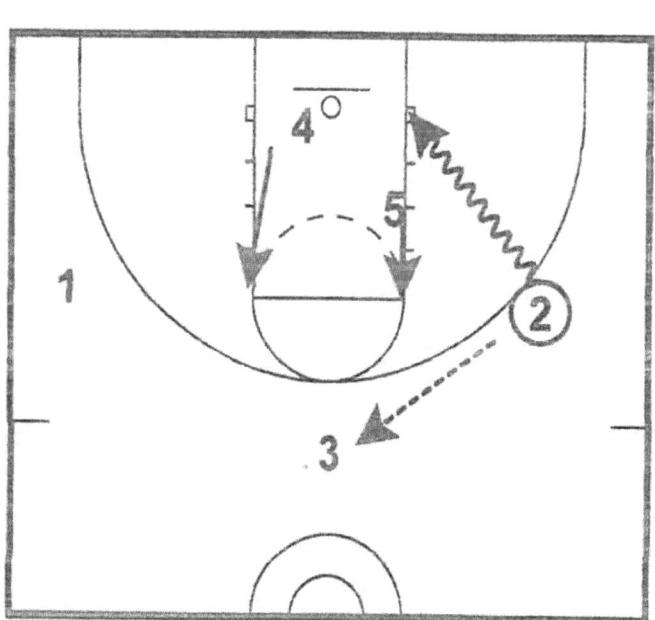

RESET**IF THERE IS NO PLAY BY 4 OR 5 THE BALL IS RETURNED TO THE TOP AND PLAY IS RESTARTED WITH A POST OR WING PASS. WINGS MAY DRIVE TO THE HOOP AT ANY TIME.

KISS BASKETBALL

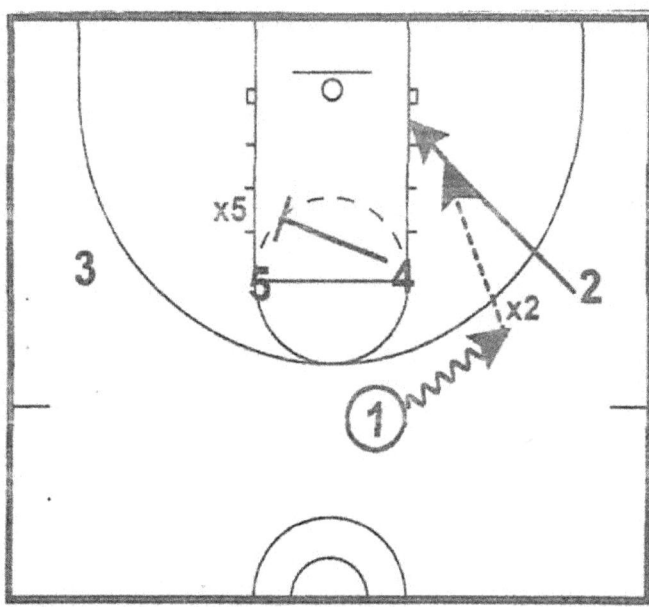

WING OVER PLAY** IF IT IS HARD TO PASS TO A WING DUE TO DEFENSIVE OVER PLAY, 1 SHOULD DRIVE AT THE DEFENDER TO FREEZE HIM AND PASS TO 2 WHO MAKES A BACK DOOR CUT.

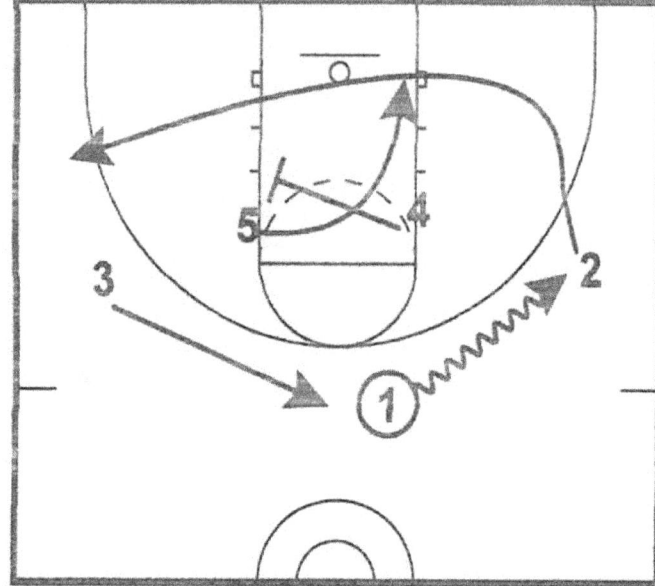

WING OVER PLAY** DRIBBLE OUT*. IF 1 CAN'T PASS TO THE WING AND YOU WANT WING OPTIONS, 1 DRIBBLES TO THE WING, 2 CLEARS OUT AND 4 SCREENS ACROSS ON X5.

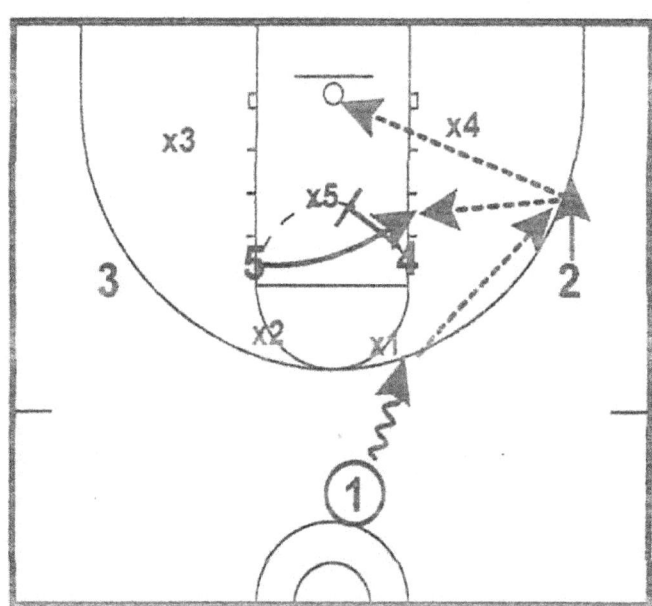

ORANGE VS A 2-3 ZONE** 1 DRIVES AT X1 TO FREEZE HIM, 2 SLIDES DOWN 2 STEPS AND GETS THE PASS. 4 SCREENS X5 AND 5 CUTS BEHIND THE SCREEN. 2 READS X4 WHO MUST COVER 5 OR 2.

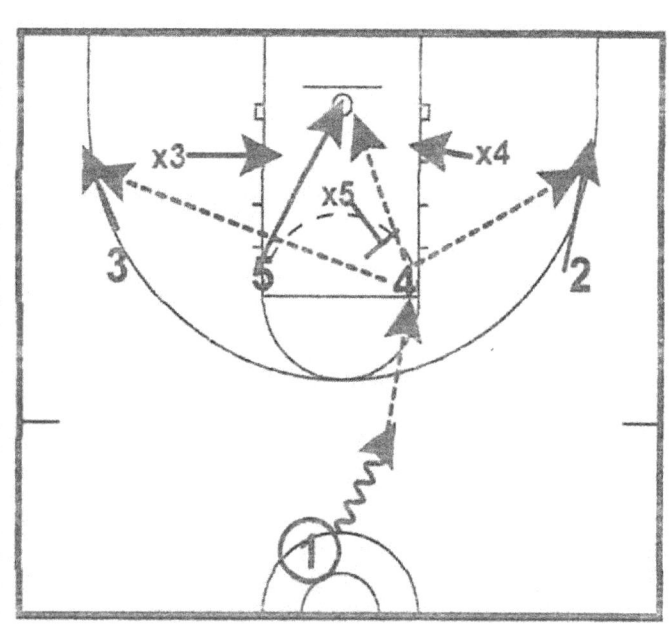

ORANGE VS A 2-3 ZONE** 1 PASSES THE BALL TO 4 WHO CAN SHOOT, 5 DIVES TO THE RIM. IF X5 COMES UP TO GUARD 4 HE PASSES TO 5. IF X3 OR X4 TRIES TO HELP, 4 PASSES TO THE WINGS WHO SLIDE DOWN.

KISS BASKETBALL

MOTION-5 OUT
A

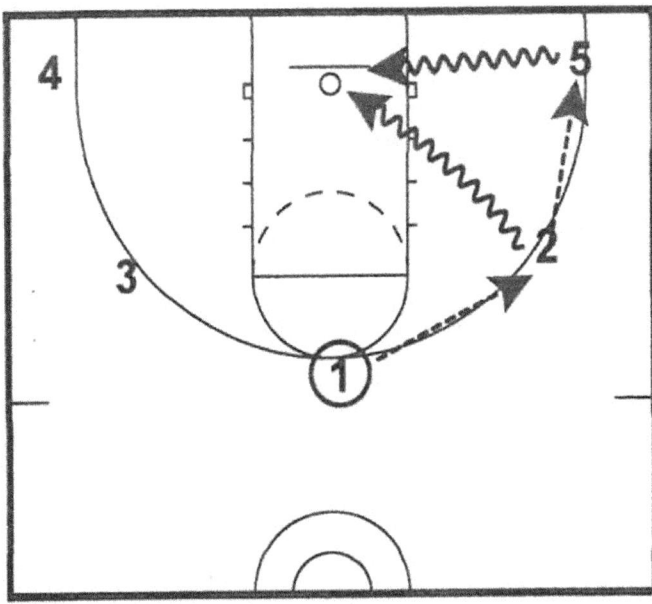

MOTION; Any player is free to drive to the hoop if he can beat their defender.

MOTION-5 OUT
A

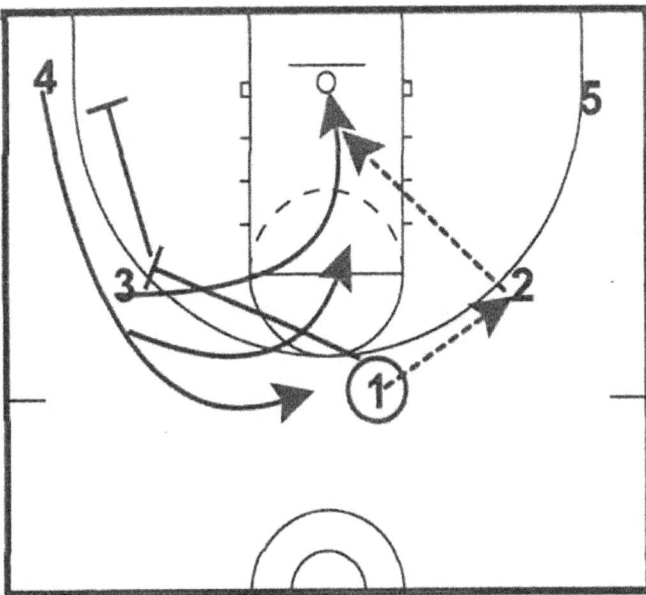

MOTION; T1 makes a wing pass and screen away for 3. 1 then screens all the way to the bottom for 4 who cuts to the hoop or replaces on top.

MOTION-5 OUT
A

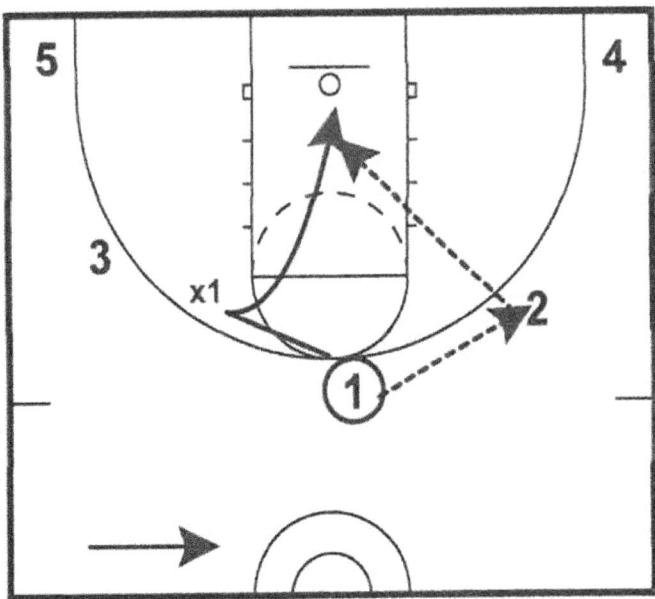

MOTION; Ever few plays 1 passes and goes to set a screen then he jabs and cuts the defenders face as he cuts to the hoop for a give and go pass.

MOTION-5 OUT
A

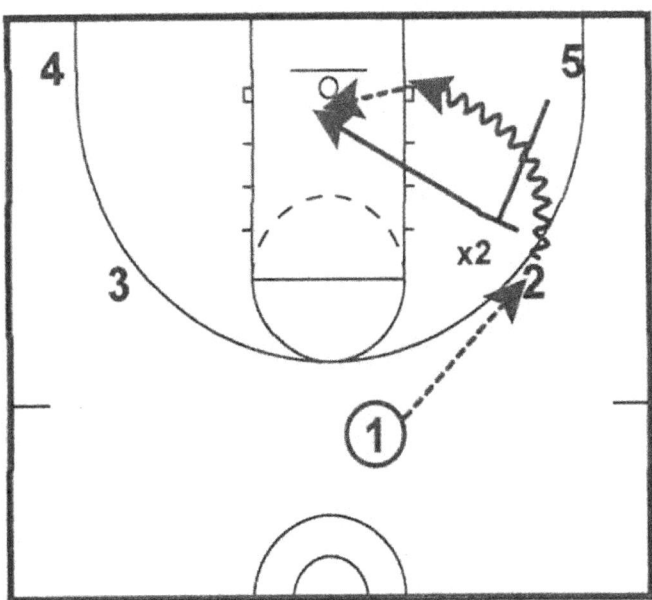

MOTION; The wing and corner can run a screen and roll.

KISS BASKETBALL

UTAH-- MAN QUICK HITTER
A

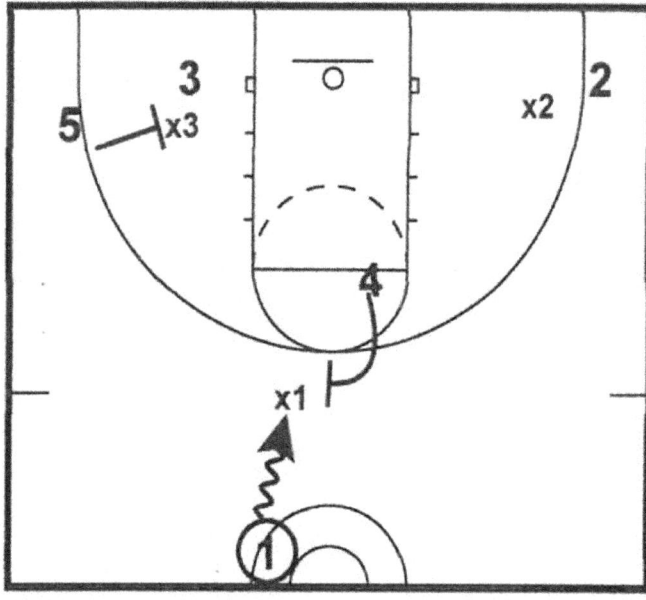

As 4 sets a screen on x1, 5 sets a screen on x3, as 1 drives his defender into 4's screen.

UTAH-- MAN QUICK HITTER
A

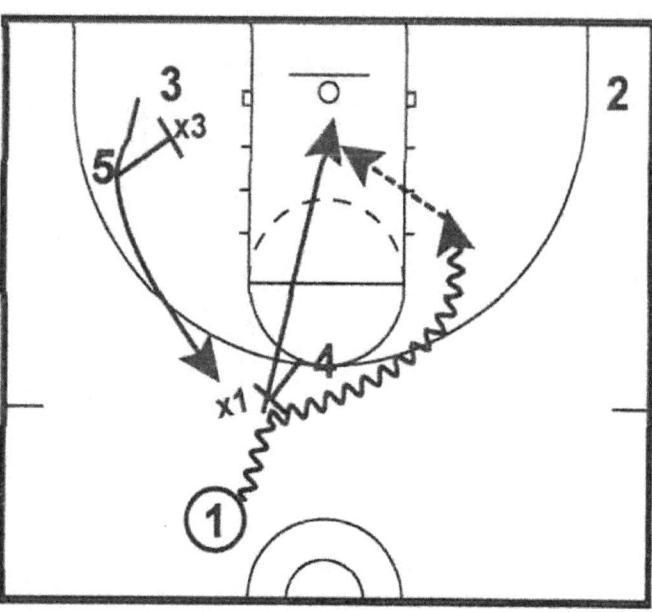

1 drives off the screen by 4 looking for a lay up, if x4 switches on to 1, 1 makes a pass to 4 for a lay up.

UTAH-- MAN QUICK HITTER
A

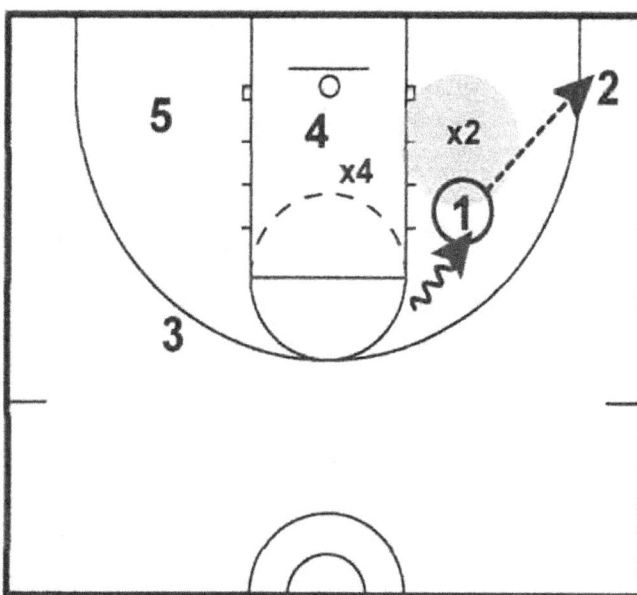

If there is no switch by x4 on to 1 but x2 slides over to stop 2's lay up, 1 passes to 2 for a wide open shot.

UTAH-- MAN QUICK HITTER
A

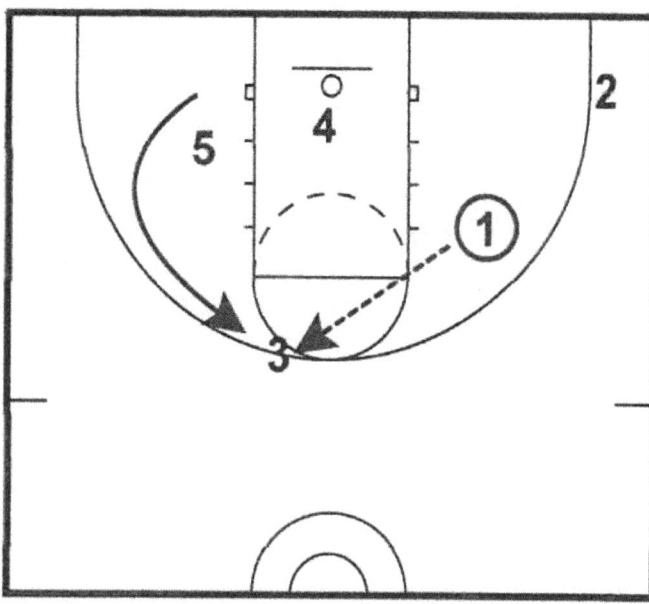

If the play breaks down, 3 coming off of 5's screen will be open it the top of the key for a shot

CHAPTER 21
ZONE OFFENSE

There are several ways to attack the zone defense, and each has its value. Some ideas used to beat zone defenses include overload, screen, flash cutters, fast passing, bombing threes, and, best of all, screening the zone.

Early in my coaching years, around 1964, I began using what I call the "TZ" or Top Zone. This offense has been successful against all types of zone defenses with little adjustment. TZ started out as a reading, faking, passing, and shooting drill. The drill was so successful that it soon became adjusted and was made into the main part of my zone offense package.

Key to the top zone offense

First, work on the basic skills of passing, shooting, screening, and faking passes to freeze the defense. For more information, see offensive skills and drills in Chapter 17. Players also must know their defined roles: where to be on the floor and what to do from that position.

False motion

It is helpful to have false motion before the play. False motion is moving the ball away from a player or area on the floor where you attack. This false motion can be from passing or dribbling to the opposite side of the floor before returning the ball to your desired player or area where you plan to attack. An example is when we run the play "Money," we start the play by going to our second-best three-point player on the left side of the floor. Then we run the same play to the right side of the floor for our best three-point shooter. Against a zone defense, we often run a stack to the side of the floor with the weakest defenders. After we pass or bring the ball down the side of the floor where the opponent is strongest. We then screen the weak side of the zone and put the weakest defender or zone area in a position where they are outnumbered two to one or three to one. This is the same idea we use against man defense. We clear the opponent's best defenders to the left side of the floor and run the quick hitter, "Utah," to the right-hand side of the floor.

TOP ZONE DRILLS

To get the players ready to attack a zone, I have them work on the TZ (top-zone) drills as shown at the end of this chapter. All the TZ drills are set up so that the offense has a one-player advantage, such as 3 vs 2 or 2 vs 1. This forces the offense to read the defense and make the correct pass after making a ball or eye fake to freeze the defense. The drills run with the offense having an advantage. When we go 5-on-5 live against a zone defense, we gain a one-player advantage with our screens and overloads.

TOP ZONE DRILLS

1. Guards 3 vs 2
2. Guards and high post 4 vs 3
3. side 4 vs 3, Bottom 2 vs 1
4. 4, Bottom 3 vs 2, Bottom 4 vs 3
5. Odd zone top 3 vs 2
6. Skip pass 4 vs 3

Strengths of Top Zone

There are many strengths to the top zone method of offense. It is simple and easy to learn. Players are placed for success, and everyone has and knows their roles. It's easy to see and correct mistakes, and you get great, open, squared-up shots after just 1-2 passes. It's flexible and can attack all zones and works with average shooters. Top Zone has great floor balance for rebounds and defends against the opponent's fast break. The TZ drills will teach and reinforce the offense while building basic skills such as passing, faking, shooting, setting screens, sealing screens, and reading the defense. All the players are facing the ball so they can see the defense and the passer. The passes are made while standing, not while on the move or off the dribble. Passes off the dribble have a much higher turnover rate. This is due to no fakes and making decisions on the move. Last of all, the top zone has options that will attack the zone's weakness.

Top Zone Rules

1. On any high post pass, the short corner player steps into the key under the basket and the wings drop down two steps toward the baseline.
2. The high post screens the top defender in any odd front defense, such as 1-2-2 or 1-3-1, and then rolls to the hoop.
3. The point guard drives at any top defender to occupy him before passing, so the defender can't defend both the ball and the offensive wing.
4. The wings always dropped two steps below the extended foul line and toward the baseline before receiving a pass, which forces a bottom defender to guard the ball.

Top Zone Options

1. Top Zone (basic)
2. Up-town (lob)
3. Downtown (baseline screen)
4. Stack (overload)
5. Money (3-point shot)
6. Horns (basic)

Problem Solving

If the top zone breaks down and the offense doesn't get a great shot, you can bet the problem is due to one of the following;

1. Players were out of position, maybe by only 3-feet.
2. The screens and seals were not installed correctly.
3. The person with the ball made a poor read or choice.
4. The offense didn't mix in the different quick hitters and use both sides of the floor.

Conclusion

The main key to beating a zone isn't making a lot of three-point shots, but making lots of shots. The TZ package depends on screens, overloads, and making good reads when the offense outnumbers the defense. If you watch games today at any level, against a zone defense, all you see is many ball reversals and skip passes; the offense ends up taking three-point shots often by poor shooters.

Top Zone is easy to run, so it is easy to scout. However, using false motion and scouting information for defensive weaknesses will override what the opponents know, and they still have to stop the offense.

KISS BASKETBALL

TOP ZONE DRILLS 1-8
A

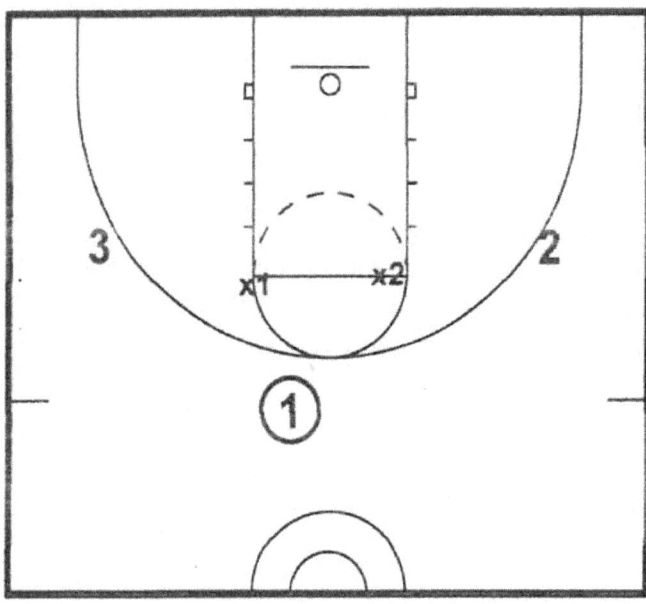

DRILL #1, 3 VS 2 TOP -1 ATTACKS ONE OF THE DEFENSIVE GUARDS, READS AND THEN PASSES OR TAKES A SHOT. KEY IS ATTACKING A DEFENDER, WINGS CAN USE SKIP PASSES.

TOP ZONE DRILLS 1-8
A

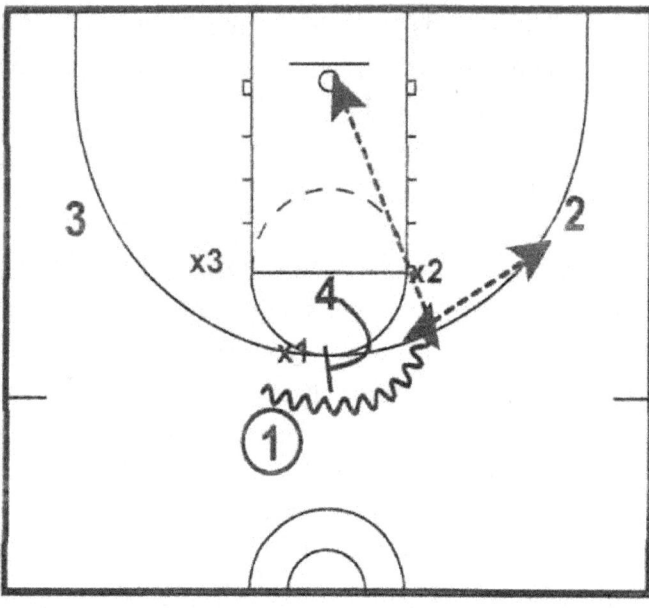

DRILL #2, 4 VS 3 ODD ZONE – THE POST SCREENS THE TOP DEFENDER AND 1 DRIVES AT A WING DEFENDER AND PASSES TO THE WING, ROLLING POST OR SHOOTS.

TOP ZONE DRILLS 1-8
A

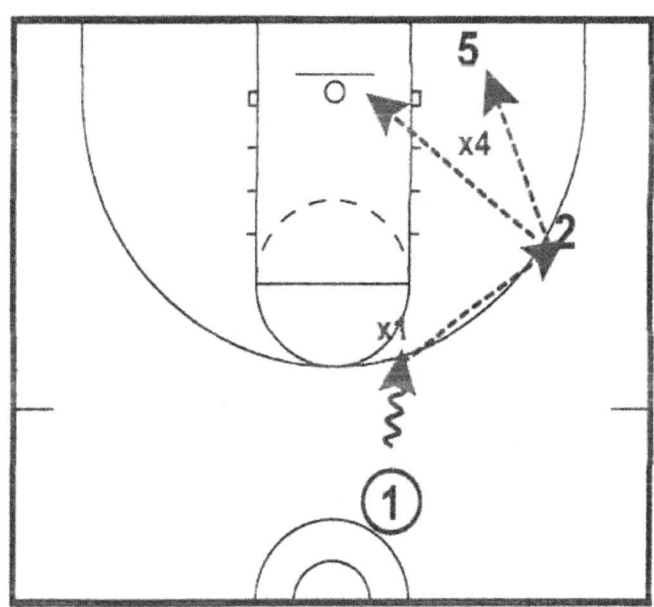

DRILL #3, 3 VS 2 SIDE L & R – 1 DRIVES AT X1 AND PASSES TO 2 WHO SHOOTS OR PASSES TO THE SHORT CORNER AFTER READING THE BOTTOM DEFENDER X4.

TOP ZONE DRILLS 1-8
A

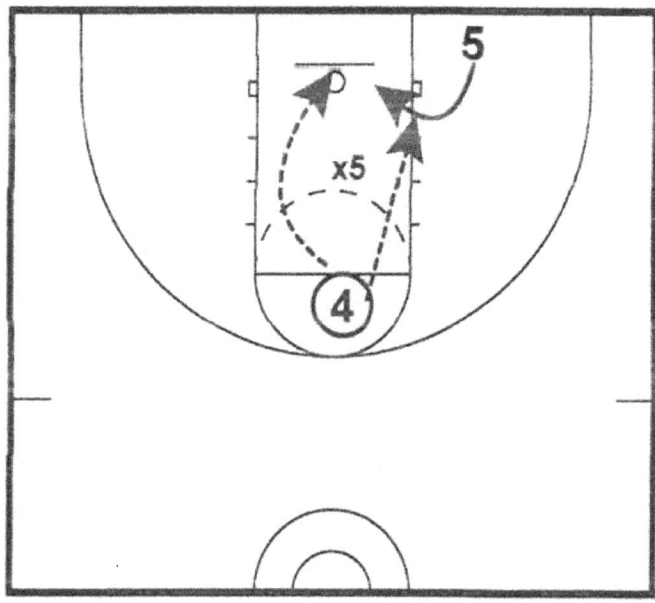

DRILL 4, 2 VS 1 BOTTOM – 4 FACES THE HOOP AND 5 STEPS INTO THE KEY. IF X5 STAYS LOW 4 SHOOTS, IF X5 COMES UP THE PASS IS MADE TO 5.

KISS BASKETBALL

TOP ZONE DRILLS 1-8
A

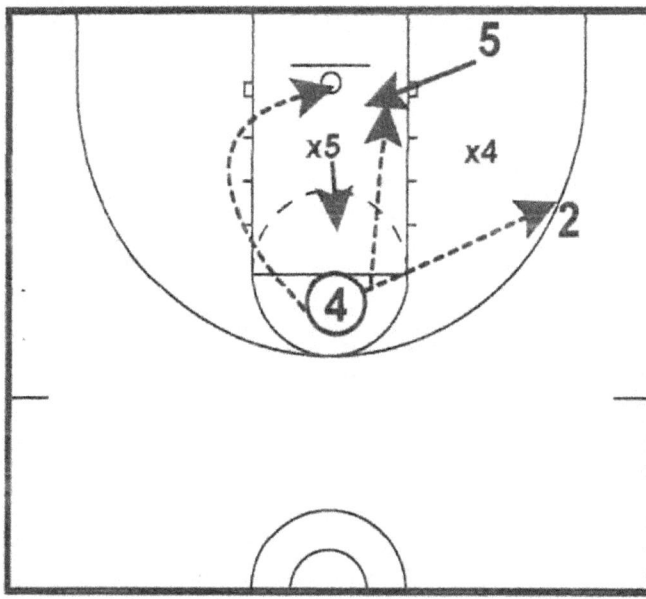

DRILL #5, 3 VS 2 BOTTOM – 4 FACES THE HOOP AND READS THE DEFENSE, IF 4 IS OPEN HE SHOOTS, IF X5 DEFENDER COMES UP, 4 READS DEFENDER X4 AND PASSES TO 5 OR 2 THE OPEN PLAYER

TOP ZONE DRILLS 1-8
A

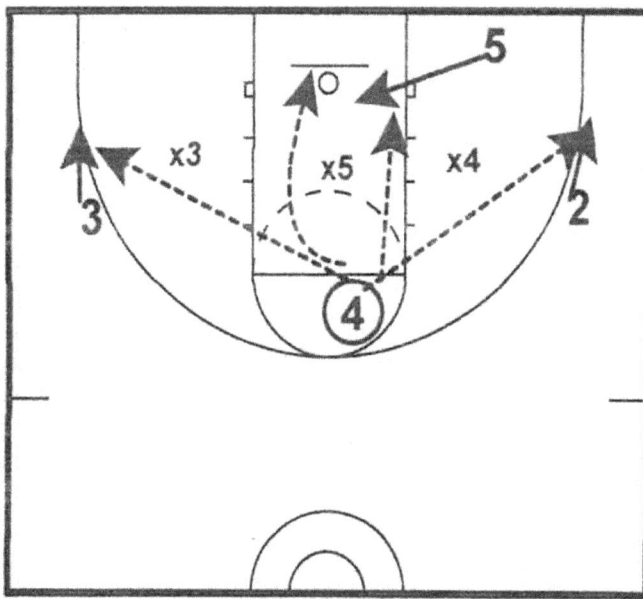

DRILL #6, 4 VS 3 BOTTOM – WHEN 4 GETS THE BALL AND FACES THE HOOP, 5 STEPS INTO THE LANE AND 2 & 3 DROP. 4 MUST READ THE DEFENSE BEFORE SHOOTING OR PASSING TO THE OPEN PLAYER.

TOP ZONE DRILLS 1-8
A

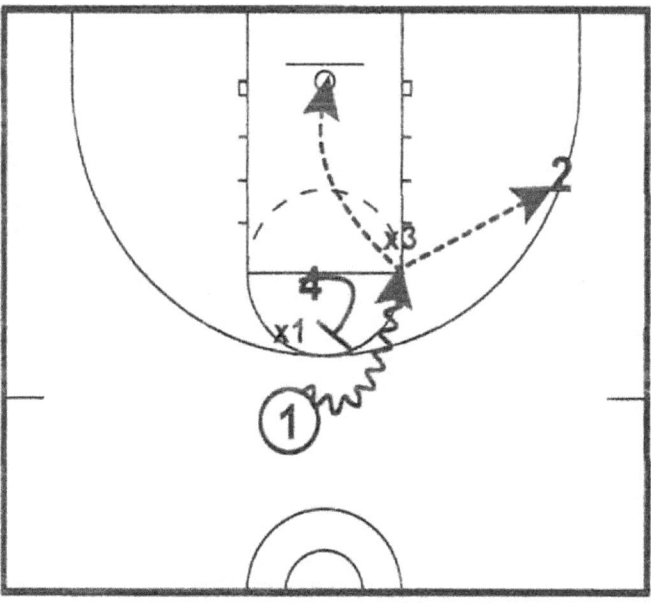

DRILL #7, 2 vs 1 ODD FRONT – 14 SCREENS THE TOP DEFENDER AND SEALS, 1 DRIVES AT X3 TO FREEZE HIM AND PASSES TO 2 OR SHOOTS IF X3 GOES TOWARD 2.

TOP ZONE DRILLS 1-8
A

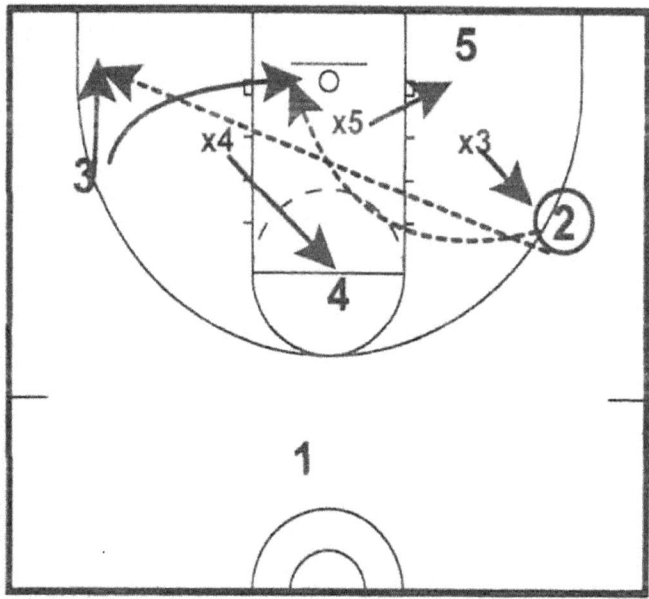

DRILL #8, SKIP PASS – IF X4 TRIES TO HELP ON DEFENSE, 3 SINKS OR GOES TO THE HOOP FOR A PASS AND SHOT.

KISS BASKETBALL

TOP ZONE BASIC
A

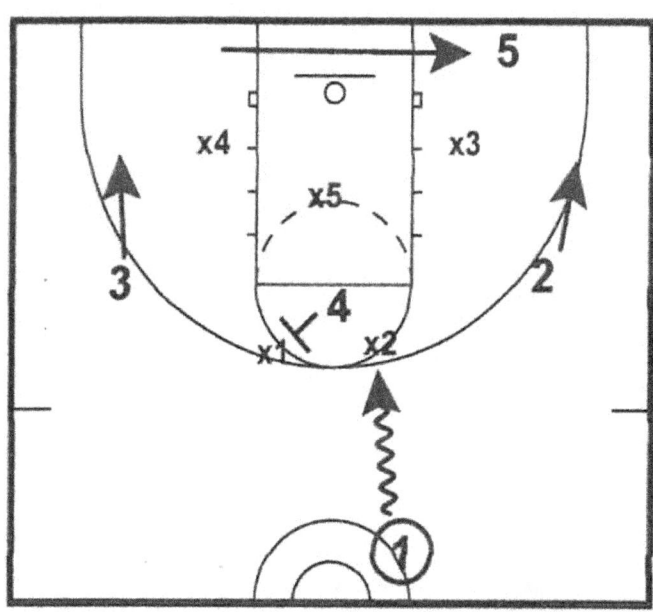

TOP ZONE vs EVEN FRONT DEFENSE; 01 dribbles at a top defender as the wings drop 6-8 feet toward the base line, high post screens the off guard and the short corner player moves to the ball side of the floor.

TOP ZONE BASIC
A

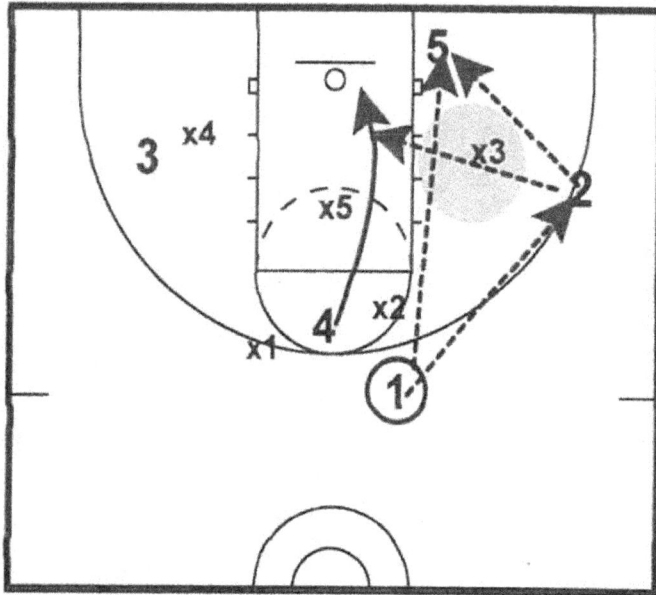

TOP ZONE vs EVEN FRONT DEFENSE; 01 passes to the open player 2-5 or 4. The passer now reads defender x3 who is out numbered and shoots or passes to the open person.

TOP ZONE BASIC
A

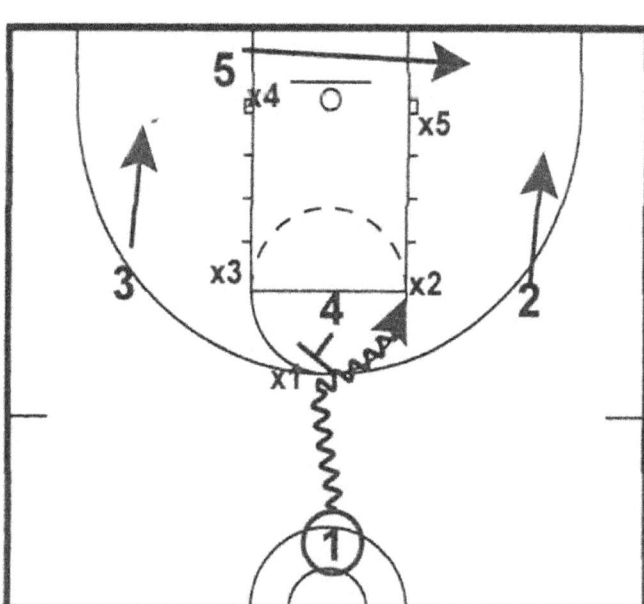

TOP ZONE vs AN ODD FRONT DEFENSE; As 04 screens the top defender and 01 dribbles off the screen, 2 & 3 drop down 6-8 feet toward the base line and 05 goes to the ball side of the floor.

TOP ZONE BASIC
A

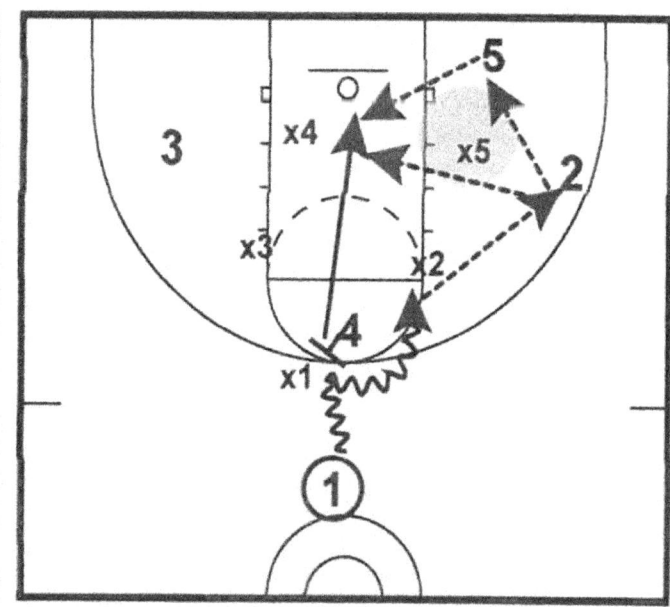

TOP ZONE vs AN ODD FRONT DEFENSE; 01 drives at x2 to freeze him and reads x5, he can pass to 4,5,or 2 who can pass or shoot

KISS BASKETBALL

STACK VS 2-3 ZONE
A

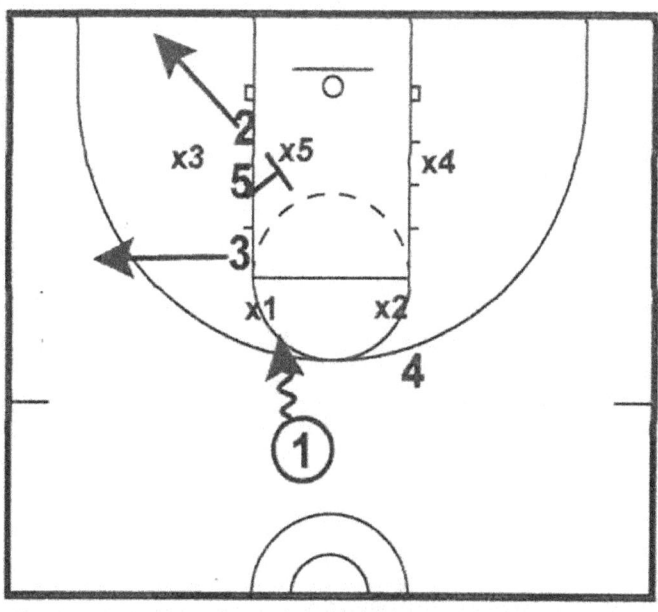

AS #1 DRIBBLES AT X1, 3 MOVES TO THREE POINT LINE, #2 MOVES TO THE SHORT CORNER AND #5 SETS A SCREEN ON X5.

STACK VS 2-3 ZONE
A

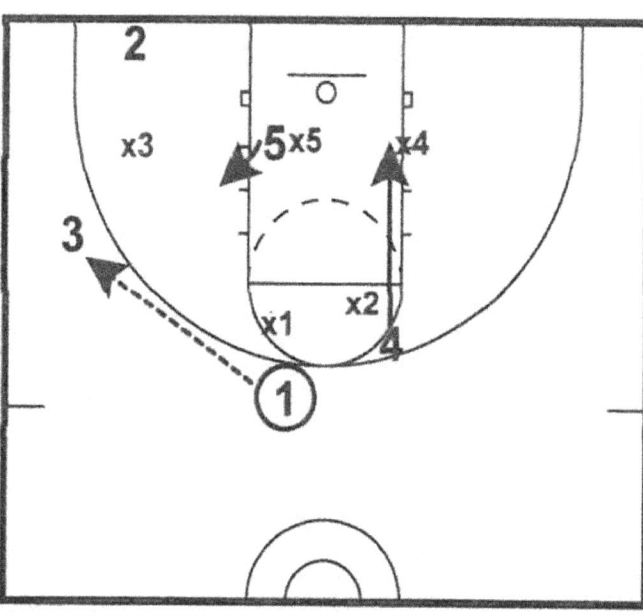

AS #1 PASSES THE BALL TO #3, #4 MOVES TO INSIDE REBOUND POSITION ON X4 AND #5 PIVOTS AND SEALS X5.

STACK VS 2-3 ZONE
A

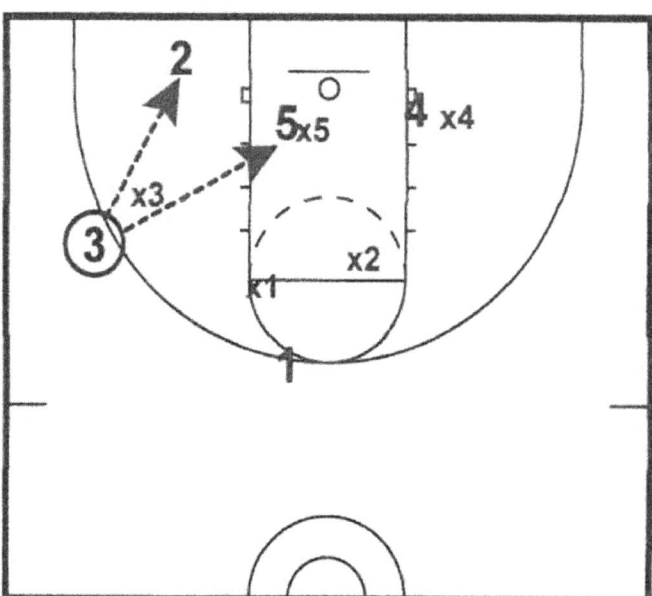

#3 READS X3, IF HE COMES OUT ON #3 HE PASSES TO #2 FOR A SHORT CORNER SHOT OR 3 PASSES INSIDE TO #5

STACK VS 2-3 ZONE
A

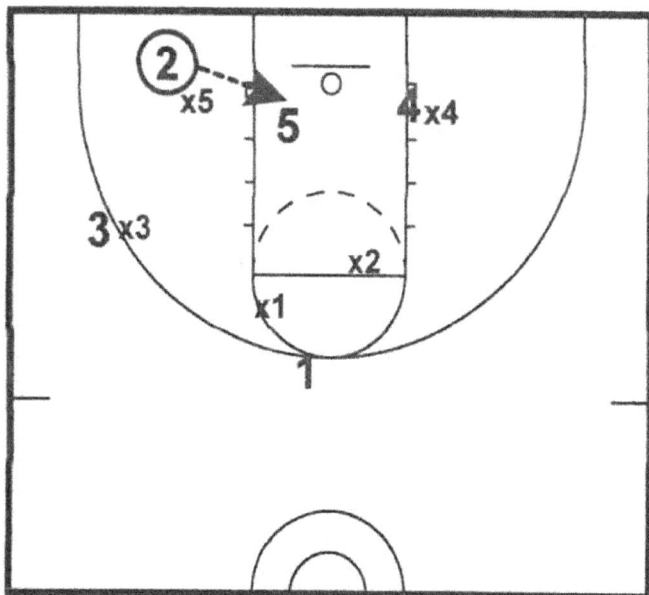

IF X5 COMES OUT ON #2 HE FAKES THE SHOT AND DROPS A PASS TO #5 FOR A LAY UP. #4 IS READY FOR A BACKSIDE REBOUND AND #1 & 3 GET BACK ON DEFENSE.

KISS BASKETBALL

UP TOWN AND DOWN TOWN vs ZONE
A

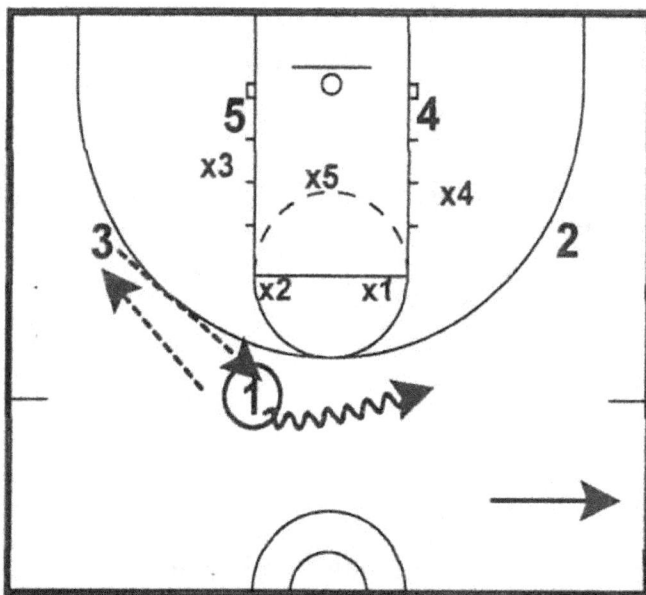

UPTOWN- 1 PASSES TO 3 AND GETS THE RETURN PASS (false motion) AND 1 STARTS HIS DRIBBLE AWAY FROM 3.

UP TOWN AND DOWN TOWN vs ZONE
A

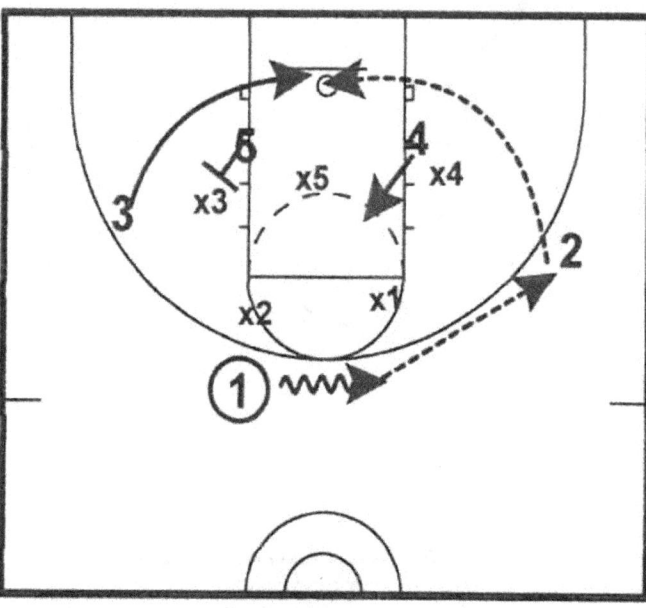

UPTOWN- WHEN 1 DRIBBLES PAST THE MID LINE AND PASSES THE BALL TO 2, 4 FLASHES UP INTO THE LANE TO FREEZE X5, OUR 5 SETS A BACK SCREEN ON X3 AND 3 OUR WING GETS A LOB PASS FROM 2.

UP TOWN AND DOWN TOWN vs ZONE
A

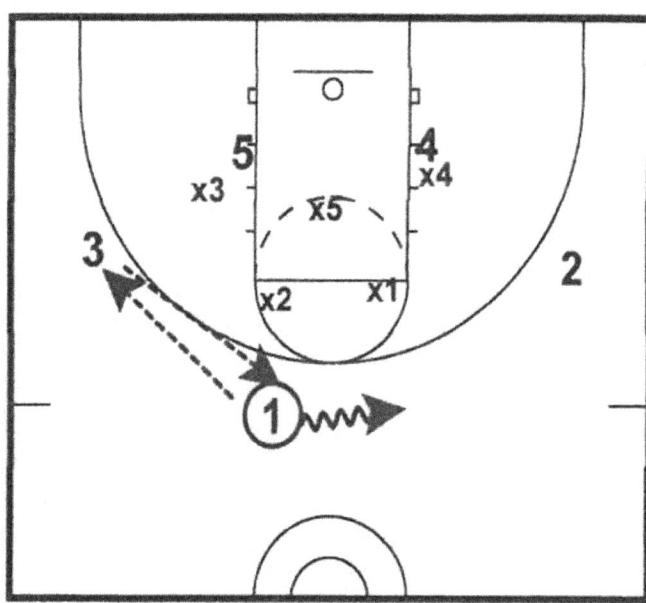

DOWNTOWN- 1 PASSES TO 3 [false motion, away from the play] AND ON THE RETURN PASS TO 1, HE DRIBBLES TOWARD 2.

UP TOWN AND DOWN TOWN vs ZONE
A

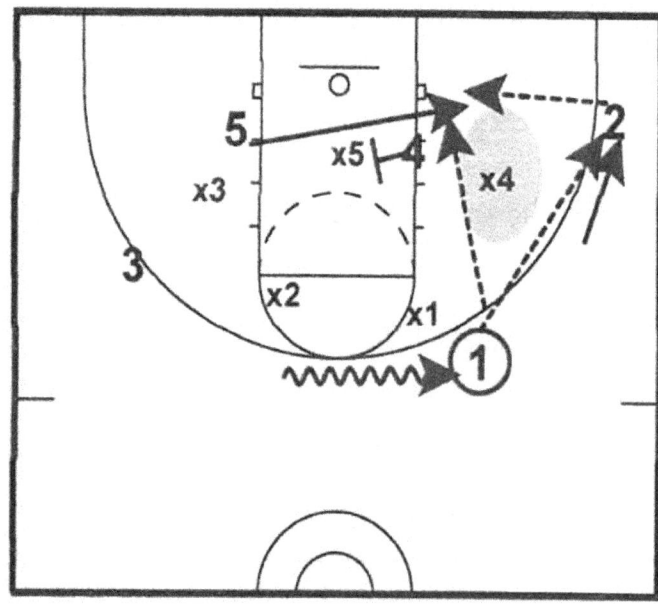

DOWNTOWN- AS 1 DRIBBLES PAST THE MIDLINE, 2 GOES TO THE CORNER AND 4 SCREENS THE MIDDLE DEFENDER X5. 1 PASSES TO 2 WHO PASSES TO 5 OR 2 SHOOTS. OFFENSE READS X4, 1 MAY PASS TO 5 IF 2 IS COVERED BY X4.

KISS BASKETBALL

MONEY VS ZONE
A

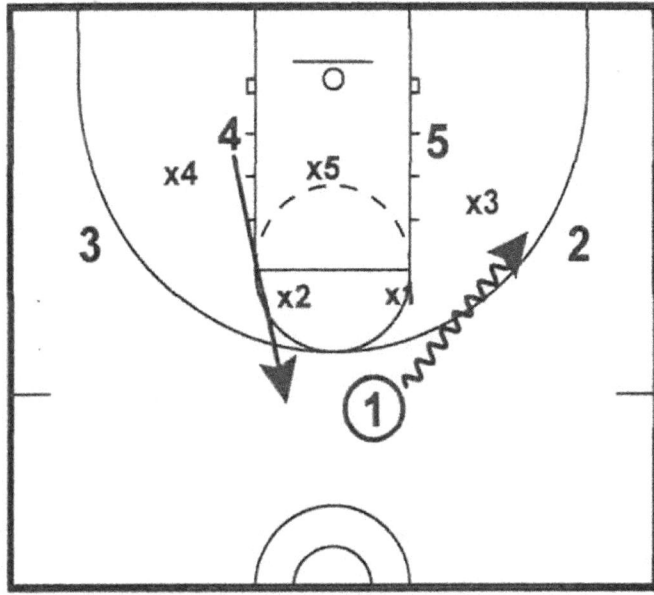

1 DOES A DRIBBLE HAND OFF TO 2

MONEY VS ZONE
A

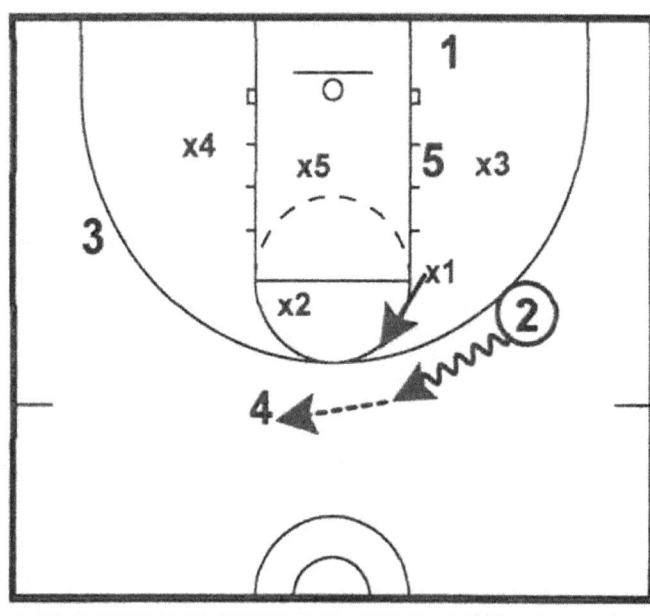

1 GOES TO THE SHORT CORNER AND 2 PASSES TO 4 AFTER DRIBBLING TO THE FOUL LINE.

MONEY VS ZONE
A

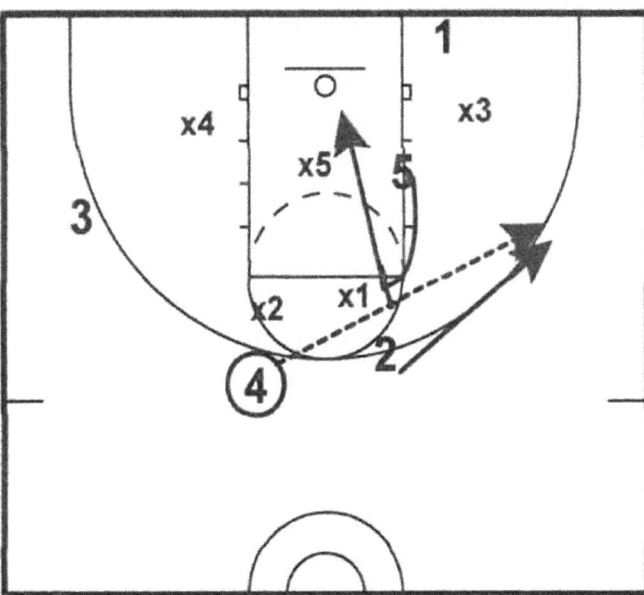

5 SETS A BACK FLAIR SCREEN ON X1 AND 2 SLIDES TOWARD THE OPEN WING AREA FOR A PASS.

MONEY VS ZONE
A

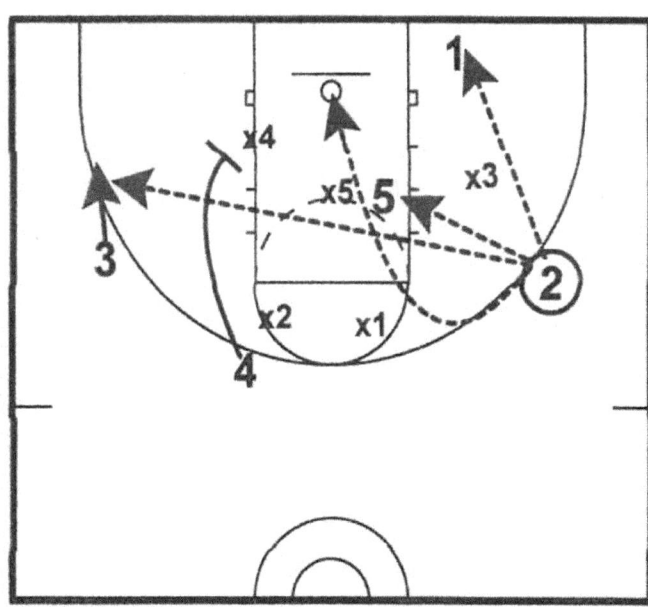

2 READS X3 IF HE STAYS ON 1, 2 SHOOTS THE 3 BALL. IF X3 COMES UP ON 2 THE PASS IS MADE TO 1 ON THE BASE LINE. 5 ROLLS TO THE HOOP. 4 SCREEN AND 3 DROPS FOR A SKIP PASS AND 3 SHOT.

KISS BASKETBALL

HORNS vs ZONE
A

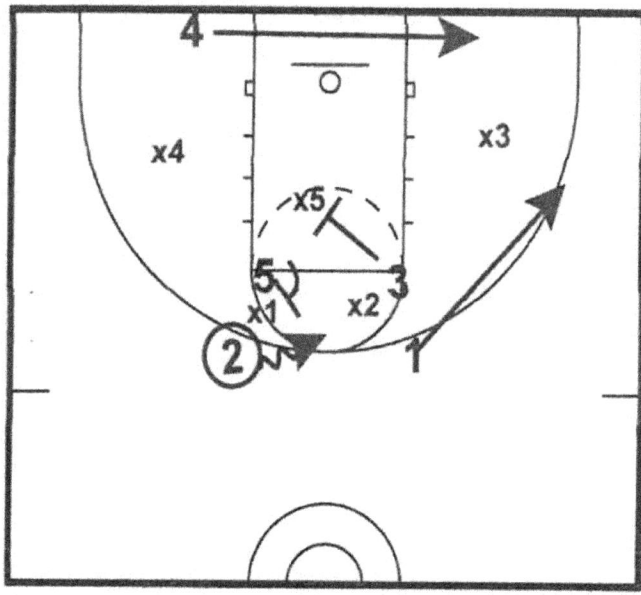

INSIDE SCREEN- 02 sets up outside the foul lane with the ball. As 05 sets a screen on X1, four things happen; 1.-The baseline runner 04 goes away from the ball. 2.-01 moves to the low wing. 3.-The away post screens the middle defender. 4.-02 drives toward the foul line.

HORNS vs ZONE
A

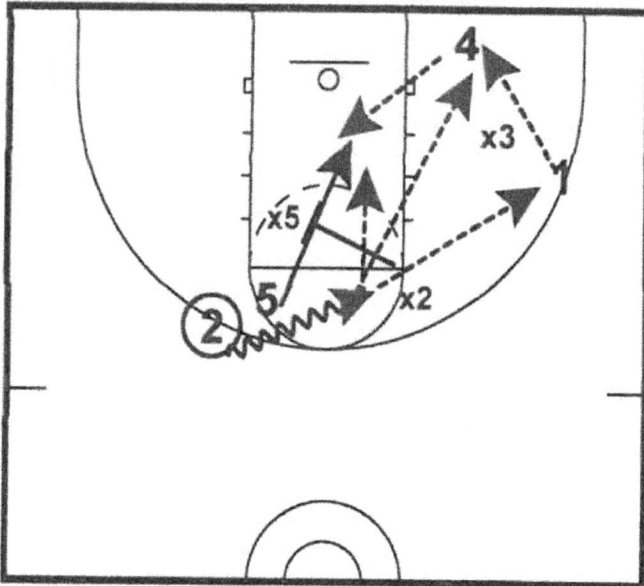

INSIDE SCREEN- If X2 follows 01 to the wing 02 can shoot, drive to the hoop or pass to 04 or 05. If X2 stops 02's drive, 02 he reads X3 and passes to the open person.

HORNS vs ZONE
A

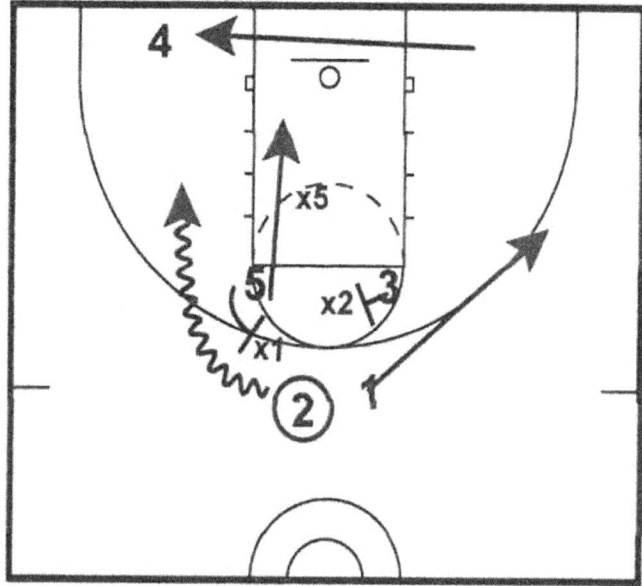

OUTSIDE SCREEN- If 02 sets up inside the foul lane, 05 sets an outside screen on X1 and three things happen; 1. 02 drives and looks for an open 15 foot shot. 2. 04 goes to the short corner. 3. screener 05 rolls to the hoop. 03 sets a flair screen on X2.

HORNS vs ZONE
A

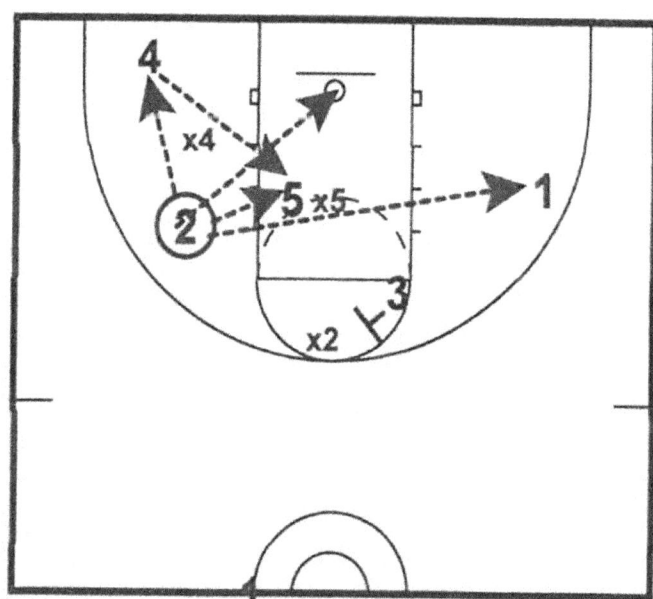

OUTSIDE SCREEN- 02 reads defender X4 who must cover 04 or him, the open person will get a shot. The person with the ball looks for 05 rolling to the hoop. If 02 has no play he looks skip pass to for 01 for a shot from the flair screen by 03 on X2.

Chapter 22
Game Point Savers

Many basketball games are close, with the final score being a difference of just a few points. This chapter will cover little things that help salvage points during a game. I like to spend a few minutes, 3-10 times a week, during practice running drills and plays on these subjects. They help your team always be thinking, not just playing and reacting.

In this chapter, we will cover plays to handle the jump ball and the opponent's free throws. We will also talk about BLOB and SLOB. BLOB stands for "Base lined out of bounds, "or when the ball is passed in bounds under the basket. It is important to have a plan for BLOB when on offense and defense. In this chapter, we will also cover. SLOB, which stands for "Sideline out of bounds," and your team must have a plan for SLOB offense and defense.

Jump Ball

First up is the jump ball. If we feel that the opponent has the best chance of winning the game's opening jump ball, we call: "Cheese." This tells us to bait the trap before the jump ball is tossed up. We bait the jump ball trap by leaving the easy and most obvious receivers open. When the jump ball is thrown into the air, we rotate all four defenders toward the open players where we anticipate the tip will go. Most of the time we are able to rotate into the path of the opponents jump ball tip.

If we feel that we will win the jump ball, we call "Break." When in Break, we line up our wing players (2 & 3) nearly out of bounds on the midcourt line. As the ball is thrown up into the air, the wings break toward the offensive hoop, running their fastbreak lanes, as taught in Chapter 12. Meanwhile, the ball is tipped to our point guard's open side. They stand with their toes on the jump ball circle, in the middle of the circle, with their back to our basket. A defender beside or behind them will guard the point guard. The winning tip is made to the point guard's open side. When the jump ball is in the point guard's hands, he turn and attack the hoop with a 3 vs 1 fast break.

When running "Break," we place our player 5 deep, near the defensive hoop, with the goal of giving up any shot, but a right-handed layup, if we lose the tap.

Over the years, we have gotten 80-90 % of all jump balls by using "Cheese" or "Break," and the end result is worth about 1.2 points per game over the course of the season. In today's game,, there is only one jump ball, which starts the basketball game. However, opening with a 2-0 lead is a great way to start a game. Drawings of "Cheese" and "Break" are at the end of this chapter.

Opponent's Free Throws

When approaching an opponent's free throws, I don't believe in blocking shots. We work hard in practice to not make fouls. As a general rule, our opponents get a few free throws. When we are on offense, I like to draw fouls, because there is such a high PPP when shooting free throws. It is essential to have a plan for both offensive and defensive situations, as well as for rebounding free throws.

When our opponent is shooting free throws, we put our 2 and 3 players [right and left wings] deep in the corners at the offensive end of the floor. This placement gets us in position for a faster attack on made or missed shots. If the other team sends two defenders deep to cover the offensive wings, this positioning makes it hard for the opponent to press full court. If the opponent only sends one defender deep, we yo-yo. Yo-yo means the ball side wing will move up toward midcourt, while the other wing stays deep near the hoop.

A quick outlet pass to the wing near midcourt can lead to a fast-hitting 2 on 1 break. The 4 and 5 players have the inside, rebounding position and should get most missed shots, and if the rebounder can't make a quick outlet pass to mid court to a yo-yoed wing. They can outlet the ball to player 1 on the sideline for a quick 3 on 2 fastbreak. Player 1 is placed on the right side of the foul line on the free throw shot and their job is to cut off the shooter and get any long rebound. Player 1 starts on the left side of the foul line on free throw shots. On a made free throw shot, they keep going toward their inbound position on the right sideline, foul line extended. While doing this, they watch player 5 who is running out of bounds with the ball. This is explained in Chapter 12.

In the last few minutes, if the score is close with a small lead, we put four players on the foul line and place the fifth defensive player on the three-point line. This will eliminate the risk of not getting the rebound on a missed shot.

Stats from thousands of free throws from all levels of play show that missed free throw shots most often come off to the right side or the front rim. With this information, the right side offensive rebounder spins behind the person trying to screen them out and moves under the basket. This movement will keep the defender from stepping into and up the lane while screening his player away from the hoop. The left side offensive rebounder moves up the foul line as far as possible from the bottom defender, who will try to screen them out on the foul shot.

When the shot goes up, the left side offensive rebounder slashes across the free throw lane to a position in front of the right side defensive rebounder. Six out of ten free throws will be made, out of the four missed shots. The left side offensive rebounder will get two or three of the missed shots. Missed shots go to the right side of the floor, and the defender on that side of the floor will be trying to screen out the offensive player. We have a 50-50 chance of getting misses off the front rim, and most misses that come off the right side of the rim. Our rebounder who spins behind his defender, on the right side, will end up under the basket. They will steal the ball or tie up the left side opponent if they get the rebound. We refer to this action as "Holy Cross" and it is performed by crossing two fingers. The person who starts on the left side rebound position slashes across the key to the right side. Over the course of a game, by running the "Holy Cross" offense, we gain about three points per game.

Each night when we shoot and record our free throws, we practice this "Holy Cross" action on missed free throws. With today's high school rules, all fouls after the 4th foul in a quarter will result in two shots, so there are very few times we can run Holy Cross, but we get half of the missed free throws.

With the placement of our wings (2 & 3) deep at our offensive end of the floor, if our opponent shoots free throws, we can get about 4-5 extra points a game. Drawings of "Holy Cross" are at the end of this chapter, and deep placement of our wings (2 & 3 men) is shown at the end of chapters 12 and 13).

Blob

BLOB Offense

As stated at the beginning of the chapter, BLOB stands for "Base lined out of bounds," or when the ball is passed in bounds under the basket and needs to be addressed in both offense and defense.

On BLOB offensive plays, we get to pass the ball inbounds from under our basket. Our first goal is to get the ball safely in bounds, one hundred percent of the time. The second goal is to score. The third goal is to have a plan for when a three-point shot is needed. Fourth,, we want to run plays that will attack both zone and man-to-man defenses. Lastly, the long-range game goal is to score three to four baskets on BLOB plays during the course of the game. This difference of three to four baskets or six to eight points is enough to win most close games.

On most BLOB plays on offense, we run what is called "Line" because it gives us good angles and vision to set screens. Most often, if the screener sets a good screen, seals, and rolls back to the ball, they are open. This is true as long as the person cutting off the screen v-cuts and scrapes off the screen. This will force a defensive switch. In a man-to-man defense, we can clear out defenders and score with a screen and roll, utilizing our best players. Against zone defense, we can seal off half of the court, out-number the defense for an open pass and shot. Diagrams at the end of this chapter illustrate some "Line" plays against man and zone defenses, as well as how to execute a three-point shot.

BLOB defense

When playing BLOB from our 1-2-2 defense, the top defender drops down under the basket between players 4 & 5. This gives the defense a 2-3 zone look. We will concede any long, deep pass toward midcourt and trap any pass made inbound to the corner area. The defense must line up by the nearest offensive player and make physical contact with the distance forearm, while the arm nearest to the ball is in a pass denial position. When the offensive player makes any slight movement, the defender physically drives the offensive player one or two steps toward the sideline with his arm bar. This defensive movement prevents any movement away from the hoop and prevents any attempts from the offensive player to move across the key to screen or get open.

SLOB

Our other acronym for game point savers is SLOB, which stands for "Sideline out of bounds," and your team must have a plan for SLOB offense and defense.

Defensive SLOB

On SLOB defensive plays, we never guard the inbounds player, allowing us to have a 5 vs. 4 player advantage. This extra defender protects the basket while the other defenders can deny without worrying about a lob pass or backdoor cut.

Offense SLOB

On the SLOB offense, we run our "Line" offense. We line up three players 10 feet from the passer and our best advantage player in the low post area. The diagram at the end of this chapter shows how we line up against tight-man defense. If we have a matchup we will win, we place that player in the low post position. For an inbounds post pass, the diagrams also show a play called "whizzer" for when there is no advantage. Reading the defense and calling a SLOB play that utilizes our strength is worth approximately 2 points per game.

If the opponent is turning up the pressure, we run a play called "Pinch." When running the pinch, and the ball is near the half-court line, we make the inbounds pass into the backcourt. This is so that there is no danger of an over-and-back call.

When the defense is in a zone or sagging man defense, we inbound with a pass into the backcourt and then attack with our secondary break, as described in Chapter 13. (Diagrams for Blob and Slob are at the end of this chapter.) Play "Pinch" or "Line"

Conclusion

Winning teams are fun to watch, especially when they win by doing small moves that their opponent had no clue were happening. If Jump ball, Free Throw, Slob, and Blob plays are practiced and executed well, your team can gain about 15 extra points, enough to win most games.

KISS BASKETBALL

JUMP BALL CHEESE AND BREAK
A

JUMP BALL CHEESE AND BREAK
A

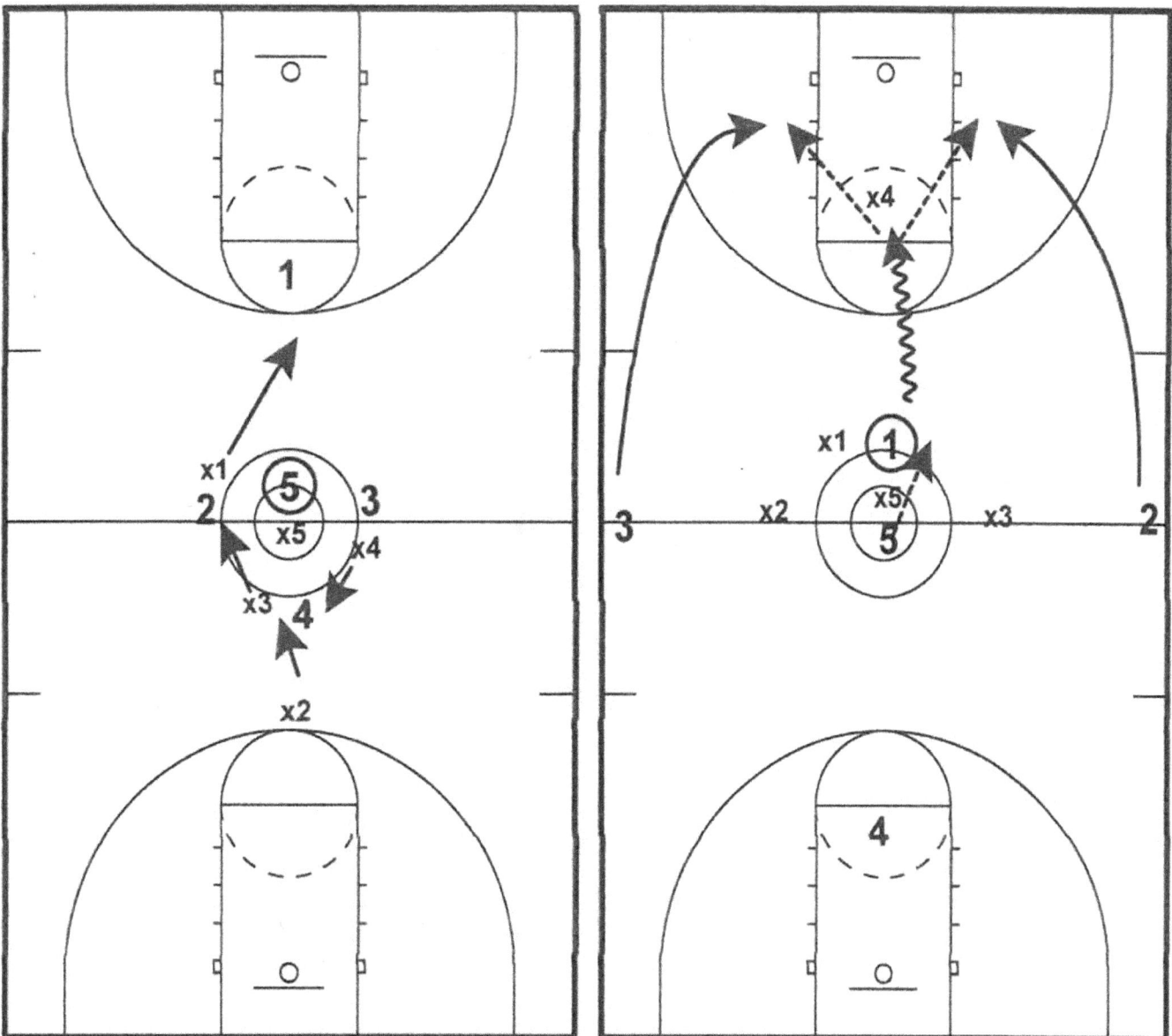

CHEESE-we will be out jumped. We show 4,2 and 1 to be open, but as the ball is in the air x2 & x4 take away 4, x1 takes the open 1, x3 rotates over to take 2. We leave 3 open because its a hard tap angle.

BREAK-We win the tap. When the ball is thrown the wide wings, sprint to the hoop. The ball is tapped to 1's open side, he turns and attacks the hoop for a 3 on 1 break. 5 can also tap long to 2 or 3.

KISS BASKETBALL

FREE THROW OFFENSE
A

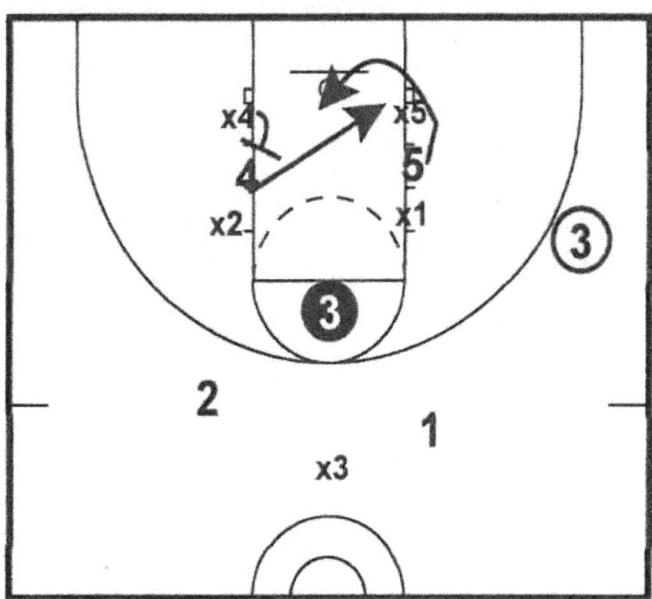

FREE THROW OFFENSE; 4 moves up the lane away from X4 on the shot 4 sprints across the lane in front of X5 who is trying to screen out 5 who is spinning under the hoop. 4 gets any miss to the front rim and right side.

FREE TRROW BLITZ
A

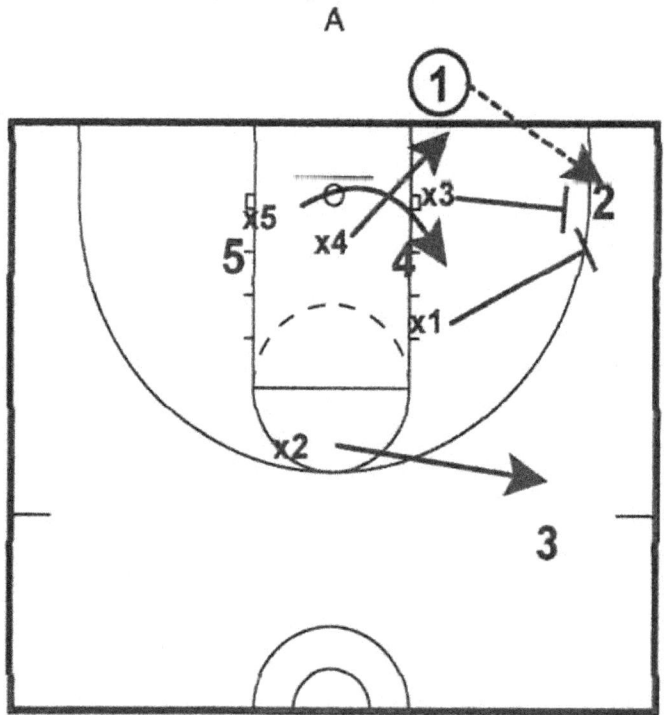

FREE THROW BLITZ . If the pass is made into the corner we double team the ball while denying close pass receivers.

KISS BASKETBALL

BLOB . #1 VS MAN AND ZONE
A

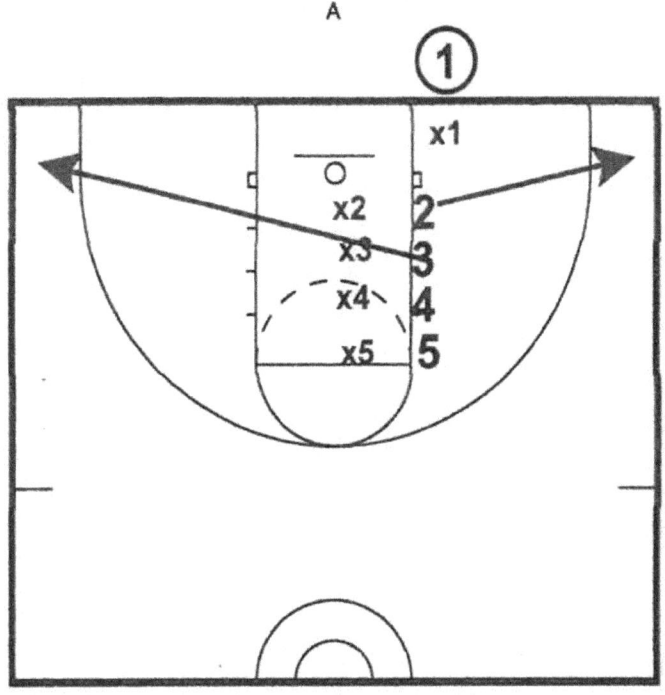

#1 (Call is any # ending in 1 such as 81, 91, 51) the players line up starting at the foul line. When the ball is slapped 2 and 3 break to the corners for a shot.

BLOB . #1 VS MAN AND ZONE
A

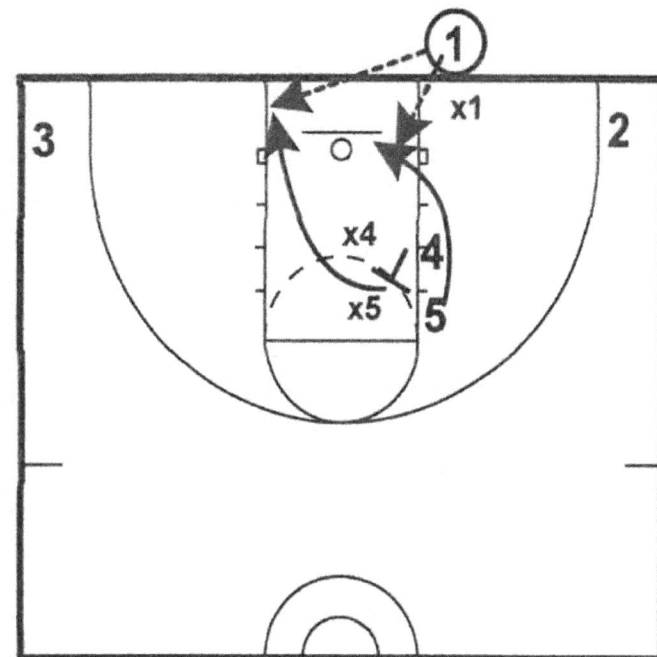

After a delay, 4 sets a screen on x5, seals and rolls to the off side block and 5 cuts to the hoop. 1 passes to who ever x4 leaves open.

BLOB . #1 VS MAN AND ZONE
A

3 point shot out of play #1. 4 screens x3, others pinch in and screen to form a wall, the best shooter steps out for a pass and shot. Passer steps inbounds.

BLOB . #1 VS MAN AND ZONE
A

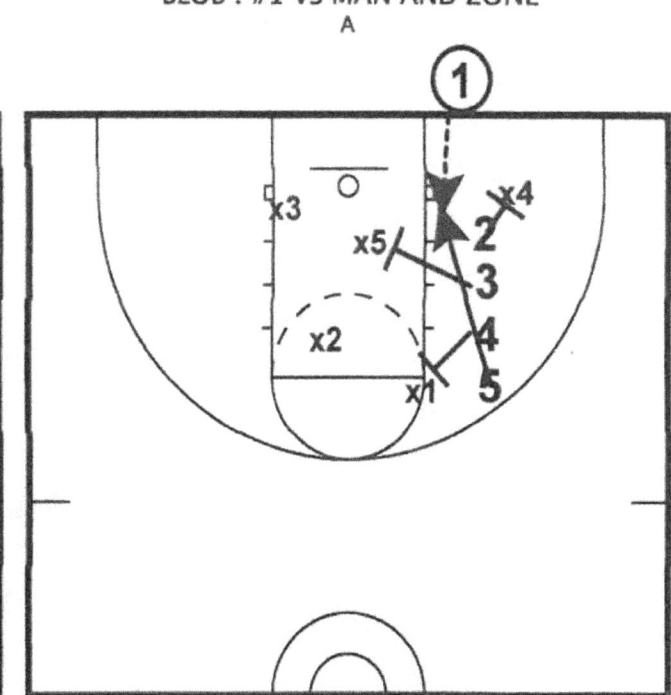

#1 vs a zone defense– 2 and 3 screen the bottom two zone defenders out, 4 screens the guard and 5 cuts down the open alley for a pass.

KISS BASKETBALL

SLOB (line, post, wizzer, pinch)
A

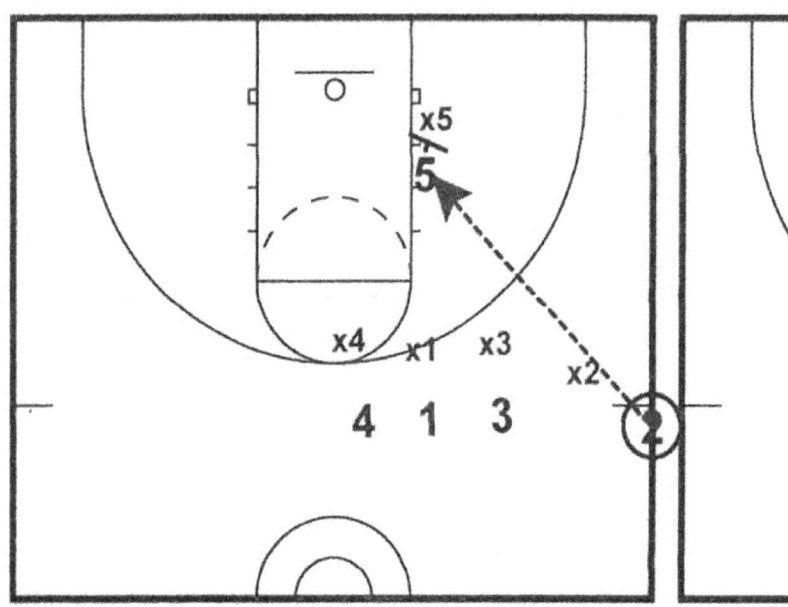

POST: If the opponent plays man defense we post our best 1 on 1 player for a direct pass from O2.

SLOB (line, post, wizzer, pinch)
A

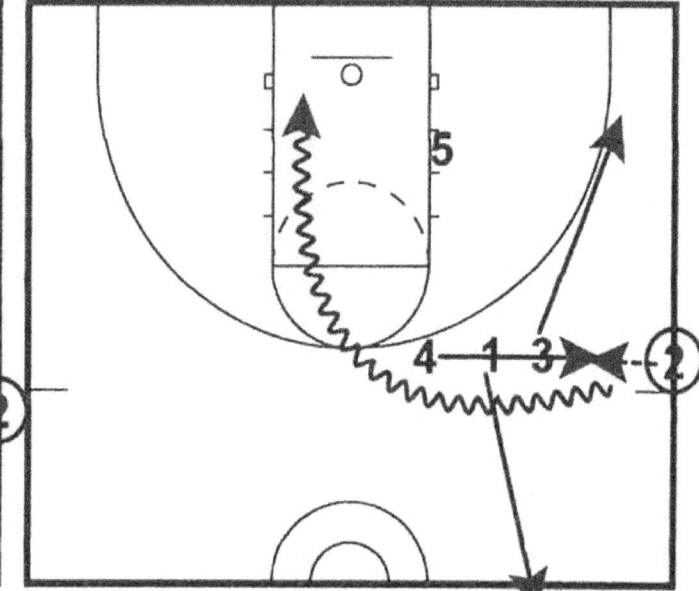

LINE: If there is no post pass, O1 and O3 split in opposite directions and O4 steps forward for a bounce pass, and he hands off to O2 who drives to score.

SLOB (line, post, wizzer, pinch)
A

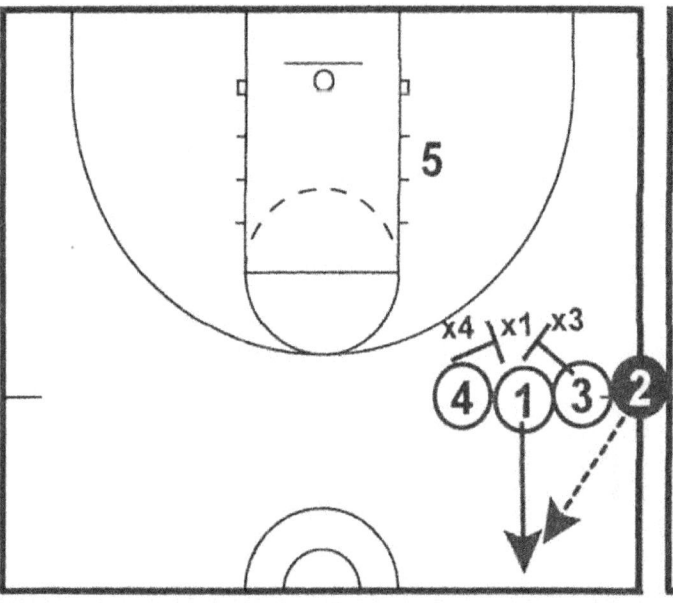

PINCH; The line players O4 & O3 set a pinch down screen for O1 who breaks back for a pass from O2.

SLOB (line, post, wizzer, pinch)
A

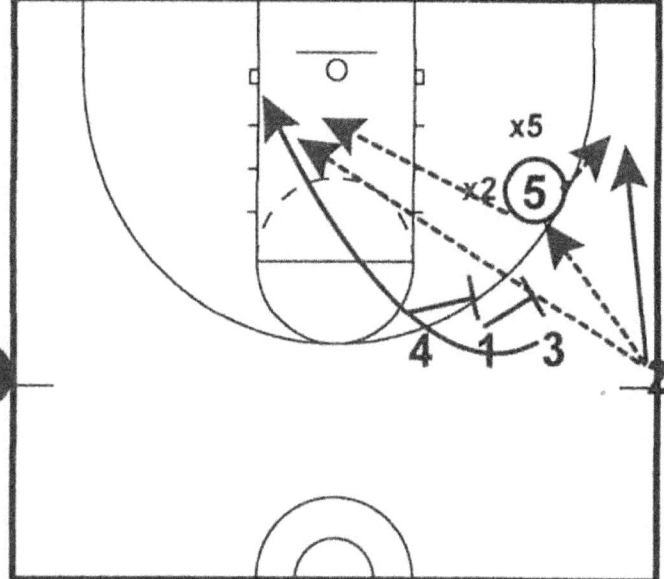

Whizzer; The post breaks toward O2 for the ball as 1 and 4 set back stagger screens for O3 who cuts to the hoop for pass from O5 or O2.

CHAPTER 23
OFFENSE VS. PRESSURE

With your fast break and half-court offense in place, the next step is pressure in the back and mid-court. The goal is to get the ball inbounds, down the floor against the pressure, and end with a score.

The following are examples of different kinds of pressure: man, man run and jump, as well as different zone formations like 2-2-1, 1-3-1, or 1-2-2 zones. When attacking any opponent's defensive pressure, the best success will come from scouting, knowing your opponent, and having practiced an offensive plan. Don't let your team be surprised.

KNOWING YOUR OPPONENT

Knowing your opponent and beating their pressure should come after you have your team drilled and prepped with your philosophy. Chapter 24 delves into the importance of stats, explaining how they can help you understand your opponent and develop a solid game plan.

Listed below are strategies a teuse can use to beat pressure by applying pressure on different parts of the floor.

BEATING PRESSURE WITH A NEW INBOUNDS PASSER

If the opponent makes it hard to inbound the pass, we break this pressure by using the Fastbreak as taught in Chapter 12. If there has been no inbounds pass, player 4 moves back toward the baseline and checks if there is no defender pressuring the ball. Player 5 still has the ball out of bounds. Player 4 points to the floor under the basket and says "bounce pass" as they run out of bounds for the bounce pass from 5. Then, player 5, who is unguarded, steps in bounds for a quick return pass from 4, free of pressure.

It's important to use a bounce pass so that the new inbounds passer, player 4, is standing out of bounds when they get the ball. Then the offense can flow into our fast break running roles, to break backcourt pressure. Player 4 steps in bounds, 15-20 feet from 5 with the ball and 5-6 feet behind the ball for a possible pressure release pass. If possible, it is good to give the officials a heads-up before doing this play, which you can only do after a made basket. (A drawing at the end of the chapter will show the new inbounds passer play)

HOME RUN

If the defense is in a full-court man press, we need a basket to beat the pressure. We do this with "Home Run", a pressure-breaking play. Player 1 takes the ball out of bounds, and the 5 steps out of bounds for a bounce pass on the other side of the floor. As 1 makes the bounce pass to 5, Player 4 sets a back screen on Defender X1. Player 1 then sprints down the floor for a long pass from 5, for a layup. The back screener, 4 holds and seals their screen, then follows 1 on a sprint down the floor. Player 1 should be open for a layup unless X4 switches on to them. If this switch happens, X4 will follow 1 down the floor after he seals his screen on X1. Player 4 should be open near midcourt for a pass. Then they will attack the basket, two on one with Player 1. Players 2 and 3 start in the back court, about 20 feet in front of 5, and run a screen and roll back toward 5 if the ball isn't thrown long.

This play has four good options.

1st 5 passes to the deep player 1 for a lay-up.

2nd 5 passes to the screener, 4 at mid court for a two-on-one break with 1.

3rd 5 passes to the cutter 2 coming off a back screen by 3.

4th 5 passes to the rolling screener 3 if their defender switches on to 2.

If options 1 and 2 aren't wide open for a pass, 5 makes the easy wide-open pass of options 3 or 4.

When running the Home Run play, Player 1 must be fast and good at making layup shots. Player 4 must be a good foul shooter, as they may draw a charge on their back screen. Player 5 needs a strong arm to throw long. Also, player 3 sets a back screen on X2, then rolls back to the passer. Player 2 delays a few seconds before cutting off the back screen toward the passer. (See the drawing at the end of the chapter for the Home Run play)

PASSING BACKWARDS

When attacking down court, the last person to pass the ball is always the trailer. The trailer must move 15-20 feet from the ball and about 6 feet behind the level of the ball. If the ball can't be dribbled or passed ahead, the backwards pass to the trailer is always open.

When the trailer gets a backwards pass, they should always dribble away from the passer toward the ball side wing player(#) who is coming up mid-court on the sideline. The person with the ball should land on a jump stop, look in the middle of the floor and deep, while making 2 or 3 pass fakes. If under pressure, pass the ball soon and, if possible, use a bounce pass to prevent a deflection.

Backwards passes are very hard to defend. Defense will sink to the level of the ball. If the ball progression down the floor is stopped with a double team, the offense will have an open trailer player advantage.. The player who makes a backwards pass now becomes the new trail person. (See the diagram at the end of the chapter on Passing Backwards)

HALF COURT TRAP

The following is how we like to beat the half-court trap pressure, while staying with our numbered break positions. The key is to outnumber the defense, so that the offense is playing 3 against 2 or 2 against 1. We want the best players making the shots and decisions. The offense is run the same on both the left and right sides of the floor. When breaking half-court pressure, the point guard picks a side, and the other players adjust.

Player 5 brings the ball toward the top defender in the middle of the floor. If 1 is on the right side of the floor, 2 goes into the middle of the floor behind the middle trapping defender. Just before 5 is under pressure, they pass to 1 and replace 2 in the middle of the floor. On the pass from 5 to 1, 2 runs to the ball sideline, 20 feet behind the midcourt trap on 1 with the ball. Player 1 attacks like they are going to dribble into the trap, but then backs up a dribble and passes to 2, who is behind the trap near the sideline.

When 2 gets the pass from 1, they attack the basket on a sprint as the offense has a 3 vs 2 defender advantage. At this point, 4 can screen for 3 and seal their screen. The offense now has a 3 vs 1 offensive advantage for a great shot, plus 5 comes down the middle of the floor from midcourt toward the foul line. (See the drawing at the end of the chapter on beating the half-court zone trap.)

Conclusion

When attacking pressure, try to clear out and go one on one with your best ball handlers. If the defense is trapping, stay out of the corners in the back court and across the half-court line. The offense will have a player advantage (5 vs 4) against traps, so if there isn't a clear pass down court, use the backwards, open pass out of the trap.

Once your team has mastered their roles in the numbered break, the players will be set up for success against pressure, because you will have two good ball handlers and scores deep, ready to attack. The defense will be spread too thin to apply much backcourt pressure. By always sending our players 2 and 3 deep, down the floor, our opponents will be trying to pressure the back court with their big players. This puts them out of their comfort zone, skill set, and exposes their lack of quickness.

With practice against different presses and staying in the numbered fastbreak roles, the offense will end up with a great shot.

KISS BASKETBALL

NEW PASSER

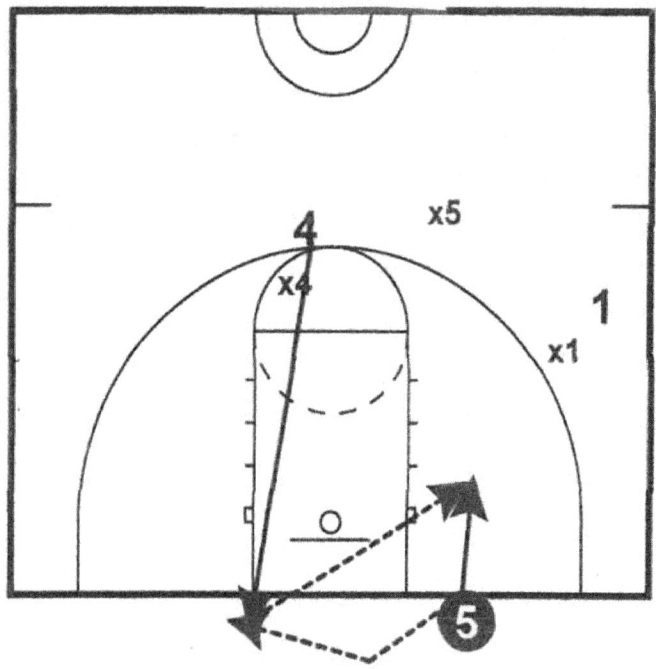

If the defense is pressing with a center fielder or no pressure on 5, 4 runs out of bounds for a bounce pass from 5 who steps inbounds for a return pass from 4.

PASSING BACKWARDS

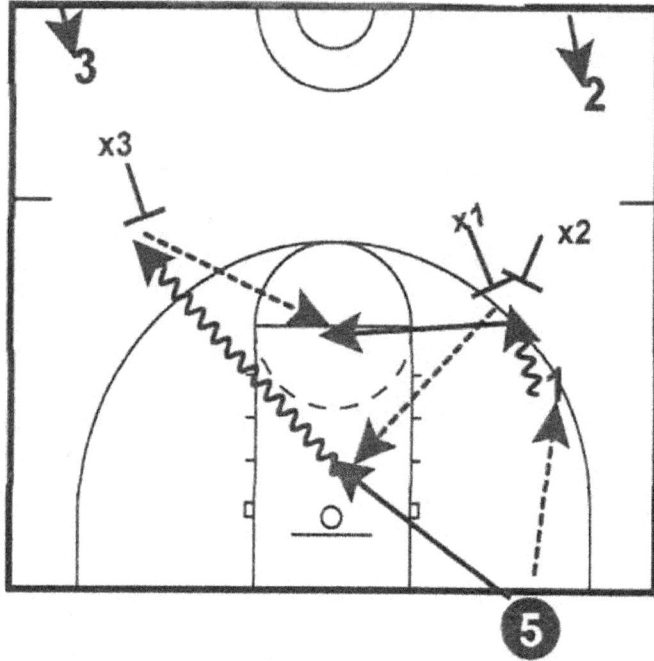

5 inbounds to 1 who dribbles into trouble so he passes backwards to the trailer 5. 5 dribbles away from 1 and up the floor into trouble so he passes to 1 who is now the trailer.

HOME RUN "SNOWMAN"
A

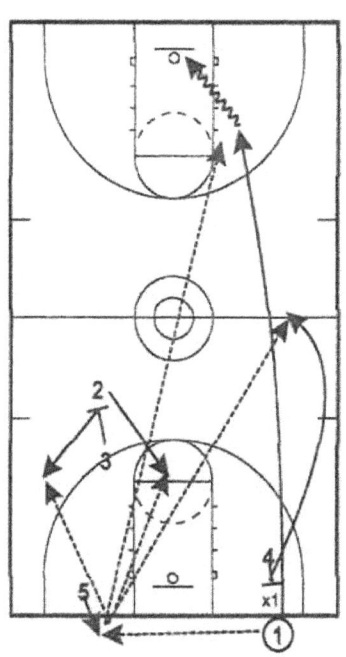

1 passes to 5 who has stepped out of bounds, 4 back screens on x1 and 1 runs deep, 4 seals his screen and also runs deep. After a delay 3 back screens for 2 and then seals and rolls back for a pass.

BEATING THE ½ COURT TRAP

21- beating 1/2 court zone

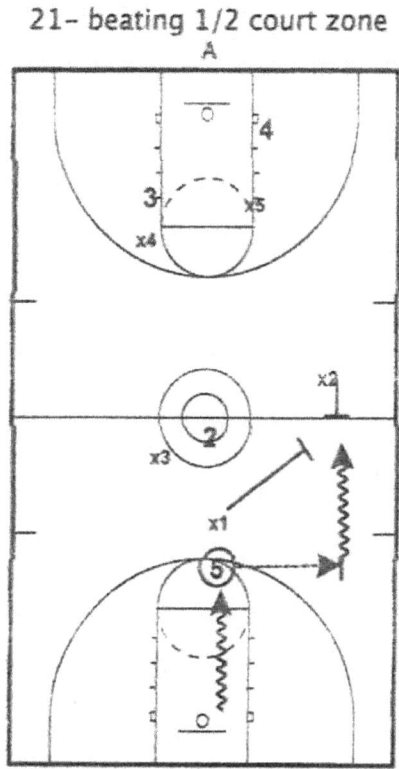

5 dribbles until he meets pressure then he passes the ball to player 1 the point guard who acts like he will dribble into a double team.

21- beating 1/2 court zone

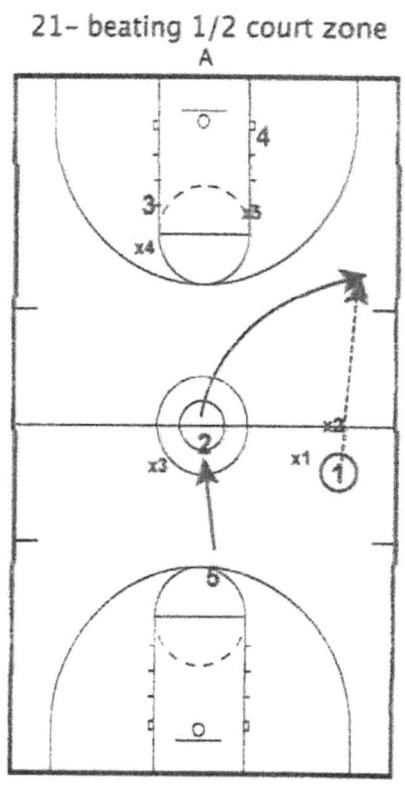

when 1 starts his dribble, 2 cuts to the ball sideline 20 feet behind the trap and 5 replaces 2 in the middle of the floor. 1 passes past the trap of x1 and x2 to 2.

21- beating 1/2 court zone

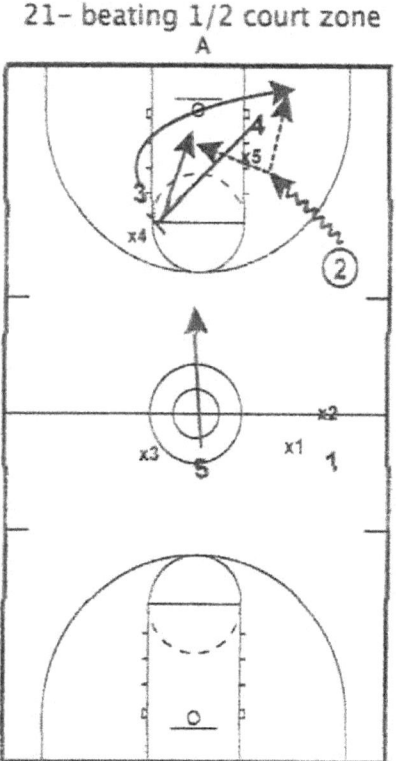

As 2 starts his hard drive at x5, 4 sets a screen on x4 and seals, 3 cuts behind x5. 2 can pass to 3 in the short corner, 4 on a good seal or take a lay up or shoot.

21- beating 1/2 court zone

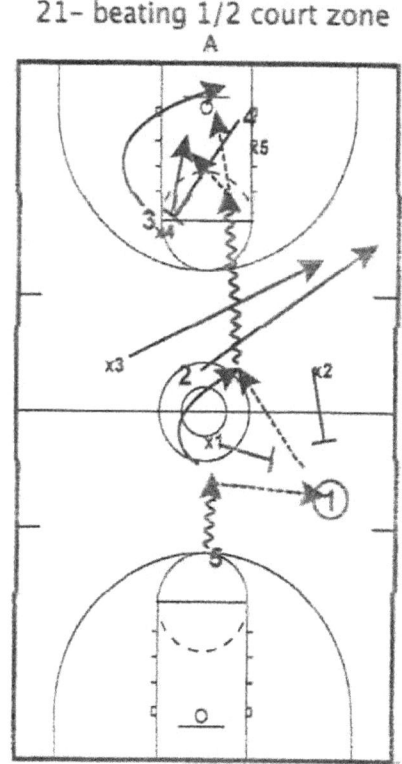

when 2 clears to the side line and X3 follows him, 1 passes to 5 in the middle of the floor, who attacks the hoop in a 3 vs 2 situation.

PART 5
CONCLUSION

CHAPTER 24
STATS

I started coaching high school sports in 1963, and I kept stats mainly to show kids where they needed to improve. At this time, there was little scouting due to the amount of travel needed to see opponents' games and limited resources to film. Scouting had to come from newspapers and word of mouth.

In 1985, I moved into the city and began filming games. This enabled me to scout opponents and collect better stats on players. Filming provided more detailed stats, which I used to evaluate my team and our opponent more effectively. This also allowed me to put together a good scouting report and produce a better practice plan. By the year 2000, I had a computer, and this opened a whole new field of statistics.

I built a library of basketball books full of analytics information, which improved my success as a coach. The game is fast, so it's easy to miss what's happening away from the ball. The film highlights who gives a second effort or full effort on both offense and defense, and who effectively screens out shots or slides toward the ball to provide gap help on drives, while also denying cutters.

Why stats are important

Knowing an opponent's player scored 20 or more points can be helpful. However, stats and film reveal not just the total points, but also how and where they were scored.

The more detailed stats you have on your opponent, the better you will know what game plan to put in place and practice. Stats will give you percentages so you can play the odds. If your opponent is 3 for 20 from the three-point line or 15% on makes over several games, then pack back your defense into the key and let them shoot 3's. If the opponent gets all of their scoring from two players, the stats and scouting report may dictate a "Triangle and 2" defense.

It's crucial to understand the opponent's average points scored and allowed while on defense. Specifically, do they run a man-to-man or zone defense? Knowing each of the opponent's individual stats helps, but watching film or live action gives more information.

Using Analytic Apps

Today, I use an analytic app to break down my game films. This saves me many hours and gives me stats that, as a coach, I can't produce on my own.

Twenty-four hours after a game, I get game film, along with both team and player stats of my team and the opponent. The team stats are given by quarters and game totals. The player stats include: minutes played, shooting % on free throws, 2's and 3's, turnovers, assists, offensive, defensive and total rebounds, the +/- points when the player was on the floor, deflections, steals, charges drawn, points off turnovers, second chance points,

points in the paint, and other stats, but best of all is the VPS. The VPS is a point value system based on a formula that assesses all the players' positive stats divided by negative stats. The VPS stat gives a score, showing the player's value for the game. I divide the VPS by the minutes a player was in the game to get a better picture of the player's value. The VPS and minutes played are listed on the app stats. PPPs, as talked about at the end of this chapter, are also produced by the app. There are many apps out there these days. I personally use Hudl, but do your own research to decide the best app(s) to assist you in gathering stats.

Evaluating and Using Stats

It is beneficial to scout with a coaching friend and ask them what they saw and how they would approach the opponent. They may point out things you didn't see. After studying the scouting tape and or stats, I make a list of the opponent's strengths and weaknesses on offense and defense.

Next, I come up with plan A for defense along with a backup plan B. I run plans A & B by the other coaches, for pro and cons. We then usually agree on the best plan, but I am open to changes based on my coach's opinions. I value my assistant's opinions, which helps build a good coaching relationship and trust. When you coach with someone for a season or two, you will soon think alike and share responsibility.

These defensive plans are worked on in practice, with the aim of taking away the opponent's offensive strength. The same plan idea is used when we work on our offense. I select plays that will attack the opponent's weakness on defense. The coaches, second team, and JV''s are used, in practice, to represent the opponent's offense and defense.

When working on the offensive and defensive plans in practice, players are informed about the practice's objectives and how they will counter the opponent. The night before each game, the players are given a detailed scouting report on our opponent's players and team, along with a list of the top 5 things we must do when we play them.

The following might be an example of five game goals:

1. Win the rebound battle, work the boards

2. Press and keep the tempo fast

3. Pound the ball inside to our posts

4. Stay disciplined and run our plays

5. Deny their two best players the ball; if they get it pushed, then left under pressure, double team if needed.

(At the end of this chapter is a sample of a pregame goal sheet)

After the game, I fill in the results beside the pregame goals, and each goal is given a grade A to F. In the next practice, the goal grades are discussed, explaining why they were low or good. The goal sheet teaches the players the value of thinking and playing toward goals.

PPP Stats

Of all the stats produced, I like the VPS stat for players and the PPP (Points Per Possession) for the team. Most stats are player stats, but the PPP is a team stat. The overall philosophy of KISS BASKETBALL works toward a PPP of 1.0 when on offense, while forcing a PPP of under 0.6 when on defense. The following is an example of three ways our offense and defense work together to help our team win the PPP battle and game.

The study of the PPP from shots taken during a game or practice proves that shooting free throws will give the highest PPP, 1.6. On offense, I want my team to get to the foul line frequently, which will help build a high PPP. On defense, we focus on minimizing fouls to lower our opponents' PPP and keep them off the foul line.

Example #2. Stats show that after free throw shooting, the second-highest PPP, 1.2 comes from shots within eight feet of the basket. When on offense, your plays should leave the hoop free of players unless you have a great post player. This makes it possible for shots to be taken by players moving toward the hoop, on cuts and from one or two dribble drives. This will produce defensive fouls, offensive free throws, and shots within 5-15 feet of the basket. Our 1-2-2 Zone defense will clog the key and prevent layups and shots within fifteen feet of the hoop. This produces a PPP of well under 1 for our opponent on close shots.

Example #3 The third-highest shooting PPP is the three-point shot, with a PPP of about 0.7. The three-point shot is worth 1.5 times more than the two-point shot, but it is deeper and harder to make, which produces a lower success percentage.

When on defense our scouting report will tell us which three-point shooters to cover and who we sag off or/and give the shot to. With our 1-2-2 zone, the opponent shouldn't make a high percentage of their three-pointers. With the Kiss offensive and defensive philosophy, we expect to win the PPP battle on three-point shots taken by .5 to 1.0 advantage. Examples 2 and 3 will be enough to win most games if the offensive and defensive goals are reached.

Conclusion

Basketball is fun to coach because it is fast paced. If it is well coached the team can improve to where it is competitive in all games, even those lost. The team may be small, slow, and have low skill, but if they give full effort during games and practice, they are winners.

Don't let wins or losses be the standard that determines the season's success or your ability to coach. Look at the big picture of your stats and compare them year to year. During my third three years of coaching, I had an undefeated team. Year 4 was one of my six losing seasons in 60 years of coaching. We only won 2 games, but the tougher season forced me to explore all the ways to improve as a coach. In my 5th year, my team only lost 1 game.

BASKETBALL REPORT CARD

Open Door vs _____

	GOAL		RESULTS		GRADE	
	ODCA	OPP.	ODCA	OPP.	ODCA	OPP.
FIELD GOAL %						
FREE THROW %						
REBOUND ADVANTAGE						
TURNOVERS						
FOULS						
PLAYERS 10+ POINTS						
TOTAL POINTS						

THINGS WE MUST DO TO WIN
1. _____
2. _____
3. _____
4. _____

DEF GRADE ___ OFF GRADE ___ LINES ___

CHAPTER 24
Three MORE FEET

I had the pleasure of coaching for several years with Steve Buhler. Steve was a good coach; he loved kids, basketball, and he was a master at his coaching craft. When our teams lost a game, we attributed it to players being 3 feet out of position. The lack of "Three Feet" soon became our joke and battle cry, as we watched game and practice film. We saw that when players weren't moving the 3 feet needed, at both ends of the floor, it hurt the team and players' success, so soon after the 3 more feet concept dictated our practice plans.

THREE MORE FEET ON DEFENSE

When a player is three feet out of position on defense, he will fail a lot, and this will destroy team and individual defense. It's the coach's job to make sure this doesn't happen.

The following are some areas where "three more feet: is important if you want near perfection from your team defense.

Stance:

When a player wants to improve quickness, rebounding, driving, jumping, shooting, etc., they must drop their bottom. Good defense requires a low center of gravity. Playing with their bottom down, each player's feet should be 12-18 inches wider or a total width gain of about 3 feet. A few minutes each practice night doing defensive slides and several duck walk trips will build leg strength to stay low and gain three more feet of width.

Quickness

Quickness can overcome size when used properly. To have quickness, players must spread out three feet, which will put them in a lower, wider position. Quickness to move left, right, or any direction requires a low starting position.

Closeouts

Most defensive players close out three feet from the offensive player with the ball. Teach the defender to close out by being up three feet. Have them overplay the offensive player with the ball on their right side. Being up three feet takes away the shot, putting the defender in a position to press any pass.

Chesting the Cutter

When guarding a passer, the defender must move three feet toward the ball receiver and the basket. Then they are in position to chest the passer if they try to cut the defender's face and run toward the basket. To chest a cutter takes balance and strength, which comes from a low, wide stance.

Gap Help

A defender nearest to the ball needs to move three plus feet toward the ball in a bluff and retreat action. This is so they won't be late giving gap help, and the driver can split the ball help seam. The end result will be a reach-in foul by the defensive gap helper or an easy drive to the hoop.

Rebounding

When an opponent shoots the ball, the defenders must move 3 feet closer to the person they are to screen out. Without this, the offense player can run past the defense, get an offensive rebound and make a score.

Weak Side Help

Defenders, who are away from the ball side of the floor, must move three feet or more toward the ball side of the floor. This way, they are close enough to give gap help on any action coming toward them or the basket. A failure to move toward the ball side of the floor will make them late with gap help.

Front the Post

Keeping the ball from entering the post will keep the post player from getting high-percentage shots. The defense must move up, three feet above the offensive post, and round them to a 3/4 deny position. From this position, the post defender can keep passes from the post player. Then the defender is free to move toward the corner or away from the hoop to give defensive help. By being up three feet, the defender is in a position to deny the player the ball.

Wing Deny

Most teams will have a few good players who can score, so the defense must overplay the passing lane to these players. This requires the defender to move up three feet and get their arm between the ball and the receiver. This denial position makes it hard for the receiver to get a pass.

Charges

Taking charges is all about moving in front of the dribbler with the ball. Or to get off your man, slide three feet into the path of the ball, as it comes down the floor or toward the hoop.

Bluffing and retreat

Players need to move their feet and slide three-plus feet in a bluff and retreat motion in order to be ready to execute gap help.

Loose 50-50 Balls

Getting 50-50 balls means extra possessions and extra shots. Players who are in a good defensive position to move the extra three feet will get the loose balls on the floor, the long rebounds, or tipped passes.

Pressuring

When playing with quick players or when playing from behind, your team must be able to press the ball with a trapping defense, in the back or front court. The success of a team's press and traps will depend on players playing up three feet on the ball and overplaying passing lanes.

Defensive conclusion

Teams that play up 3 more feet will soon force the offensive opponent to run their offense 6-10 feet further from the basket or beyond the three-point line. Now dribble drives will take 2-4 extra dribbles when going to the hoop, which uses up time, so that the defense can move over to stop the drive. Passes are now longer, so there are more steals, or it takes two passes to get a shot near the basket, not one pass.

THREE MORE FEET ON Offense

It's fun to watch your team score off of a play, such as a back door, screen and roll, lob, or after coming off of a double staggered screen. Close to 50% of high school players' shots are not square to the hoop, or the shot is rushed, the shooter has poor form, or the shooter is three feet out of their range.

Getting Open

Outside players need to v-cut 3 feet toward the hoop and then move out to the three-point line for a pass. So that they do not drift 3-6 feet off the three-point line to get open for a pass, if they do this, the offense may sputter, and players are now out of three-point shooting range.

RUNNING THE WING ON A FAST BREAK

By running three more feet outside the three-point line, the wing will be in an easy position to see the pass. Also, the ball is moved down the floor faster, and the offense is spread.

POST POSITION

If the post is set up three feet too low along the foul lane, they will be out of position for low-post moves and a quick score. Many post players set up so low that if they make a baseline move, they are behind the backboard or are unable to use the backboard for a bank shot.

SCREENS

When cutting off screens, offensive players need to move within three feet of the screen and then V-cut off the screen, as they cut or scrape off the set screen, to get open. The cutter should rub shoulders with the screener.

Screen setters need to roll three or move feet toward the hoop, or the defense can switch the screen with no penalty, and the offense will lose its 2 1 player advantage. If the screener can shoot a deep ball, they should often step away from the hoop by three or more feet and look for a step-back pass.

DRIVING INTO TROUBLE

Drivers most often dribble, with their head down and three feet too deep. They are so close to a defender that they have no shot, and if they pass, it will be under pressure. The driver should pull up three feet from the defense and take a wide-open mid-range jumper.

PASSES

In Pass Fakes, the passer needs to fake a pass away from where they want to pass the ball. Then they need to move the ball three feet to the other side of the defender so that they can make an easy pass to a desired receiver. Also, passes made three feet too low, high, or to the wrong side will lead to a bad pass, which often leads to another bad pass.

Cuts past the defender

The offensive cutter needs to jab three feet away from their desired cut. Then they complete their v-cut with a cross-over step, and run past the defender; they just move out of their way with a 3-foot jab step.

BODY BALANCE;

Players need to spread their feet three feet wide and bend their knees so that they have the body balance to not be knocked over. This also puts them in the position to jump, drive, or make a basketball move, and they will take up more space on the floor.

SCREENING OUT ON SHOTS

Failure to move out three more feet and banging into the offense when screening out will allow the offensive players to crash the boards.

OFFENSIVE REBOUNDING

Offensive players most often step back three feet when they take a shot and just watch or turn and go back on defense. The result is that the offensive player is too far from the basket to get offensive rebounds.

Offensive Conclusion

Teams that are physical and make an effort to gain a position three feet closer to the hoop on all activity at the offensive end of the floor will have a greater chance of victory. Their shots are closer to the basket and have a higher percentage of being made. There will be more opportunities for offensive rebounds. As the offense scores more, the execution will be easier and the team will look well-coached.

Conclusion

Three feet more drills all season will produce a team that keeps getting better as the year goes along. Playing three feet up requires good practice plans. Practice must be positive, and players must be held accountable for failure to be up three feet; if not, they will drop and do 5 quick pushups, after they tell the coach what they did wrong.

Three feet up practice drills are the solid foundation that is stable and season-lasting. Coaching with Steve and working toward three more feet made basketball so much fun. During the 8 years I coached with Steve Buhler, any time in a game something would go wrong, we would turn toward each other and say," They should have been up three more feet." This always ended up in a good laugh, as we thought a lot alike.

CHAPTER 26
CONCLUSION

This book is heavy on defense and fourth-quarter offense because those are the most typically undercoached and practiced parts of basketball. When these two areas are practiced and played well, it helps players play smarter basketball as the season advances.

Before finishing this book, I want to share a few last ideas on the KISS philosophy, such as tips on how to make players thinkers and share how the coach can build rapport with players, with the use of awards, constructive feedback, and helping players with their health, for the coach to show different ways to coach the game.

Make Players Thinkers

Educating your team about basketball will give you thinkers on the floor. When players become thinkers, they will be better at their roles, have more confidence, and feel that they are a part of the team, because they have input. Players who are thinkers will be able to make the adjustments needed during time-outs and on the floor. This way, the team has an increased chance for success and plays better as the game progresses. To develop, thinkers explain in detail why every drill is run and how it works, explain team and game goals, ask questions, and let the players help make decisions.

It's best if the coach doesn't do all the talking and make all the decisions. Players should decide how they want to do a pregame warm-up, what color of socks they will wear, where the team will eat after the game, etc. Little decisions like this will build team chemistry and encourage decision-making skills and problem-solving. As you do this through the season, turn more decisions over to the players.

During a time out, have players problem solve with you. Ask questions like: how are the opponents scoring? After players tell me the answer, I ask: What can we do about it?

When we need to score, I will ask: What offense do you want to run?

Current Coaching

Coaching kids in this era is different from the 1950s and '60s. In the past, if a player left their uniform at home, they didn't play in that game. If they were late to practice, they ran lines. If they didn't give a full effort, they carried a gold-painted brick all day at school. Comments like "don't be a wallflower" or "grow a pair" are total no-nos today. Today, if you tell a player to quit moving like a slug, the player may feel hurt or that you don't like them. Some players will tell their parents you called them a slug, and the AD will hear that you are picking on their kid. The coach is under the microscope by everyone, mainly the protective parents, and the administration, which fears lawsuits.

Player discipline has changed; however, if players play for a coach who believes in discipline and is fair, they will respect the coach and remember the lessons they were taught for a lifetime. That is why a strong rapport is necessary, and clear expectations and boundaries are created.

I have both the players and parents sign a contract of expectations to make the season run smoothly. I also have a list of parents, dos, and don'ts. I feel the contract and parent list help to set boundaries. (copies are at the end of this chapter)

Rapport with Players

It's important to not only build good team chemistry but also, as the coach, create a strong rapport with players. The basketball season is long, and you will have a lot of contact with the players throughout the year. This close contact with players will make you like a parental figure, so you must be ready to hand out both discipline and lots of love.

Be honest and loyal to the players, walk your talk. Build a good relationship with each person so they will know you care about them. There is a lot of truth and wisdom in the old saying from Theodore Roosevelt, "People don't care how much you know, until they know how much you care about them." The coach must give full effort and commitment, and perform like they have the best job in the world. Encourage players in their physical and mental effort and progress. Talk about ways to improve or how they can get better more often than you talk about wins or losses.

Awards and Constructive feedback

To build team chemistry and motivate players, stats and awards are needed. I bought a large brass bell and mounted it on the end zone wall, and ran a wire from the bell to just under the basket. When a player drew a charge or made a three-point shot during a game, the Jr High kids would ring the bell 3-4 times and then hang a large letter C or 3 on the wire. The goal was to get several letter "C"'s and "3's" on the line each home game. One time, late in a game when we were up several points, a sub center drew a charge, and he was so excited and proud that he jumped up and ran over to the bell, which he rang several times. The end result was a technical foul from the official, but it was a good team laugh, well worth the T-foul.

During the years we have worked extra hard on drawing charges, I have had two different players draw over 25 charges during a season, and had several who got into the teens. Most players don't get 5 charges during their entire time of playing on the varsity, let alone 5 during a season. If most players got a charge, it was due to the fact that they couldn't get out of the way in time. At the end of each season, at the basketball awards ceremony, I would call all the players up front if they didn't get a charge during the season in a game, and would give each one of them a red towel. We called this the "OL'E" award, named after bullfighters who jumped out of the way of a charging bull while using their red cape. Some parents didn't like their son being called out, but I saw it as being part of a non-charge club that if you didn't want to be a part of it, get tough, gap help, and take charge, don't be a wallflower.

Today's officials make it hard to draw a defensive charge; out of three nice charges, they will give you one charge, call one a blocking foul, and there will be one non-call. In spite of the officials' calls, I feel it is important to keep working on charges for several reasons; It makes players play in a low charge-taking position so they can move quick, keeps them from being afraid of stopping drives, and trains them to be in position to give gap help. Because the bell is also rung several times when we make a three-point shot and a large number three is hung on the wire line, I have the players who made a 3 or charge during the game sign the 3 or C on the wire line, and I hand them out on awards night. Overall, the bell has been a lot of fun; it has improved defense and three-point shooting, plus the fans and players like to hear the bell as it means success.

Award

After each game or a week of practice, I hand out paper awards called 'HARDWOOD' and "DEFENSE." The Hardwood award can include any of the following: effort, hustle, attitude, desire, citizenship, leadership, improvement, or academics. The defensive award covers rebounds, charges, steals, gap help, deflections, and shutting down an opponent. (Samples of these awards are shown at the end of this chapter.)

Constructive feedback

In a short postgame meeting, if we win, I have the players pick out 3-5 things that went well, and if we lose, we list 3-5 things that need more work to upset the same team next time we play them. After a loss, I compliment the other team and hold back on remarks or evaluations because everyone is emotional, and you are not in a position to make a good evaluation.

To get full effort, so that offense and defensive plans will work, the coach must give out 3-5 positive comments for every correction, because some players see even constructive corrections as negative comments.

Player health

Basketball is played during the wintertime when kids get colds and run down. I like to hand out chewable vitamin C tablets when a player makes a top-level play on offense or defense during practice. You can buy a large tub of Vitamin C in different flavors for next to nothing, and you can reward players while keeping them healthy. Kids today often stay up very late at night and eat a lot of junk food. The coach must talk about taking care of your body with good food and rest.

Conclusion

Now that you have finished this book, you should have a better understanding of pre-season planning and how to create and apply a defensive and offense philosophy based on PPP. With the KISS system, you should have the practice drills, plays, and tips for being more effective and efficient as a team. Also, communication and organization tips for your team, which help you talk better with each other and coaches.

The KISS system focuses on Knowledge, Interest, Scouting, and Strategy. In this book, we help you as a coach with the Knowledge needed for you and your team to be successful. We share ways to keep coaches and players Interested and engaged, which should show in performance. We also explain how scouting your own team and an opponent helps you to build a game plan and learn your team's strengths and weaknesses. This all helps you create and adapt a strong strategy for your practices and games.

If I had this book back in 1963 when I started coaching, it would have increased my knowledge and sped up my learning, much faster than the many years of trial and error I experienced. I hope you have been able to learn from my experience and value the many little choices and changes that produce winning basketball.

Today, at age 83, I still operate with the KISS system to keep basketball organized down to the last minute of practice. In 61 years of coaching, the KISS system has produced 55 winning seasons, 989 wins, at a 70+% success rate.

I hope you continue to find this KISS basketball guide helpful, as it is time-tested and has helped me for 61 years. Regardless of your team's ability, age, or experience, reading and using this book can help your team grow stronger as they reach their full potential, and give the coach joy and success.

OPEN DOOR BASKETBALL

1. I will abide by the school drug and alcohol policy.

2. I will set solid academic goals throughout high school and never create problems for the team because I fail to take care of my academic responsibilities.

3. I will work hard in practice, be loyal to my teammates, to my coaches and to the program.

4. I will overcome the urge to complain, think negatively, act selfishly, cause dissension or engage in any other unnecessary behavior that disrupts team chemistry.

5. I will become an ambassador of our program, going out of my way to make friends and family feel good about our program.

6. I will show frequent and genuine appreciation for those who work on behalf of our program (managers, administrators, etc.)

7. I will not make excuses for my play, but take responsibility for my actions and learn from my mistakes.

8. I will refrain from using obscenities during practice and competition.

9. I will accept the decisions of the coaching staff regarding playing time and I will support my teammates when I am not in the game.

10. I will strive to be a role model for the younger athletes in our community.

Parent's Signature_____ Date_____

Participant's Signature_____ Date_____

Coach's Signature_____ Date_____

You will not receive a uniform until this paper is returned with two signatures.

HARDWOOD PLAYER AWARD

To. _____

For the week of _____

* EFFORT *HUSTLE *ATTITUDE *ACADEMICS
* CITIZENSHIP. *IMPROVEMENT *DESIRE
*LEADERSHIP.

_____ Coach

DEFENSIVE PLAYER OF THEN WEEK

DATE _____

COACH _____

Working with Young Athletes

Do's and Don'ts

Probably since the beginning of sports history, there have been parents who were enthusiastic, shouting, supportive, critical, loving, pushing, caring, and demanding, on the sidelines or in the stands. Most of the time, this is crucial to the performance, good or bad, of the child's athletic endeavor. After working with young athletes, their parents, and their coaches, we were asked to come up with a list of what works and what doesn't work for the parents of aspiring young athletes. The following are the most powerful dos and don'ts for parents to support their child most positively and beneficially.

The Do's

Allow your child to be interested and to want to play whatever sport he or she chooses. Provide the opportunity of many choices and support his or her choice, even if it is not yours. Support your child's choice to play no sport when he or she is most comfortable with that option.

Teach your child to respect his or her coach. Do this primarily by show. In respect to the couch, yourself. It is vital to the child's progress and performance that he or she listens to and trusts the coach's advice and instructions.

Be willing to let your child make his or her own mistakes and learn from them. When your child makes a mistake, ask what they think they could have done differently, what they learned from the experience, and if they would like any feedback (not criticism or blame) from you - what you saw, what you think they might have done differently, and what you think they might have learned.

Be interested and supportive, light and playful, understanding and open-hearted. Be accepting and tolerant of your child's learning process and his or her physical abilities. Acknowledge and enjoy your child's. Young athletes' participation and successes-even the small ones. Opinions, Be willing to be wrong and model flexibility of your own, move off your position. Listen to the

The Don'ts

Don't try to relive your youth through your child. Just because you wanted to be or were on a sports team of your choice, does not mean that sport will be your Childs choice. Accept that your child may not excel in that or any sport.

Don't blame the equipment, coach, other players, referees, or even the weather if your child or the team does not do well or win. Blaming others teaches non-accountability to kids. They do not learn to look at what they could have done differently or learn from their mistakes if they learn to blame others.

Don't push, push, push. Children who are pushed beyond their capabilities may lose their self-confidence, become resistant and resentful toward their parents, become unsure of themselves and their abilities, and stop trying. They may also exhibit a disturbance in eating and/or sleeping habits.

Don't expect perfection or tie your ego or image to your child's performance. Perfectionism is a very hard expectation to live up to. Laying guilt on a child because their performance made you look bad is highly destructive. Your child is not responsible for your ego or your reputation in the community.

Remembering this simple list may assist parents in remembering that youth sports are to be enjoyed by children as well as parents. Most children play sports because they have fun playing. When sports become work and drudgery, children lose interest and some of the joy in growing up. Remembering to be a little less serious about life helps all of us enjoy athletic competition.

STACEY GEIKEN

Reprinted with permission from the recently published book Visual Athletics by Kay Porter, Ph.D., and Judy Foster (Wm. C. Brown Publishers, Trade and Direct Group, 1990). The book describes the use of visualization for high schools and colleges, as well as for individuals in all areas of athletic competition

Quick Guide
Charts, Diagrams, and Plays

Part 1: Preparing for the Season

1 Selecting Players

2 Type of players

3 Preseason Planning

Pg 1 Sample first three weeks of practice plan

Pg 2 Sample day one week one practice plan

4 Fundamental Skills: an overview

5 Player Scouting

Pg 1 Coach evaluation form

Pg 2 Player/Team Survey

Pg 3 Film/In-game Notes Example , Key, and Blank

Part 2: Defense skills, drills, and strategies

6. Defensive Philosophy

Pg 1 Defensive Survey

7 Defensive Skills and Drills

8 1-2-2 Zone Roles

Pg 1 12-Tight defense.

Pg 2 Corner and Wing Trap defenses.

9 . Defensive Plan B, C, & D

Pg 1 Plan B Triangle +2 defense.

Pg 2 Plan C - Z-Man defense.

Pg 3 Plan D - Double-Z defense

10 Half Court Trap-Paw

Pg 1 Paw the half court trap defense.

11 Full Court Man-CF

Pg 1 Man Centerfield press.

Pg 2 Man Centerfield Drills

Part 3: player roles and fast break

12 numbered break

Pg1 passing options

13 Teaching running role

14 Sprint break

Pg 1 secondary break vs man defense

Pg 2 secondary break vs man defense

15 Keys to sprint break

Part 4: Offensive skills, drills, and strategies

16 Offensive Philosophy

17 Offense skills and drills

18 Delay pointers

Pg 1 Vegas clock milker play

19 Stall

Pg 1 delay blue 6

20 Man offense

Pg 1 Orange A play

Pg 2 Orange A play

Pg 3 orange A play

Pg 4 Motion 5-out

Pg 5 Utah man quick hitter

21 Zone offense

Pg 1 Top zone drills

Pg 2 Top zone drills 1-8

Pg 3 Top zone basic

Pg 4 Stack vs 2-3 zone

Pg 5 Up town and down town vs zone

Pg 6 Money vs zone here

Pg Horns vs zone

22 Jump ball, free throws, and SLOB and BLOB

Pg 1 free throw offense and blitz

Pg 2 jump ball cheese and break

Pg 3 Blob play

Pg 4 Slob: pinch, post, line, wizzer

23 Offense vs Pressure

Pg 1 Home run "snowman" passing backward/new passer

Pg 2 beating half court zone

Part 5: Conclusion

24 Stats

Pg 4 Basketball Report Card

25. Three more feet

26. Conclusion

Pg 1 Player agreement

Pg 2 Hardwood award

Pg 3 Defensive Player award

Pg 4 Thoughts for parents

References

Mark Twain Quote in Part 1

Articles referenced/shared in Chapter 23/24

Any photo releases needed

Steve Houidini. Dave. Magician. Terry. Guru

60 YEARS OF WINNING BASKETBALL WITH KISS

Some happy Basketball guys, after a great year & cutting down the nets.

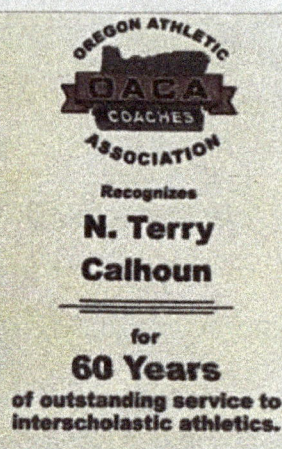

OREGON ATHLETIC COACHES ASSOCIATION

Recognizes

N. Terry Calhoun

for

60 Years

of outstanding service to interscholastic athletics.

WALK THE ROAD TO VICTORY

Thrill of winning district – on to state

late 3 lifts Damascus

Year 20 with the Barlow Bruins

22-4 record.

TOUGHNESS

23-1 league champs

1959 4th place at State.
Captain Terry Calhoun

1963-4 TO 2024-5 YEARLY WINS

Year WINs	WINs	WINs	
1963-4---16	1985---17	2005-6---18	*** 6 losing yrs.
1964-5---12	1986---12	2006-7----7***	
1965-6---22	1987---22	2007-8---17	55 winning yrs.
1966-7---2***	1988---17	2008-9---15	
1967-8---21	1989---20	2009-0---22	Total games
1968-9---15	1990---13	2010-1---25	1403
1969-0---13	1991---12	2011-2---17	
1970-1----9***	1992---12	2012-3---15	Record
1971-2----9***	1993---16	2013-4---15	989-414
1972-3---19	1994---23	2014-5---19	
1973-4---16	1995---19	2015-6---25	winning %
1974-5---15	1996---15	2016-7----9***	.704
1975-6---16	1997---16	2017-8---14	
1976-7---17	1998---14	2018-9---13.	61 year of
1978-9---19	1999---15	2019-0---16.	Coaching BX
1979-0---20	2000---14	2020-1---8 covid yr.	
1980-1---16	2001---21	2021-2---18+10 (JVB+V GIRLS)	
1981-2---18	2002---20	2022-3---19	
1982-3---17	2003---14	2023-4---22	
1983-4---16	2004---13	2024-5---23	
1984-5-----9***			

    61 years of coaching basketball has been a ton of fun. Win totals will happen and it's just a number that will grow if you coach enough years. The total depends on many different variables and most are out of your control, league strength, nonleague games, sickness, injures, grades, officials, etc.

    The key question is, did you help your players physically, mentally and spiritually as you taught discipline, commitment, hard work, loyalty, love of teammates, leadership and giving 100%, the life time skills needed for success.

www.ingramcontent.com/pod-product-compliance
Lightning Source LLC
Chambersburg PA
CBHW081233170426
43198CB00017B/2745